D0065599

PR AS IN PRESIDENT

Also by VIC GOLD

I DON'T NEED YOU WHEN I'M RIGHT,
The Confessions of a Washington PR Man

PR AS IN
PRESIDENT

VIC GOLD

Garden City, New York 1977

ISBN: 0-385-12334-5
Library of Congress Catalog Card Number 76–51690

To Mac, Dave and, again, Dale

flack ENG. 1: STROKE, BLOW, FLAP 2: a recurrent sound of striking (as of a loose tire chain on a frozen road) *slang: PRESS AGENT*

PR AS IN PRESIDENT

The Mediascopic Eye in a Campaign Overview*

It reminded Frank Mankiewicz, another Retired Flack with an eviscerated political psyche, of the picture of the Quaker on the Quaker Oats box looking at the picture of the Quaker on the Quaker Oats box. As this Retired Flack saw it, coming from grits not oats country, it was more like the cow's head on the old Pet Milk can forty years ago.

Rerun the film, let's look at it again:

On screen, the image of Jimmy Carter, newly nominated Democratic Presidential nominee, is seen sitting in front of the television trinity in his Americana Hotel suite. Not one, not two, but three screens, ABC, NBC, CBS. Two of the screens reflect the face of his wife being interviewed at the convention hall. The third is the same screen we're watching.

If you voted for the first time in 1976, you won't remember the Pet Milk can of my youth because the company has stream-

* *me'-di-a-sco'-pic* fr. mediascopia, a psycho-optical illness common to Americans in the latter half of the 20th century, the primary symptom of which is the recollection of current history as a blurred montage of media images, e.g., flashbacks, replays, Fast Forward Speeds, close-ups, cutaways, headlines, fantasies, and interpretive commentaries. Cf. Wicker-Severeid Syndrome.

lined its trademark, dropping the metaphysical imagery for a simplistic cartoon bovine more suitable to a simplistic audiovisual age. But as symbolic merchandising, the old label was one of a kind. Much better than Mankiewicz's Quaker.

The image was the message. The image told us: *Though processed, the product inside this container is as pure as that squeezed out of your friendly neighborhood cow.*

So much for commercialism. It was the image-*within*-the-image, at once grotesque and paradoxical, that transcended the ordinary sales pitch for a thinking label-reader. To a prepubescent flack, it asked the question: *In a world of symbolic merchandising, where does imagery end and reality begin?*

There was, you see, the real can, with its wraparound label. And on the label a replica picture of the *can*, but with this cow's head poking out. On scale, the head was the same size as the can from which it poked, leading the prepubescent mind to infer that it was either a shrunken head or a cow with a dwarfed body. In either case, because the image on the can was a reproduction of the image on the can, then the image on the image . . .

There was a lesson there for one who would mature in a Supermedia Age. The closer I looked in 1936, the smaller the cow got. The closer I looked in 1976, the more distant the candidate got. Imagery begets only imagery, so that an infinity of images, on a label or a television screen, cannot bring the viewer closer to, only further removed from, the reality of a product.

A month later, I was in Kansas City when Jerry watched Betty dance with Tony.

That was the night Ford won his party's Presidential nomination. But his flacks—Press Secretary Ron Nessen in the lead—weren't given to metaphysical imagery. They banned live television coverage from the Presidential suite. They even banned print reporters from the Presidential suite. The only exceptions were newsmagazine photographers. Dirck Halstead of *Time* (a friend of the President's personal photographer and most influential public relations advisor, David Hume Kennerly) was able to capture the imagic moment when Jerry Ford, shirt-sleeved without tie, saw Betty on the network trinity, with the superimposed message on the lower third of the screens: FORD WINS.

2

Zoom in the following midday on the empty floor of Kemper
Arena, where two professional image specialists—one representing the Republican National Committee and Jerry Ford, the second the convention pool producer for the three major networks
—are in a huddle alongside the podium. They are negotiating the
technical details of the climactic night ahead: the precise timing,
special lighting, and sound that will bring the closing session of
the 1976 Republican National Convention to the televiewing
public in a style consistent with the needs of both network TV
and the Ford campaign.

Not collusion, only mutually beneficial collaboration. The
same kind of conference had preceded each session of the Democratic National Convention. A modern convention is produced
of, by, and for the television cameras. To disregard that fact of
supermedia political life, as did Barry Goldwater's unruly delegates in 1964 and George McGovern's unscripted followers in
1972, is to risk maiming a Presidential campaign at its inception.

The Goldwaterites, angered by the media, shook their fists at
the TV cameras. Viewed on screens across the country, their
fury came through as a personal threat to the American family
room and neighborhood bar. McGovern's 3 A.M. acceptance
speech, after raucous hours of convention haggling, was considered ruinous to his election chances, in that (1) he had blown
prime-time, proving to anyone who until then had doubted it
that (2) he was incompetent to run the country.

These were the specters from the past that frightened convention managers and network schedulers alike in 1976: the nominee
must have his audience; Walter must have his sleep.

The evening before, when Reagan's delegates overran their
allotted time for spontaneous demonstration, Ford's PR team had
filtered word through the media galleries that it was a plot to
prevent the President's nomination from showing at prime-time.
What worried Bill Carruthers, Ford's audiovisual coordinator,
was that a sequel to that scene, planned or spontaneous, could
push the President's acceptance speech into early morning hours.

Carruthers was scripting the evening's ceremonies to prevent
such a recurrence. Tight time limits were put on the ceremonials
of nominating Bob Dole as Ford's Vice-Presidential running

3

mate, as well as Dole's acceptance speech, then being drafted by a White House staff member. Carruthers had also prepared a documentary film puff on Jerry Ford's life-and-times—a dramatic counterpart to the Carter film shown to the Democratic Convention a month earlier. (Ford's audiovisual expert had produced a similar film for Nixon in 1972.) But showing this film would hardly be a time waste, since it represented several hundred thousand dollars' worth of freebie network advertising. Additional time between the Dole speech and the President's arrival at the auditorium would be filled by Cary Grant's introduction of Betty Ford, who would appear on the convention dais for the first time.

It would not, however, be the first time Betty had occupied center stage at the convention. In that area, too, Carruthers had been a busy collaborator in his employer's behalf. Two evenings before, he and George Murphy, the erstwhile dancer-Senator responsible for convention floor special effects, had choreographed the pas-de-deux that enabled Betty Ford to upstage Nancy Reagan in the Candidates' Wives Royal Entrance Competition.

Opening night of the convention, Nancy had edged Betty in inspiring orchestrated bedlam on the floor. To prevent that embarrassment the following night—more than an embarrassment, really, since the media was measuring crowd enthusiasm for the wives in gauging Ford-Reagan delegate strength—Carruthers and Murphy called in show business reinforcements. The scenario:

Mrs. Ford would arrive at the auditorium early to take her seat in the special VIP guest box with her family and guests, among whom was Tony Orlando. At the moment Nancy arrived to take her seat, Murphy would signal the convention band to break into the Orlando theme, "Tie a Yellow Ribbon Round the Old Oak Tree."

Orlando, who was to Ford at the 1976 convention what Sammy Davis, Jr., was to Nixon in 1972 (though not black, Tony was the next best thing—a show biz ethnic with a black supporting cast), had a VIP seat in the Ford family box. On cue, as the band went into his theme, he leaped to his feet, took Betty by the hand, and began dancing in the aisle.

As Carruthers had figured, the network cameras swung away from Nancy Reagan to what *Newsweek* would describe in its

4

convention coverage as a "spontaneous" dance exhibition in the Ford section. This bit of upstaging, reported *Time*, represented a "triumph" for Mrs. Ford over "her rival." Every little contest counts.

Now, as he huddled with the network pool producer over the final evening's live coverage, Carruthers had another Reagan hitch to smooth into his Ford scenario. The evening before, when the President visited Reagan at the Alameda Plaza, Reagan had agreed to address the convention on closing night. Carruthers' problem was where to fit the Reagan speech into his closing night ceremonies.

Custom would have the losing candidate go to the rostrum before the winner. The nominee's address was always both the climax and coda to the party convention. This year, however, Republican Convention scenarists had pressing reasons to depart from custom.

First, Carruthers and other members of the President's PR team envied the dramatic success that Bob Strauss and Jimmy Carter achieved following Carter's acceptance speech at Madison Square Garden. The Democrats had first brought all elements of their party to the platform in an audiovisual smörgåsbord of milling unity. Then followed "Daddy" King's moving benediction, to bring the convention to a kneeling ovation. Contrary to traditional PR wisdom which dictates, *Never risk topping your candidate*, King's prayer-speech enhanced rather than detracted from Carter's acceptance. Carruthers wanted a similar all-factions smörgåsbord on his closing night platform, with network cameras focused on a Republican Party unified behind Jerry Ford.

A second, more crucial, reason for Carruthers' desire to depart from custom was Ronald Reagan's ability as a crowd-mover. Scheduled prior to Ford, Reagan, even in brief remarks (he planned to give a truncated version of what was to have been his acceptance speech), could make the President's address anticlimactic. Not to forget the commotion a solo Reagan appearance would inevitably create.

Carruthers' solution was a stroke in unorthodox convention scheduling. He decided to cast Reagan as the "Daddy" King of the Republican Convention. Reagan would speak *after* the President. If Ford's acceptance was good, then Reagan's speech would be a tidy unifying coda. On the other hand, if the President reverted to type (despite elaborate rehearsals) and delivered a less-than-inspiring speech, then Reagan's message might salvage the event. It would bring the audience to its feet and the final on-camera scene would be a Republican Party love feast.

LOGISTICS: At a signal given following Ford's speech, as the assorted items in the smörgåsbord gathered on stage—Dole and his wife, Rockefeller and "Happy," the Ford family, et al.—the convention's master spotlight would beam to Reagan's box. The President would then wave to his defeated challenger, inviting him to join the throng. Reagan would accept the invitation. Then, when he reached the dais, Ford would call on him to deliver the convention coda.

It would all appear to be the President's spur-of-the-moment idea. And that was the way we saw it happen, in living color, on the screen, on the screen, on the screen . . .

But wait: in the contrived event (before we see it), there is a glitch. It seems that no one has informed John Rhodes, the convention chairman, of the planned scenario. So that when Reagan appears in his box, to the roar of his followers, Rhodes asks him to come to the podium to say a few words *at that moment*. Reagan refuses. Word spreads along media row that a bitter Nancy has persuaded her husband to forego any display of party unity. It has been a tough year and Nancy, they say, owns the mean streak in the family. Rhodes sends word again: Won't Ron please say just a *few* words? *This isn't my night*, Reagan tells interviewers, stalling. *It's the President's night*. Again he refuses.

Thank God, Carruthers is thinking, that at least we've got a losing candidate who knows how to follow a script.

FAST FORWARD SPEED *September 1976*

ABC-TV, with Barry Jagoda, titled "Media Advisor" to Candidate Jimmy Carter:

Q.: What strategy are you planning in preparing your candidate for the debate?

A.: Naturalness. We're stressing *naturalness*.

6

Programmed spontaneity, calculated naturalness. From the beginning, this was to be the most public relations-oriented Presidential campaign in history. Not simply because Gerald Ford, from the day he assumed the office in August 1974, had operated the most public relations-oriented Presidency in history (yes, more so than Kennedy, Johnson, Nixon). Not simply because post-Watergate federal election spending laws placed a premium on pure flackery, as distinguished from paid advertising exposure, so that campaign schedules had to be built around media events that could thrust the candidate's visage and message into voters' homes at minimum cost.

More than that: the news media, under the pressure of their own accelerated needs—news now, not twice a day but every hour on the hour—would be active participants in the games the flacks would play. Newsmen would become absorbed not merely in covering the candidates, but in the mechanics *of the campaign. In-depth interpretive reporting, the print medium's reaction to television, had reached the point where it was no longer adequate to report merely* what *the candidates did and said each day. The* what *would at times get less space and time than the* how *and* why.

Inevitably, a symbiosis had to develop between the candidate's flacks—the behind-the-scenes operators who could furnish how *and* why *material—and the media. Kansas City was not the first nor would it be the last occasion when the spotlight of publicity beamed where the professional collaborators of manufactured news, explicitly or osmotically, agreed it should beam. The media were no longer observers. They were active players in campaign scenarios. There would be newsmen covering the campaign; newsmen assigned to report on the coverage of the campaign; and, full circle, the phenomenon of newsmen covering the activities of the campaign's media experts. Meaning, newsmen reporting on the very process by which they, and the public, were being manipulated. To the end that very little was left to the imagination of the American people—but much to their nascent cynicism about the process by which they choose a President in the Supermedia Age.*

7

THREE QUICK CUTAWAYS

". . . Carter learned his lines for 1976 not as advertising copy but on the stump in the early months of 1975 . . . Lines that went well were kept. What fell flat was dropped. 'We used to say that's a C performance or that's a B performance or that's an A performance,' Rafshoon recalls. 'We knew instinctively in our minds what made an A and what made a B.'"

JOSEPH LELYVELD,
The New York Times Magazine,
March 28

REAGAN LOOKING
TO TELEVISION
TO SOFTEN IMAGE

". . . Reagan advisors say the television broadcasts are designed to 'reposition him on the issues' that they expect to dominate the Presidential election campaign . . . There also will be an attempt to make it easier for voters to identify with his conservative ideology. Where he has spoken in the past of the 'free enterprise system' he will now stress 'jobs' . . ."

JACK GERMOND, *Washington Star,*
June 27

FORD'S STRATEGY FOR THE FALL:
PROJECTING A "PRESIDENTIAL" IMAGE

". . . The basic strategy for the President's role in the fall, urged on him by advisors who are acutely aware of his limitations as a campaigner, was contained in a lengthy memo submitted to Mr. Ford about two weeks ago. Its basic thrust has largely been accepted by the President, campaign and White House aides said . . ."

EDWARD WALSH, *Washington Post,*
August 17

PERSPECTIVE   *Plus ça change, plus c'est la même chose*

"This wild political year, so unpredictable in every other respect, has authenticated the trend toward the politics of style. Not that issues have disappeared from American politics, but the way a politician handles himself on the issues seems to have more impact on voters than the specifics of his position. A candidate's bearing is more significant than his promises. Personality overshadows policy. Charm, or the lack of it, cancels out much of the usual stuff of political debate . . . Television has removed the middleman between politicians and voters and intensified a one-to-one relationship between the candidate on the tube and the voter in an armchair. Politics threatens to become a spectator sport, subject to all the vicarious thrills of contest and climax . . ."

> PENN KIMBALL, writing in *Saturday Review*, June 8, 1968, the year Richard Nixon was elected

"The networks' image of American politics (that is, politics as a game and the campaign as a horserace) formed the basis of the great majority of television news stories about the . . . Democratic campaign. The contenders were engaged in a horserace for a political prize, and they employed certain strategies and tactics to gain support from various sectors of the population which would move them along the track. Such reporting makes the campaign an exciting and dramatic contest—but it also encourages the view that American elections are little more than a struggle among individuals seeking personal gain and power . . ."

> MARC PLATTNER, writing in *The Alternative*, November 1972, the year Richard Nixon was re-elected

UPDATE *Plus c'est la même chose, plus c'est la même chose*

WINTER BOOK, 1975

"The preliminaries are over, the primaries are about to begin. The largest Presidential horse race in the Party's history is underway."

> *The Democratic Review*, Autumn 1975

January, 1976
  "A-a-a-a-n-d THEY'RE OFF!!!"

> *Time*

February

"The game of President-making has become a kind of Winter Olympics in New Hampshire—a quadrennial sport in which the players and their entourages often outnumber the crowds."

Newsweek

March

"With your help and support I'll stay in the saddle four more years."

Candidate GERALD FORD

"The ball game is in the second inning and the score is 10 to 9."

Candidate RONALD REAGAN

"The football game is in the first quarter and it's a long way from the goal line."

Candidate GEORGE WALLACE

April

"I think that Coach Carter, frankly, is blaming the umpire before the game is over."*

Candidate HENRY JACKSON

"Never underestimate the importance of momentum* in these Presidential elections. Once that avalanche starts down the ski slope, get out of the way."

Candidate MORRIS UDALL

May

"Ford has real momentum—real momentum—President Ford has real momentum."*

Pollster LOUIS HARRIS,
ABC-TV, post-Oregon

June

"DOWN THE HOME STRETCH"

Newsweek

(* first recorded mangled sports metaphor of campaign)
(* 120th recorded use of "momentum" in campaign)
(* 121st, 122nd, 123rd, recorded uses of "momentum" in campaign)

July–August
"The name of the game is delegates."

> Used by WALTER CRONKITE,
> CBS-TV, twelve recorded times

"The name of the game is delegates."

> Used by JOHN CHANCELLOR-DAVID BRINKLEY,
> NBC-TV, eight recorded times

"The name of the game is delegates."

> Used by HARRY REASONER,
> ABC-TV, ten recorded times

September
"THE KICK-OFF"

> *Time*

"It was like a bad baseball game, where after seven innings everybody wants to go home."

> Candidate GENE MCCARTHY,
> quoted after first debate

October
"Jimmy Carter moved into New Mexico today like a prize fighter moving in for the knockout."

> SAM DONALDSON, ABC-TV

Pregame Warm-up December 1974– December 1975

The Retired Flack, a veteran of two national campaigns, two dozen state and local election contests, 378 media events, 745 photo opportunities, not to forget countless balloon rises at political rallies, will sit this one out. He travels to San Francisco and meets a Long Shot. He travels to Montgomery and sees a Front-runner. He returns to Washington and watches the Process in Gestation . . .

December 1974   Breakfast with Jimmy

FOR AMERICA'S THIRD CENTURY, WHY NOT THE BEST?

The slogan has a subliminal message. The candidate's cover photo on the four-color slick brochure is angled to give him a certain look, to evoke a memory. There is something reminiscent about the upfront puff hairstyle, the deep-browed eyeset, the gonial swell.

Jimmy Carter and his public-image advisors would remind us of John F. Kennedy—just as fourteen years ago Kennedy and his PR men stirred memories among Democrats of Franklin D. Roosevelt, with the slogan: A TIME FOR GREATNESS.

There was brash arrogance about the Kennedy slogan, and there is brash arrogance about Jimmy Carter's. For a junior Senator from Massachusetts with a middling record as a lawmaker to suggest his potential for GREATNESS presumed a lot; for an out-going one-term *Governor* of Georgia to hit you boldface with the suggestion that he represents THE BEST presumes even more. But brisk understatement in campaign slogans is a luxury that can be afforded only by known quantities. I LIKE IKE was good for a war hero with a 99.9 percent recognition factor. Outside Georgia, Jimmy Carter's nonrecognition runs to 98 percent. A little brashness, if it attracts attention, could be all to the good.

For that matter, Carter isn't doing that well *inside* Georgia, where, according to Reg Murphy, there is no heavy run on I LIKE JIMMY buttons. The challenge for Carter's imagectomists was capsuled two days ago, when he announced his Presidential candidacy in Atlanta. Reaction varied between stunned silence and patronizing smirks. Before the Governor left his own state capital to fly here for his first public appearance as a Presidential campaigner, he was welcomed to national politics by the Atlanta *Constitution* headline:

JIMMY CARTER IS RUNNING FOR WHAT?

Murphy, the *Constitution*'s editor, claims that there is a disease which afflicts one-term Southern governors when they undergo the trauma of leaving the mansion after a lifetime single-mindedly spent getting there: they go berserk. Some turn to drink. Others to delusions that they can handpick a successor. Yet others to odd variations on the theme of freezing time, staying close to power. Carter's immediate predecessor, Lester Maddox, the Ax-Handle King, for example, threatened to run for President in 1968 but was persuaded to settle for a quiet readjustment to society as Lieutenant Governor.

In Georgia, it seems, the disease is even inheritable: when Eugene Talmadge died as Governor-elect in 1947, his son Herman ("Humman") stormed the mansion, ringed it with National Guardsmen, and refused to surrender it to a pretender claimant, the Lieutenant-Governor-elect, M. E. Thompson. For some time, Georgia had two governors, until the courts ruled against Humman and Divine Right; a demonstration of judicial *lèse majesté* that Georgia voters corrected at the next election.

But that was the raucous politics of Old Georgia and the Old South. This December morning, two weeks before Jimmy Carter's term as Governor expires, two years before the Presidential election, I am attending a group breakfast of a dozen or so people gathered in the upper reaches of the San Francisco Hilton to meet and break sourdough with another self-advertised exponent of the New South.

THE NEW SOUTH: that perennial Atlanta Chamber of Commerce puff phrase. When Henry W. Grady was editor of the *Constitution* ("Covers Dixie Like the Dew"), he delivered his address by that title to an elite group of Eastern Establishmentarians, the New England Society of New York, December 2, 1886; Grady's Yankee audience was captivated by an Atlanta journalist's depiction of a benighted region finally come to terms with the verdict of Appomattox; a Deep South which, two decades after Sherman's March, had put aside magnolia memories and racialism in favor of industrial and social progress.

Created in Atlanta by Atlantans, the New South has since become a stock public relations image resurrected for gullible Yankees, going on nine decades, whenever Georgia elects a Governor who is either a racial moderate or, in the alternative, doesn't wear brown shoes with blue suits. Either case, the idea is to attract Northern capital—industrial plants, branch offices—to Georgia and the Southeast.

Carl Sanders, the man Carter defeated in the 1970 Governor's race, was featured in the Eastern press as a New Southern leader, a liberal-moderate on race. Reg Murphy contends that Carter beat Sanders on just that score, with a blatant appeal to the Ax-Handle King's white racist constituency. Jimmy Carter, says Henry W. Grady's (and Ralph McGill's) successor as editor of Georgia's largest newspaper, speaks with forked drawl.

But didn't Carter restore Martin Luther King's portrait to the State Capitol, after Maddox had it removed? And doesn't Atlanta's black community support Carter? Murphy says that restoring King's portrait to the Capitol wall was cosmetic, the kind of calculated gesture Jimmy Carter is skilled at making whenever he wants to cover up some ugly political truth about himself.

"Jimmy Carter doesn't have any credibility left in Georgia," claims Murphy. "He's traveled the state too many times. He's made too many promises to too many people. After four years, they've compared notes. He's through in Georgia. This Presidential thing is a monumental ego trip."

> *I'd rather be a lamppost on Lenox Avenue*
> *than Governor of the State of Georgia . . .*

The invidious old Harlem comparison comes to mind as the Ego Tripper approaches, escorted by his personal aide for this occasion, Peter Bourne.

Who is Jimmy Carter? Is he Henry Grady's New South redeemer? Reg Murphy's sonofabitch? It makes no difference, at least not today. He is the only Presidential candidate within three thousand miles, and the Retired Flack is pressed for column material.

Jimmy Carter wears black shoes with his blue suit. This could be New South progressivism or simply a hangover from the years he spent at Annapolis where, the Governor lets drop (within five minutes after our introduction), he not only attended, but graduated. He also studied under Hyman Rickover.

Carter's association with Rickover quickly surfaced in all early campaign conversations with what he considered the "conservative" press. His purpose: to let interviewers know that what we had here was no mere branchhead peckerwood. When, however, talking to younger, non-Establishment members of the media, he spoke of his admiration for Bob Dylan, Greg Allman . . .

DAVID NORDAN, Political Editor, *Atlanta Journal*, October 1976:

"*Carter is no doubt like a lot of country boys who stumble on an education and a bus ticket out of places like Plains. They spend a lifetime mindlessly trying to convince themselves, the Mailers and the smart set who read* Playboy *interviews that they really are intellectuals and they don't hail from Tobacco Road . . .*

"Carter, as Governor, hardly let a celebrity pass through Atlanta without inviting him or her to the mansion. He is one of the most unabashed name-droppers in America, and he'll quote some obscure philosopher you never heard of quicker than a cat can scratch . . ."

Carter is a small man, crisply turned out for a full day's campaigning. There will be a press conference later in the morning, speech to the North American Congress on Alcohol and Drug Problems, the host organization for his visit, then a meeting, I have been surreptitiously informed, with a wealthy prospective contributor. (Jimmy, confides my informant, "excels at one-on-one sessions.")

By one Retired Flack's subjective political public relations criteria for Presidential candidates, the Governor grades, on initial impact, six on a scale of ten: fair handshake; nice political smile, Southern gentlemen genre (broad, yet self-effacing); but an accent which, like my wife's, hits strangers as incomprehensible, i.e., soft-Deep Southern spoken with a clipped, rapid inflection. Southerners are not supposed to speak quickly, as George Wallace has learned the hard way; it violates the rules.

For the moment there are five of us, separated from the other guests at the breakfast, Bourne having slipped the candidate aside to talk to me, the only journalist around.

We are off in a corner, sipping orange juice, launched into such earnest political topics as Southern accents and Hyman Rickover, the Wit & Wisdom Of. There are (1) Gus Hewlett, executive secretary of the host organization; (2) Bourne, the British-born Carter aide who handed me that brochure the afternoon before, and asked whether my wife and I would be interested in coming to "meet Jimmy at breakfast"; (3) my wife, Dale, an expatriate Alabamian who, having retained her accent through fifteen years of exile in Washington, D.C., is comparing notes on regional phonetics with (4) the soon-to-be-ex-Governor of Georgia, for whom (5) I, the Retired Flack, suddenly feel sorry.

Jimmy Carter reminds me of some of my erstwhile Southern

political clients who kept playing the game after their legs and timing had gone, e.g., Gordon Persons, an Alabama Governor during the early 1950s, who ended his career running for probate judge; "Big Jim" Folsom, a two-term Governor, who spent his next decade qualifying for offices, moving rung-by-rung down the political ladder, losing all the way.

Carter seems to deserve better. One-on-one, the man, despite Reg's low opinion, projects a reserve which, in another era, would be described as dignity. He is nevertheless making a fool of himself Lester Maddox-style.

Gus Hewlett has introduced me as a Washington PR expert in a former life (although of the wrong party) with two national campaigns under my belt. The first with Goldwater in '64 (L), the second with Agnew in '72 (W).* Unsurprisingly, Carter does not appear anxious to solicit my advice. Not simply because I am of the wrong party, however. I recognize the symptoms of the politician who has made his move and couldn't care less what any "expert," Democrat or Republican, might tell him.

"I'm not running as a regional candidate. I'm not out to stop George Wallace, or anybody else," Carter says. "I'm in this to win."

Carter knows that if he picks up a telephone and calls fifty political public relations "experts" around the country, they will fill his ear with advice he doesn't want to hear: either some paraphrase of the *Constitution* headline, or a suggestion that if he's serious about national office he ought to think in more practical terms . . .

Vice-President Carter? Possible. With the right handling, a Southerner *could* become the Democratic Vice-Presidential candidate in 1976, especially if he were able to sabotage his fellow Southerner, George Wallace. But Carter should understand that no ex-Governor of Georgia can become a Presidential nominee, even if there weren't a nonrecognition factor to overcome. No. He can't because he is going up against a prejudice bigger than the one John F. Kennedy faced in 1960. Much bigger, more complex: if Jesus Christ Himself returned to proclaim Roman Catholicism the True Faith, Christianity could survive; but if He

* But later forfeited.

spoke His parables in a Georgia accent, St. Patrick's would convert to a mosque within a week.

"Kennedy image?"
The afternoon before, Peter Bourne went blank at the suggestion that his candidate's brochure is pregnant with subliminal meaning. This wasn't too surprising. Amateurs committed to a cause refuse to acknowledge that manipulation plays any part in their candidate's Campaign to Win Men's Minds. And Bourne, intellectual though he is, seems to have all the inner faith of those dedicated zealots of the 1964 Goldwater crusade: the Hot-Eyed Ones fervent in the notion that though all politicians are bred in sin, theirs was somehow the product of an immaculate conception.

Peter Bourne is anything but a hot-eyed zealot. He is buttondown, very proper, possessing the manner and accent of an Oxford don. So much so that if, as Gus Hewlett says, Bourne is a key advisor, this tells me something special about Jimmy Carter: Southern governors I have known don't include that sort of baggage in their immediate entourage; advisors, that is, who look and sound strange in Opp, Alabama, or Winder, Georgia.

An M.D. graduate of Atlanta's Emory University, Bourne is a clinical psychiatrist specializing in drug and alcoholism treatment. He and his wife, Mary King, began working for Carter during the 1970 Governor's race, then joined his administration in Atlanta. Since 1972, Bourne has lived in Washington, D.C., first as a federal official in the drug-alcoholism field, more recently as an independent professional consultant. He has been Carter's political advance man, making contact with the National Capital political-press Establishment: the provincial candidate's ambassador-without-portfolio to the outer world.

It was Bourne who first interested Carter in the drug-alcoholism treatment field. As a result, says Hewlett, Georgia now has one of the better treatment programs in the country. And it was Bourne who months ago arranged for the Governor's appearance in San Francisco; fortuitous scheduling for a Presidential candidate who wants to give his campaign a national rather than mere regional look.

"Well, it's possible someone might see a resemblance," Peter

Bourne told me after re-examining the Kelly green Carter brochure. "But there's nothing contrived. Not at all. Jimmy doesn't care for that sort of thing. Jimmy is just himself."

ALL CARTER MATERIAL COMES IN GREEN: *brochures, buttons, bumper stickers. The same bright green he used in his winning Governor's race, says Alex Wilson, graphics man for Carter's Atlanta ad agency, Gerald Rafshoon & Company. "He won with it then, he felt good about it, so we kept it," adds Wilson. Besides, in the Bicentennial red-white-blue year, "it's distinctive."*

"Greening," for freshness, rebirth: "Carter didn't want anything too sophisticated," Wilson later tells John Twohey of the Washington Post. *"He wanted good graphics. But nothing that looked too much like Madison Avenue. Nothing too slick."*

Jimmy Himself informs me that the brochure was produced by "Jerry Rafshoon's people." If there was any intent to suggest a physical resemblance to John F. Kennedy, says the candidate, he isn't aware of it.

The right answer. Smart candidates treat questions about their public relations/advertising as they would questions about personal toilet habits. It's something that happens on the other side of a closed door. Nobody's business but their own or their proctologist's.

Does the President piss from a standing or sitting position? Psychology Today *wants to know.*

Even in a sunshine age, there are limits. Discretion is the better part of political public relations. (But I wonder how Open Door Jerry Ford would handle that question?)

"I have my own style," Carter is saying. The slogan? It goes back to his days under Rickover. There was, it seems, this traumatic session between Hyman the Master and Jimmy the Apprentice.

"Have you done your best?" asked the Master.

"Not always," replied the Apprentice.

"Why not?" snapped the Master.

Carter says that this Question changed his life. Got him to thinking. And that's how Peter Bourne's candidate would have me believe his slogan was born. I'm not buying. But Jimmy Himself does make it sound convincing.

"I don't get to talk to national columnists," Jimmy Carter is saying, "unless they're either going to or coming from Montgomery. We operate a correspondent's way-station in Atlanta."

"You know what they say in Birmingham, Governor. They say, if you die in Alabama and go to hell . . ."

"You'll have to lay over in Atlanta." Carter finishes the line and grins.

Despite his mocking complaint, Carter knows that operating out of Atlanta has given him a large edge over other politicians of his region competing for national attention, much as it gave Ellis Arnall and other Georgia governors in past years. An edge, for example, over Reubin Askew, who works out of Tallahassee, neither a transportation vortex nor regional headquarters for major news media.

It took George Wallace to get the big Eastern correspondents to transfer to Southern Airways, off the Miami route. Wallace's emergence as a national figure—more important, national threat—has worked to Carter's advantage in terms of national publicity. Traveling correspondents from points North and East arrive in Atlanta directly from George's bone-dry mansion—where iced tea and hot rhetoric are the standard guest fare—to be greeted by the Governor of Georgia with a good stiff shot of Scotch (straight from Jimmy's personal den cabinet, the one opened with a special key). Then, over lunch or dinner, they contrast the Voice of Montgomery with the Voice of Atlanta.

Nothing says more of the impact of the modern news media on the national political structure than the fact that a lameduck Governor of Georgia—one who doesn't spend his idle hours riding bicycles backward at circuses—can believe that he is a viable candidate for President; a belief based on Jimmy Carter's not merely comprehending the new rules of Supermedia Politics, but understanding that nothing is so attractive to Yankee correspondents (or Southern newsmen gone North, like "Scotty" Reston, Tom Wicker) as a progressive-talking, racially enlightened "New South" political spokesman.

Ninety years, almost to the day, and Henry Grady's line is still

21

selling to gullible Yankees. But could it be that all Jimmy Carter is really angling for is a new paper mill for Sumter County, Georgia?

January 1975   The Front-runner

"A thirteen-year-old Alabama junior high student hasn't known any Governor except George Wallace," Frank Lee tells me en route down Interstate 65 to Montgomery from Birmingham. "It's like our generation and Franklin Roosevelt."

Lee has been Wallace's public relations-media pro since 1961. he is making a tangential connection between the inaugural we are about to witness and what will be a Wallace campaign theme in 1976.

The polls show Alabama's Governor as the front-runner for the Democratic Presidential nomination, the favorite (excluding Ted Kennedy, who says he isn't running) of a plurality of party rank-and-file. But what the rank-and-file remember is George Wallace, a hyperkinetic, mobile bundle of political instinct, jabbing in the air at power-crazy federal judges and pointy-headed bureaucrats.

That was the candidate cheered by the blue collars of Milwaukee and Detroit in 1964, 1968, and 1972. But there is an image lag and what Wallace's team now has to work with is a wraith of the Old George. Their candidate still jabs. His references to power-crazy judges and pointy-heads are still pungent, his political instinct intact. But something vital is gone.

Ninety percent of successful political image-making consists of doing the best with what you have. Shaping the material at hand to advantage. You have a disability—political, moral, physical? First, try to joke it away, provided you have a candidate who can deliver a punch line. So George has this one-liner: "I'm not like some folks in government," he tells his audiences, "I'm only paralyzed *below* the neck." He delivers it well, it tickles the crowd. But they laugh nervously. The joke doesn't answer those inner doubts, can a man in a wheelchair help blue collars send a message to Washington?

Something more is needed. A reassuring image out of history. Just as Jimmy Carter's imagectomists would project his physical qualities to suggest JFK, George Wallace's staff would use his

physical disability to remind us of a Great President-in-a-
wheelchair.

George Wallace, as his followers once knew him, is no more.
But might he be *perceived* as another FDR?

THE SEMANTICS OF MODERN AMERICAN POLITICS
1976

perceive\per-śēv\ *vt* ME *perceiven*, fr. OF *perceivre* fr. L *per-
cipere:* 1. to attain awareness and understanding of. 2. to become
aware of through the senses. With its nominal form (*perception*),
the most overworked word of the recent Presidential election year,
testimony of the impact of the image-making arts on the consciousness of journalists covering the 1976 campaign (e.g., "Reagan's
selection of Schweiker as a running mate is *perceived* as an effort
to . . ." In former years, Reagan's selection would have been
"*thought* to be, etc."). Supplanting prizewinning cliches from
previous campaigns: *credibility* (1972), *peaked* (1968), *mainstream*
(1964), *charisma* (1960).

When we arrived at the State Capitol, I find out there won't be
an Inaugural Ball this year. *Hard times, unemployment lines,* explains Billy Joe Camp, Wallace's press secretary. *A ball would be
inappropriate.*

Vintage George Wallace, playing to his populist constituency.
Taking a page out of the book of his favorite President: in 1933,
FDR did not attend his Inaugural Ball. *Hard times, it would have
been inappropriate . . .*

This will be Alabama's fourth consecutive Wallace inauguration, counting the ceremony in January 1967, when George's
first wife was sworn in as surrogate Governor. Never one for
frills, Wallace has turned what was once Montgomery's quadrennial social gala into a drab affair, routine as the extra point kick at
one of Bear Bryant's football games up the road in Tuscaloosa.

Bring back Big Jim Folsom, complains a frustrated state Senator in the lounge of the Governor's House Motel. Big Jim, roar-
ing through the night for "champagne for the ladies, Bourbon-
and-branchwater for the gents," leading countless choruses of his
favorite, "On Top of Old Smoky."

23

Frank Lee is vice-president of the Birmingham firm of Luckie & Forney, the largest advertising/PR agency in Alabama and, outside Atlanta, one of the biggest in the Southeast. Forty-eight years old, a native Alabamian, Lee has been senior account supervisor of all of Wallace's winning gubernatorial campaigns and two of his Presidential races.

Lee's forte is campaign administration: mobilizing and organizing the assortment of technical skills that go into the production of a modern media promotional campaign. He does not lack the PR showman's touch, either, having supplied Wallace's winning 1962 slogan, "Stand Up for Alabama"; later enlarged, to fit the candidate's expanded political horizon, to "Stand Up for America."

Luckie & Forney bills $10 million a year, primarily from industrial and commercial, not political clients. The State of Alabama tourism account is an exception, the plum that falls to the image-makers who handle a successful Governor's race. Luckie & Forney, and Frank Lee, have won four straight during the past decade and a half. They have done well by George Wallace, and he by them.

Nevertheless, says Lee, the agency has opted out of any more Wallace Presidential campaigns. National races put too much manpower drain on what, by New York standards, is a small- to medium-size firm. George will use another Alabama agency for time-and-space purchases in 1976. But if extra technical help is needed on television production, Lee will be on call.

"I don't know whether George plans to run in the primaries or as an independent," Lee says of Wallace's 1976 plans. "I doubt whether George himself knows."

But the Wallace for President organization, operating out of Montgomery, is taking in campaign funds, geared to go either way.

"They never really stopped after 1972."

Lee imported me to provide color commentary for the statewide inaugural telecast. As a certified Washington expert I am to supply Alabama viewers with profound Brinkleyesque insights into "the national significance" of the event. Profundity on ice: contrary to the blurb in Luckie & Forney's tourism brochure about the tonic quality of Alabama year-round climate, this January morning in a makeshift outdoor TV booth in the Cradle of the Confederacy is as brutal as anything endured at a Washington inauguration.

It is lip-numbing cold. The script calls for a Wallace inaugural address lasting thirty minutes. However, Lee says it all depends on whether Wallace is inspired to depart from text, to speak "from the heart." We light a candle that George is by now sated with making inaugural speeches and cuts it short.

Years ago Lee told me that Wallace despises written speech texts, preferring to speak from notes; or, when he really gets wound up, to wing it. This is high-risk politics for most national politicians, but George has the sure semantic radar of a populist leader who knows his peepul. He seldom, if ever, blows his act with a careless line delivered from a podium. He can dance verbal jigs around the Sunday afternoon TV panels, leaving the sharpest interviewer at a loss.

Circa 1968 Wallace versus Wallace
People say you're a racist, Mike tells George in a CBS-TV interview.
Well, snaps George, they say the same about you.
Me? Whoever said that about me?
Why, replies George, the Kerner Commission, that's who. They wrote that America was a racist society, that all whites were racist, and furthermore . . .

Television, however, is not the communications medium George Wallace was born to. Nor radio, where, on a national hook-up, his disembodied south Alabamese does his cause no service. He remains, by instinct and early training, the basic American spellbinder, a twentieth-century politician who retains the oratorical flourish of the pre-electronic age, when public speakers were graded on an ability to be heard, without benefit of microphone or sound amplifier, by the most remote, half-deaf citizen on the outer fringe of the county courthouse lawn.

The style is overheated, strident, the antithesis of everything McLuhan preaches about effective communication in the cool electronic age. Wallace has worked at mastering the televised studio speech, speaking at a slower clip, enunciating more clearly (hitting those "g's" at the end of his gerunds; the absence of which, except for Walter Cronkite, downgrades a public speaker among Middle American television-radio audiences).

But the Wallace that is remembered is not the TV studio speaker. It is the Wallace of the TV filmclips during the 1960s, sending his message.

"Now some writers make sport of my sayin' Pres-i-*dent* instead o' *Pres*-i-dent. But you know, there are more peepul in this country that say Pres-i-*dent* than *Pres*-i-dent. And they're the peepul gonna vote for me."

GEORGE WALLACE

Jimmy Carter, as I recall, says *Pres*-i-dent. There are other differences between the two Southerners—beyond the artificial labeling of Old/New and the superficial similarity of their careers.

Both come from small Black Belt communities, but Carter carries the soft accent of Black Belt aristocracy. He is the scion of a family that owns the town, while Wallace is of more modest stock. Jimmy graduated from Annapolis—along about the time George was a World War Two Air Corps sergeant.

Wallace despises Carter, George *perceives* Carter as a Judas goat for *his* constituency, a tool of the Democratic Establishment in Washington. That two-faced sumbitch, says George, I'll clean his plow like I did Terry Sanford's. Meaning Wallace figures to whup Jimmy in Georgia the way he whupped Sanford in his home state of North Carolina four years ago.

Twelve years and three Presidential elections ago, Wallace stood at the top of the Capitol steps for his first inauguration. He took the oath on the gold star where Jeff Davis was sworn in as President of the Confederacy. George promised his peepul "segregation forever." Confederate flags waved. The bands played "Dixie."

If there has been any national significance to this fourth Wallace inaugural, I intone, wrapping up my Brinkley imitation

26

at the end of the long, frigid morning, it is not in the forgettable rhetorical meringue of the Governor's forty-minute address. It is in the absence of the Stars and Bars, or the rendition of even one chorus of the Confederate anthem. Instead, a black singing group, personally selected by Cornelia Wallace, sings uplifting spirituals. The new Wallace Cabinet is on the platform as he takes the oath. It includes the first black Cabinet official in Alabama history. But most significant of all, if by "national significance" is meant George Wallace's Presidential campaign, is the fact that he is sworn in and makes his speech standing in that special apparatus, at the *foot* of the Capitol stairs.

Afterward, the Governor goes to his office and receives all visitors. Anyone who wants to shake his hand. The line snakes around the Capitol for blocks. George, with Cornelia beside him, sits for six hours more, shaking hands, greeting old friends.

"Six hours!" a Wallace staffer points out the next morning. "Don't tell me the Old Man doesn't have the stamina . . ."

"Southern governors didn't seriously run for Presidential nominations. Southern governors didn't carry preferential primaries in Yankee states. Southern politicians didn't address Harvard assemblies. Southern governors didn't debate the issues with students in the March snows of Nebraska.

"Wallace did."

> GEORGE WALLACE, speaking of himself
> in the third person, past tense,
> July 1976

January 1975 The New Jackson

Congressman Andrew Young is hosting a reception for Atlanta's black Mayor, Maynard Jackson. A late-arriving Senator moves quickly through the crowd, takes the honored guest by the arm and leads him—250 pounds of profusely sweating politician—to the outer lobby. Maynard Jackson pulls a damp handkerchief from his breast pocket and wipes his forehead. The Senator asks some aggressive bystanders pushing to get into the act to move aside, please, this will be a two-man shot.

Flashbulb . . . The Senator apologizes to Maynard Jackson for having a previously scheduled engagement, shakes the Mayor's hand one more time, and departs, photographer in tow. Total time elapsed, entry-to-exit: ten minutes.

"I think," says a House staff aide, checking his watch as the Senator's retinue moves down the corridor, "we just saw Scoop shave Hubert's record for a quick drop-in photo opportunity by a minute and a half."

July 1975

What we have here is a well-bankrolled effort to *communicate*. There is a New Scoop Jackson being rehearsed and readied for the 1976 primaries. The old unsparkling model, remembered for its ability to mesmerize small audiences into semicoma in 1972, is undergoing radical imagectomy.

To date, however, the operation is only a partial success. There have been minor complications. Recently, following Scoop's effort to lure Warren Beatty and other glittering West Coast activists to his cause, some of the Senator's hawkish friends warned him against sacrificing too much old substance for new fluff.

Jackson in the past has been a Senator who disdained "phony PR." But given his setback three years ago he has gathered around him more flacks than you can shake a *shtik* at. There are:

Steve Ross, a Miami pro, responsible for Jackson's "public presentation"; Lloyd Wright, former PR chief of the American Association of Retired Persons, the "media director"; and last, but most important, Bob Keefe, overall campaign director, a canny publicist with a decade-and-a-half experience on Capitol Hill handling Democratic senatorial races.

Much professional talent, maybe too much. Whenever there is talk of a New Anybody on the national political scene, it testifies to some intrinsic, rather than cosmetic, flaw in the Old Model. Jackson operates under the same handicap that buried Bob Taft's Presidential campaigns in the 1940s and '50s. He has intellect, experience, a substantial legislative record, but somehow doesn't connect. There is an element missing, a spark, the ability to project beyond a narrow constituent base. It is an element that money can't buy. In 1952 there was a "New Taft," with a cadre of public relations professionals. They tried to reshape his public image, peddle him as "Fighting Bob." It didn't sell. PR Law No. 6: You can't squeeze blood into a turnip.

Now Scoop, responding to professional advice, has hired a speech instructor to help him get the lard out of his words; gone off the starches to slim down, if not for health's sake, then for the camera's; had an operation to correct a drooping eyelid; even let his hair grow out, letting it lap ever so slightly over the ears. (Not too radical an imagectomy, understand.)

We shall see. Two minutes into any speech, "Fighting Bob" would always revert to Robert Alphonso Taft. PR Law No. 7: You can't teach an old pol new tricks; though the corollary is, if the money is right, flacks will try to find a loophole.

"I have only one opponent for this nomination. My opponent is George Wallace. *Period.*"

HENRY JACKSON, mid-1975

Late 1975 (Uh, Senator Jackson . . .)
SARGENT SHRIVER: "We'll take the primary route as Jack Kennedy did in 1960" . . . LLOYD BENTSEN: "The Roosevelt candidate of the seventies" . . . MORRIS UDALL. "One or more of the group of center-left candidates has to stand out in New Hampshire and Massachusetts and move from there to successes in New York and Wisconsin" . . . MILTON SHAPP: "The federal government must be run on a business-like basis, with executive leadership and managerial skill" . . . BIRCH BAYH: "I want to kick some tails, to get things moving."

August 1975 Ronald Reagan Is a Radiclib
The Party of Principle supports:
. . . Repeal of all laws interfering with the right to commit suicide as an infringement of the ultimate right of an individual to manage his or her own life.

Plank of the Libertarian Party
platform, adopted in convention,
New York City, 1975

Like a semi-rehabilitated addict, the professional image-maker who leaves the business fights a visceral instinct to manipulate men and events: the hubris that first led him to become a political PR man. Temptation is everywhere.

Some never fully recover. Jack Valenti, who flacked for LBJ, is now president of the Motion Picture Producers Association, one of the sweetest six-figure sinecures ever devised by bourgeois man, and yet Valenti drools at the idea of getting back to campaign life. Like a shot of coke in the nose, he tells *Rolling Stone*. That's what political show biz is.

This Retired Flack has more painful memories. A difference in clientele, but mine were more like a rabies series in the belly button. When losing with Goldwater is your fondest recollection . . . I will sit this one out. And the next one. And the one after that.

Yesterday morning the Retired Flack takes a phone call from the friend of a forty-six-year-old Charlottesville, Virginia, lawyer running for President.

"Who?"

"Roger MacBride," my caller repeats. "He was nominated by the Libertarians a few weeks back. 'CBS Evening News' carried it. Roger needs help."

Yeah. I remember the segment: a political convention held in the summer of 1975 to write a platform and nominate a national ticket for an election to be held autumn of '76. We start these things earlier every quadrennial. But if an ex-Governor of Georgia can announce for President in December 1974, why shouldn't something called the Libertarian Party go the whole route six months later, if only to get coverage they won't get a year from now?

"I'm out of the practice," I remind my caller. "But for curiosity—*why* do you want me to talk to Roger MacBride?"

"He needs help from somebody with national PR experience."

He says it out loud, without euphemisms. The hookers' union has been legitimatized.

When I began my career in the "profession" in the early 1950s, political candidates shrank from any public mention of "PR."

Even references to the use of public opinion polls were off-limits. The first national pollster imported into Alabama for a political survey was instructed to keep his client's identity secret. In those days, political PR men were spirited into a state and stashed incognito in a motel on the outskirts of town, kept around only for late-night meetings with the candidate and his staff.

But by the 1960s a new political breed felt no need to hide their use of modern techniques of mass persuasion. They would in fact come to be graded by the media itself for their demonstrated skills in using those techniques. In this new sophisticated age, public opinion polls would become PR weapons to intimidate the opposition and give credibility to a campaign. A candidate for Senator in the Midwest has hired Spencer-Roberts? Then he has to be taken seriously. Lou Harris polling for a gubernatorial candidate in Texas? The candidate must have something going for him. After all, didn't Harris work with *Kennedy?*

By 1972 a Presidential campaign would be faulted by newsmen (while they at the same time expressed scorn for PR technology) because of the candidate's inability to control his party's convention for prime-time exposure. Inept McGovern, said the media critics. Doesn't he know how to manipulate us? Because if he doesn't (the ultimate implication of the criticism), how can he possibly hope to *manipulate the country?*

In the seventies, even speechwriters have gone public. The "ghost" is up front, before the cameras. Candidates once insisted that they wrote all their own speeches, every word. Another myth shot to hell. The ability to attract top-drawer speechwriters, like the ability to retain the best in PR/advertising talent, points up the caliber of the campaign—especially on the Presidential level. Now candidates—not only Establishmentarians, but fringe candidates as well—openly seek the services of members of the "profession."

ROGER LEA MACBRIDE: Four years ago, my caller advises, he gained minor historical footnotoriety as the Virginia Republican elector who exercised his option for independence, casting his vote not for Nixon-Agnew but for the Libertarian Party ticket of John Hospers of California and Theodora Nathan of Oregon.

31

But the price of political independence comes high. Afterward embraced by the tiny Libertarian Party (3,671 votes in '72) in the four states in which Hospers-Nathan were on the ballot), Mac-Bride was nominated this year by acclamation.

"As I say, I'm finished with political PR," I repeat to Roger MacBride's friend, "but tell me: do the Libertarians consider themselves America's third, fourth, or fifth party?"

"Talk to the man. Find out for yourself."

It will be a waste of time, MacBride's and mine. But temptation is Temptation. Why fight a visceral instinct in a dull season?

So I meet Candidate MacBride, next afternoon, in the lounge of the Federal City Club (my choice), three blocks from the White House. This, I think as we shake hands and sink slowly into our nineteenth-century Eastern Establishment chair cushions, is about as close as he'll ever get to 1600 Pennsylvania. Unless some sympathetic U.S. Senator gets him a Wednesday morning tour pass.

MacBride begins a Libertarian spiel over midafternoon Cokes (his choice). I am quickly corrected on one semantic misconception. He is not a "conservative" on the order of past candidates I have worked for. Libertarian conservatism, it develops, embraces a compound of principles acceptable to both Goldwaterites and McGovernites.

It is a mind-bending parlay. Here I see the leader of a party that takes in followers of the two biggest losers in American Presidential election history.

"Goldwater and McGovern followers have more in common than most people realize," MacBride informs me. "Both movements were grass-root. Both were opposed to big impersonal government. The McGovernites called it the System, the Goldwaterites, the bureaucracy . . ."

The Libertarian standard-bearer is a horn-rimmed cherub, low-keyed without the surface intensity that usually radiates from candidates who run on Principle. Intense, but not wholly out-of-touch. Compared to Jimmy Carter, for example, who actually believes he can become President, Roger MacBride talks common sense. His ambition is only to expand his party's base. He wants the Libertarian ticket on the ballot in thirty key states. What is important, he says, is getting the Libertarian message through to the people of America. Roger MacBride's political future is secondary. He is only a Symbol of the Principle. But could such a candidate be a harbinger? Can Roger MacBride serve the Libertarians in the 1970s as John C. Frémont did the Republicans in the 1850s?

Instinct stirs the Retired Flack's imagination. I am, however, quickly snapped back to reality: Roger hands me a copy of the party platform. I assure him I will read it, but point out that platforms are relics of a former political era, not really crucial to modern national campaigns.

MacBride says that he understands that fact of political life, but deplores it. "*We* take our platform seriously," he says. Then he commences to speak affectionately, as if on first-name terms, of "the Founding Fathers"—particularly Jefferson, with whose spirit, I am impressed, he is in daily communion. Jefferson, as MacBride views his Charlottesville neighbor, was a "proto-Libertarian," one of the original American political advocates of small, manageable government.

This is an idea whose time has come, gone, and returned. Even liberal Democrats are making speeches these days that sound like Goldwater's 1964 texts. Anti-Big Government rhetoric is the rage. The best new political PR act in town is to run against politics and politicians. Post-Watergate, the manipulators have their candidates shedding the perks of political power. Smart young governors, Brown of California and Dukakis of Massachusetts, spurn limos and manses, speak only of cutting down the size of government. It is the political PR of antipolitical PR.

But such acts are best carried off by professional politicians; accomplished actors, not sincere amateur performers like Roger Lea MacBride. The Libertarian candidate's unique virtue as a Presidential candidate is that he suffers from delusions brought on by innocence, not megalomania. If such a man can go through a campaign retaining that virtue, he will achieve something few Presidential candidates—even third, fourth, and fifth party losers —have ever accomplished.

This then is the counsel the Retired Flack offers the nominee of the Party of Principle: Roger, I say, why go the way of the Nixon balloon hype, and Kennedy imagery? If you're really sincere about standing apart from the two major parties, bringing America back to fundamental truths, put aside professional flackery. Just be your own straightforward eighteenth-century self.

MacBride seems impressed, by my reasoning, yet troubled. "If a party can't relate to the national media in 1976," he sighs, "how can it hope to reach the people?" This is the dilemma of an ideologue trying to express traditional values in a form acceptable to modern audiences—like the dilemma of the twentieth-century clergy: Should the service be in Latin or English? At what point does compromising the technique of communications compromise the substance of the message itself?

Have faith, I assure MacBride. Look, you're not running to get elected. Only for an ideal. Why not make the Grand Gesture your own way? Deal with the media directly as Roger Lea MacBride. Don't screw up a pure act with a professional middleman.

It is the Bicentennial year: "Sam Adams," I remind the candidate of the Libertarian Party, "didn't use professional PR counsel." A fatuous non sequitur. But as we part, the thought seems to comfort Tom Jefferson's friend and neighbor.

We will have an open, we will have a candid administration. I can't change my nature after sixty-one years.

> GERALD FORD, *introducing his first*
> *White House press secretary*
> *to the news media, August 1974*

It begins unrehearsed, unscenarioed, early morning, of a humid Potomac summer day. A newsgirl delivers the *Washington Post* at a two-story red brick frame home in the northern Virginia suburbs. Steve Ford and his father are preparing a breakfast of melon, cold cereal, muffins, coffee. With the sound of movements outside, Steve Ford starts from the kitchen toward the front door.

Wait a minute, Steve, says Jerry Ford, I'll get the paper, I've done it other mornings. Why should this one be any different?

Across the narrow street, newsmen and camera wait to catch the elder Ford when he leaves the house to travel across the Potomac. The men behind the cameras are the quickest in the business, experienced on the White House beat. But this once, they're caught with their lenses down. Not a single photograph or film clip freezes for history the bracing sight of the man who within hours will become thirty-eighth President of the United States as he swings open the door, steps outside and picks up his morning paper. In a bathrobe.

It is an Era of Good Feeling at 1600 Pennsylvania Avenue, the first in more than a decade: a honeymoon between a White House press corps starved for access and a President with a ravenous appetite for coverage.

Jerry Ford has been a Congressman for twenty-four years. Now he is suddenly thrust into a political office where the market on publicity is bullish, not bearish. As a House member, Ford was on the twenty-four-hour mimeograph-handout run, hustling media attention wherever, whenever, he could get it. Paul Miltich, his Capitol Hill press secretary, was competent to handle his Michigan press constituency. But now Miltich has been replaced by Jerry ter Horst, Washington bureau chief for the *Detroit News*, an experienced and respected White House newsman.

PRIORITIES: The new President's first three job appointments on taking office are (1) a personal photographer, (2) a new press secretary, (3) a chief speechwriter.

Within a month Ford will add to this public relations cadre (4) a professional gagwriter, who will provide one-line openers for the President's speeches, and (5) a television advisor, the first in a succession, to work fulltime at improving his skills in audiovisual presentation.

The New President's flacks are fond of pointing out that their boss, unlike his PR-conscious predecessor, doesn't even wear makeup at televised news conferences. Encouraged by a favorable press, they promote this image of Just Plain Jerry, the uncosmetized President; despite the fact that Ford, far from eliminating or even curtailing the massive public relations superstructure created by Nixon, is rapidly expanding it. Measured in terms of paid flacks per carpeted square inch, this will be the most image-conscious White House in history. In time the uncosmetized President, in addition to his press office, will have a cadre of television production aides and not simply one but two $40,000 gagwriter-speech consultants on the Executive payroll.

And yet, in the aftermath of Johnson and Nixon, Vietnam and Watergate, after a decade of escalated war between the news media and the White House, the national press is concerned about its own public image. It is a disquiet that runs through the higher levels of news media management, both electronic and print, an apprehension fed by the ancient inhibition against *lèse majesté*. There is even an undercurrent of this feeling among hardened White House newsmen, a feeling that they should now demonstrate to the American people that the national news media are not bloodthirsty zealots eager to destroy the country's institutions, but good, patriotic Americans, just doing a job. Give us a Nice Guy President, they seem to be saying, we'll cover him as a Nice Guy President.

So we have Just Plain Jerry. If he did not exist, he would have to have been invented. It is an image that the media, as much as the new President's retained imagectomists, seem eager to sell to the public. Just what central casting ordered for a post-Nixon White House scenario: a Middle American ex-football player, with a Brueghel-peasant look and manner.

Never mind that in addition to enlarging the White House PR operation, Just Plain Jerry embraces, rather than diminishes, the panoply and perks institutionalized by his predecessors: the limos, helicopters, round-the-clock "historical" photography; the media royalization of the "First Family." No. What the American people need, *want*, is the image of a President with an unassuming, *uncontrived* life- and work-style. This is the image the media seek to project in their coverage of the White House. And they will do it, if necessary, by contrivance.

CANDOR: When it is learned during those first days that Jerry Ford over the years has prepared his own breakfast, the White House camera corps wants only to capture this image of an unimperial President. A delegation takes the matter up with Jerry ter Horst, the new press secretary, who takes it up with his boss.

Gosh, says Just Plain Jerry, *it's sure nice those fellows want to take my picture fixing breakfast, but there's this problem: I don't fix my own breakfast anymore. The folks who work in the White House kitchen, they'd take it personally. It's a big kitchen, you see, very mechanized and—*

Ter Horst relays this news to the photographers, knowing they'll understand the turndown. The press secretary—experienced as a conscientious, no-nonsense reporter—is an innocent in the world of political flackery. Like his boss, he thinks that simply because a President doesn't actually prepare his own breakfast, *ergo,* there's no way to *photograph* a President preparing his own breakfast.

But: *Look Jerry,* the White House photographers tell Ter Horst, *there's really no problem. None at all. Until a few weeks ago the President prepared his breakfast. Right?*

TER HORST: In his Alexandria home. Not in the White House.

Jerry, the photographers plead (*thinking Jesus, bring back Ron Ziegler, he'd get the point*), *look at it this way, man: Why should the incidental fact that the President doesn't actually prepare his breakfast anymore deprive the American people of seeing the real Jerry Ford? He still would if he could. Right? Believe us, our editors want it. It'll play big, all over the country.*

TER HORST: I don't know whether the President would go for a publicity stunt.

Let's call it a photo opportunity . . .

Well, says the President, *it's not as if it's our publicity stunt. I'd hate that. I don't like any phony image-making fluff. But, if that's what the press wants . . . and you say the networks are interested too?*

Next morning the President of the United States showers, shaves, slips on suit pants and a shirt (no tie, the casual homey

37

look) to be photographed and filmed for history, popping English muffins into a toaster, nibbling melon.

AIDE DOUBTFUL THAT FORD
WOULD GIVE NIXON PARDON

Headline, *The New York Times*,
August 10, 1974

October 1975

FORD'S 1976 DRIVE IS FOUND
LAGGING: NEW AIDE CHOSEN

Headline, *The New York Times*

"We're going to move like hell now. Things will look a lot better a month from now—to you and to me. We have problems in New Hampshire and problems in Florida but we intend to win both, because it's going to be a miserable spring with blood in the streets if we don't."

STUART SPENCER, *pep talk to the team on being named director of the President Ford Committee*

ALL THE PRESIDENT'S FLACKS

Campaigns come and campaigns go, but the Stu Spencers of the game survive. Sometimes longer than their clients. At forty-eight Spencer has the calm sanguinity of an aging professional PR man, the controlled optimism that comes from having been there before, knowing that win or lose there will be another campaign, another candidate down the road. Today's client could be next campaign's opponent; today's opponent next campaign's client.

This year, Stu has the biggest of all possible political clients. He is in hog heaven, with all the campaign resources power can attract. He has a candidate the news media is lusting to cover and an opportunity to alter the major events of our time. Presidents worry about their place in history. Their flacks luxuriate in the prospect of shaping it.

EXCEPT: Jerry Ford, Spencer's client, is in the dumps. Doesn't *anything* work around this place? A few mornings ago even his English muffin toaster blew a fuse.

Ford staffmen are arguing with each other at the White House. Ford staffmen are arguing with each other at the President Ford Committee. Ford staffmen at the White House are arguing with Ford staffmen at the President Ford Committee. Rumsfeld is telling the President, as well as any friendly newsman who will listen, that Kissinger is making Jerry look bad, taking all the credit for himself in foreign affairs. Kissinger is telling the President, as well as any friendly newsman who will listen, that Jim Schlesinger is a pain in the ass, especially at Cabinet meetings, where he takes up everybody's time with pompous, pontifical lectures. Schlesinger is complaining, to any friendly newsman who will listen, that he can't get to the President to complain because Rumsfeld is isolating Ford, making him inaccessible to outside advice.

Now, Ron Nessen . . . *Nessen* agrees with Rumsfeld about Kissinger, with Kissinger about Schlesinger, and with Schlesinger about Rumsfeld. Nessen does not like Rumsfeld's having moved Bill Greener in as deputy press secretary to second-guess his operation. But that is only half of Nessen's problem. There is also swinging David Hume Kennerly, who is insinuating to the President, at every private photo opportunity, that Nessen isn't up to the job of Presidential press secretary. If he were, why would the President be slipping in the public opinion polls?

This is the butcher block side of PR hog heaven. There being no such thing as a non-imperial Presidency—that is, a President immune to the influence of sycophants and flatterers—justification of Jerry Ford's every decision is as endemic to his White House as it was to those of his immediate, egocentric predecessors. Reassurance by subordinates is the working politician's Librium, what makes Presidents sleep easy after they have laid down their *awesome burden* for the day. No sensitive Cabinet or staff member—unless he is endowed with an independent income

39

—tells a President, "*Boss, you just blew it.*" (Not more than once. And to advise him *before* a decision about which he has already made up his mind that he is *about* to blow it, is to invite gratitude for candor and, if done more than once, exile to a Central American ambassadorship or private life.)

Only one White House staff member disagreed, before or after the fact, with Ford's decision to pardon Richard Nixon. He resigned, allowing the President to name a new, more flexible press secretary. But if Jerry ter Horst was right about Ford's mistake in pardoning Nixon, Ron Nessen is paying the professional price for that mistake. Since the prevailing wisdom around the White House is that the pardon was the correct thing to have done, it follows that any slippage in the polls is due to the press secretary's failure to tell the President's story.

Because flacks are hired to prevent such public misperceptions, Nessen has been open to criticism for his "failure." Together Kennerly, Rumsfeld, Kissinger, not to mention key Ford advisors outside the White House staff—his so-called "Locker Room Cabinet"—have exploited the press secretary's vulnerability. But Jerry Ford has already lost one press secretary and doesn't care to dump another. His response to criticism of his formal White House press operation has been to bolster his image-making apparatus in other areas. He has hired different, if not better, speechwriters, and spent more time with Bob Orben, his show biz gagwriter, and Bob Mead, his TV advisor, practicing "Presidential" speech delivery.

He has also reverted to the habits of the peripatetic Minority Leader of the House, heading out to Andrews Air Force Base two or three times weekly to board his great white bird, leaving the snakepit of 1600 Pennsylvania behind. To fly the friendly skies of *Air Force One*, thirty-five thousand feet above it all. Then to earth, to breathe the comfortable air of hotel suites filled with visiting politicians; to walk the airport fences, cheered by adoring crowds of Republican fieldworkers.

That is the non-imperial President's answer to bad reviews.

EXCEPT: Howard "Bo" Callaway is worried that Jerry might be spending too much time on the road running for President when he should stay in Washington, being President. Callaway, who resigned as Secretary of the Army to run the Ford election campaign, believes that Presidential image-making begins at home. "Bo" insists, in his machine-gun Georgia delivery (this, it appears, will be a campaign loaded with fast-talking Georgians), that the best place for Jerry to milk the advantage of incumbency is in the Oval Office, where former Presidents have been known to hang out on weekdays.

Kennerly, the President's photographer (in title) and chief public relations advisor (in fact), thinks otherwise. A restless artist with a camera, Kennerly is hungry for new settings in which to demonstrate his creative touch. In the early months of the Ford Presidency, the Oval Office was a challenge. But by now every imaginable shot has been taken in the White House, including that memorable one of the President and Rumsfeld in formal dress, yukking it up at the time of the *Mayagüez* incident.

Some of Ford's critics thought this was poor political PR, but Kennerly viewed it with a true artist's eye. He thinks the picture was superb *politique vérité*, because it caught the President in an "off guard" moment—"off guard," as in "spontaneous"—acting as a leader in a time of crisis. Jerry Ford, always on the job. Even during tuxedo hours.

Kennerly makes no secret of his admiration for the Kennedy style. Bearded, Guccied, single, twenty-eight, he considers it his chief mission to bring a touch of panache to the staid Ford White House. He has taken over the Big Brother introduction of the young Fords, Jack and Susan, to the world of Andy Warhol and Candy Bergen: the In Crowd at 1600 Penn meets the In Crowd at Elmo's; Grand Rapids meets Radical Chic, on a stylistic if not political level.

To young Jack, Kennerly has made the gift of acquaintance with Bianca Jagger, whose husband Mick and *his* flack wholly approved when a photograph appeared in *Time*, showing the President's son with arms wrapped around Rolling Stone's All-American Girl, the pair brooding moodily across the south portico at the Washington Monument; to Susan, the gift of camera lessons and the right introductions for special stringer assignments for *Time* as a lensperson covering major events.

"I can't conceive of myself as a celebrity in the traditional sense."
Jerry Ford's photographer,
interviewed by the Washington Post *in 1975*

If Kennerly's conception of what makes for good Presidential and First Family imagery isn't always enjoyed by Jerry Ford's natural constituency, it's appreciated where it matters. The Boss considers his photographer "like another son, a member of the family." Jerry thinks David is the pips at taking his picture, which, after all, is image-making at its most basic level. And because Kennerly is so with-it and has strong contacts with major media (he worked with United Press International and *Time*, winning a Pulitzer for feature photography in Vietnam), Ford looks to him more than to anyone else when matters of Presidential imagery are under discussion.

What Kennerly likes—and given his familial access to the President, he makes his point frequently—is to photograph Jerry Ford "among the people, at the grass roots." Out traveling the countryside, Ford has possibilities for warm, human interest shots that are limitless. There are the shining, uplifted faces of the young, the old, the halt, the lame, the blond, as they strain to reach across airport fences and Secret Service arms to touch their President's garments. That, argues David Hume Kennerly, is the essence of successful political image-projection on today's media market: the color event, the humanized Leader.

To Just Plain Jerry Ford this PR advice has the ring of verisimilitude. It also sounds right.

EXCEPT: Those damned perverse public opinion polls. Despite all the marvelous pictures Kennerly has taken for the White House walls and the wire service photos that regularly appear on front pages across the country—the President shaking hands, getting hugged, wearing a variety of hats, dedicating buildings, dancing ethnic dances—the public opinion surveys aren't reflecting the success of extended Presidential travel.

On the road, Ford can see, hear, feel for himself how popular he is. Everywhere people cheer, smile. But the polls continue to go from bad to worse, a decline leading to all the suggestions the President is getting to rid himself of Nessen. Or Rumsfeld. Or Kissinger. Or Schlesinger. Or Kennerly. Or Callaway.

Callaway, feeling the reverberations at the President Ford Committee, has responded to criticism of his operation by replacing his No. 2 man, Campaign Director Lee Nunn, with Spencer, the Los Angeles professional. "Bo" touts his new pro as "the best PR man in the country to take Ronald Reagan apart."

Stu Spencer is a big name in Republican campaign PR, a disciple of the school of political flackery originally developed on the West Coast during the 1930s by Clem Whitaker, Sr., and Leone Baxter. Retaining Spencer, according to Callaway, is a double coup:

First, Ford still nurtures the hope that Reagan can be frightened out of running by a show of Presidential strength in those areas where Ron might hope to run strong. Callaway, a Georgian, was named campaign manager to undercut Reagan's Deep Southern base. Nunn, a Kentuckian, was hired to handle the Border States. Now, with Nunn out (he didn't get along with "Bo"), the President's campaign committee is raiding Reagan's home base, California.

Second, and more important for added psychological value, is the fact that Spencer was senior partner of the Spencer-Roberts agency that handled Reagan's first gubernatorial campaign in 1966. Two years later, Spencer was a member of the Reagan PR team that tried to wrest the Republican nomination from Nixon at Miami Beach. It wasn't a bad try, Stu recalls. Good enough, in fact, to break a sweat on Nixon's upper lip in the late stages. But Ron made his move too late.

Spencer is sanguine. But not so sanguine as to believe that his former client will make the same strategic mistake in 1976.

July 1976   If at first you don't succeed . . .

FORD CAMPAIGN ORGANIZATION
HIT BY FACTIONAL STRIFE

Headline, *The New York Times*

"Just as political events have begun to favor President Ford's bid for the Republican Presidential nomination, his campaign organization has succumbed to factional strife.

"Frederick Slight, the campaign research director, resigned quietly three weeks ago, citing as one of his reasons the lack of communication within the President Ford Committee, and between it and the White House . . .

"Stuart Spencer, the deputy chairman and key political strategist, is reportedly so irked by the dissension that he is said to be giving serious thought to resigning soon after the Republican National Convention . . ."

WHITE HOUSE REVAMPS PR

Headline, Washington Post

"Over the last two years, if we had a major problem here it has been an inability to tell our story. I don't think we have done a very good job of that."

White House aide, backgrounding
the press after another reshuffling
of the Ford White House press staff

October 1976

It is twelve-twenty, moving into the rush hour at the Sans Souci, the Washington *haut* lunchery where the power elite meet to eat. Here on a given midday, the casual tourist—say Charlton Heston or Eva Gabor—can observe three generations of White House staff members and assorted other political celebrities scattered about a small dining room, hovered over by the world's most politic *maître d'*, Paul DeLisle: White House Past (Nixon, Johnson), White House Present; and White House Future, which in the case of Democratic candidates sometimes overlaps with the first category.

Joe Califano of the Johnson White House is a Sans Souci regular. Pierre Salinger and George Reedy, press secretaries for Kennedy and Johnson, drop by when they're in town, as does Ron Ziegler, and, between prayer breakfasts and church dinners, Chuck Colson. Ron Nessen is seen here frequently, either pumping or being pumped by editors and columnists. Robert Redford has been by with Mary McGrory, inhaling the atmosphere in preparation for a scene set here in his *All the President's Men*. The Sans Souci is to American Celebrity in the political seventies what Romanoff's and the Stork Club were to the tinsel-and-tickertape days of the forties and fifties.

Today, among the others, there is Franklyn Nofziger, who worked awhile with the Nixon White House but whose heart, even then, was out West with Ronald Reagan. Nofziger has just ordered his usual: *cervelles aux capres*. Brains with capers. The meal, if that prole term can apply to the cuisine served with light sauce and heavy accent in DeLisle's domain, describes precisely what Reagan expects from his most experienced flack during the coming year. For the moment, however, Nofziger's thoughts dwell on immediate problems, looming obstacles in the way of a Reagan Presidency. "We take them one game at a time," he says, "and the game right now is New Hampshire."

Just the sort of metaphor one would expect from a Republican PR pro who, except for a two-year stint in the propaganda catacombs of the Nixon White House, has spent the last decade in the service of the Gipper.

"Two at a time," David Keene corrects him. "Don't forget Florida."

Keene is a twenty-eight-year-old Wisconsin lawyer who came to the Reagan campaign from Jim Buckley's Senate office. He is a rare young conservative: an ideologue, yet a political pragmatist who can get along with the news media.

"If Ford blows those two, the ball game's over," Keene says, picking up the Nofziger autumn spirit.

"Maybe Stu Spencer can straighten him out," I say, looking for a reaction.

"*Stu Spencer?*" Nofziger perks up. "Is Stu in town? Gee, I wonder why he hasn't called me."

Nofziger is the sole remaining loyal Reaganite from the original team of flacks that handled the gubernatorial campaign against Pat Brown in 1966. A former Washington correspondent for the Copley newspaper chain, he moved to Sacramento in 1967 to become Reagan's communications director. He is a right-wing eccentric, but not in the flaky sense: the one member of Goldwater's 1964 press entourage who, when his colleagues took to wearing tie tacks engraved EASTERN LIBERAL PRESS, had his clasp labeled WESTERN TORY PRESS; then regarded as one of the toughest correspondents in the National Capital, Nofziger, like Spencer, is now considered one of the most accomplished Republican PR specialists in the business.

"Spencer-Roberts took care of the organization," explains Nofziger when asked about the public relations operation of Reagan's 1966 campaign. "I took care of the candidate."

In 1968, Nofziger worked at Miami Beach alongside Spencer and Clif White, of Draft Goldwater renown, in the losing effort to nominate Reagan. Now, according to rumor, the Ford White House is said to be lining up White, out of New York City, as an independent PR consultant, to help Spencer in the campaign against Reagan. Knowing Nofziger's low acidic boiling point, I press him on the subject of his former co-workers.

"What do you think of your apostate colleagues?"

"*'A'-past-eight?*" Nofziger looks at his wrist. "By my watch it's only *'a'-past-twelve.*"

Stu Spencer has this nervous tic alongside his right eye. Under pressure he blinks compulsively. Lyn Nofziger's occupational tic is pun-*spritzing*. "To tell you the truth," he continues, operating his own internal laugh machine as he goes into spasm, "I don't have any *idea* what White did for Ron in 1968. I think we sent him to Delaware. You know, so we could claim *the Clif Whites of Dover.*"

Just as one ignores Spencer's tic while talking to him, the sensible conversationalist ignores Nofziger's. Both Keene and I understand that any notice of our luncheon companion's affliction will only aggravate the condition. Keene concentrates on thickly buttering a slice of French bread. I comment that he is picking up weight in the campaign, then wave aimlessly at a nameless acquaintance across the room.

"Every time Ford flies out for another speech," says Keene, ignoring Nofziger's convulsive *heh-heh-heh,* "we gain two percent in the polls."

The treatment works. Abruptly Nofziger recovers from his fit. "*That's right,*" he says, plucking the olive from his Tanqueray martini. "No matter how hard they try to palm him off as *President,* Jerry Ford comes through as the Congressman from Grand

Rapids. Stu Spencer can't change that. Spencer and White can't change it. A PR man is only as good as his material. You can cover a klutz just so far. Sooner or later the klutz shines through."

In the specialized world of political kingmaking, Dave Keene can be classified as senior political field man working toward a graduate degree in campaign management. He is also as articulate a press spokesman, and as competent a speech or statement draftsman, as any political campaign aide bearing the title "press secretary." If called upon, in fact, Keene could step into a campaign press secretaryship; just as Nofziger, for his part, could step out as press secretary to take up a senior campaign field position. Despite being a lawyer, not an advertising or PR specialist, Keene, in brief, is a campaign flack.

The old division of campaign responsibility, the compartmentalization of political operations between backroom pols who made substantive and tactical political decisions and front office flacks who merely handled the press, has disappeared. Because in a Supermedia Age appearance *is* reality, every top-level aide in a Presidential campaign must possess some degree of public relations skill.

Much as anything, this blurring of old distinctions—the fact that those closely associated with the candidate both reflect and shape his image in the public eye—accounts for the passing into history of the potbellied, cigar-smoking backroom boss of stereotypical political legend. In selecting their campaign managers, the candidates of the 1970s look for political sagacity in lean, articulate, mediagenic young men, with an understanding of news cycles.

In this regard, Keene's superior, John Sears, the newest member of the Reagan team, is the prototype of the modern Presidential campaign manager-flack. Cool, buttoned-down, Sears has that special talent for stroking the working press, simultaneously selling himself and his candidate.

It was the talent that first brought Sears, now forty-three, into politics at the Presidential level. A graduate of Notre Dame, he was a young member of the Manhattan corporate law factory

47

headed by John Mitchell and joined by Richard Nixon in the mid-1960s. When Nixon was first laying in supplies and young aides for his 1968 rerun at the Presidency, Sears's self-contained manner and low-keyed ability to bullshit on any political topic made him a natural for a key campaign assignment.

Nixon, still uncomfortable with members of the news media, was nevertheless anxious to erase public recollection of that embarrassing 1962 "farewell" news conference at Los Angeles, when he quit politics with his revealing self-pitying blast at the press. He calculated that the best way to put that issue behind him was by opening his campaign with an informal approach to media relations. He would have no "press secretary" in New Hampshire. What he would have instead was John Sears, and occasionally Pat Buchanan, keeping newsmen happy with brilliant insights on dull campaign days.

Sears's popularity with correspondents covering the New Hampshire primary that year helped salve his candidate's relationship with the press. But after Nixon's election, camaraderie with the media enemy was looked upon, by the President and Sears's old law firm superior, Mitchell, with disfavor.

In the Nixon White House, 1969–70, Sears was a prime suspect whenever inside White House speculations appeared in the widely read Evans & Novak column; and not always without cause. For, having escaped the dreary prospect of a lifetime of anonymity as a Manhattan bond attorney, Sears, like others before him, had become a victim of Potomac Source's Disease: an irresistible itch to be quoted by the news media, with, or in terminal cases even without, attribution.

In the Nixon administration, symptoms of the disease were easily detected since most Nixon White House appointees shared the President's abhorrence of the Washington press corps. Those few members of the team who remained accessible to friends in the news media paid a price. Some had their phones tapped: Sears, like Bill Safire, was among this number. Nevertheless, though repeatedly warned not to fraternize with the enemy and to refer all newsmen's inquiries to the tender loving care of Ron Ziegler, Sears found it impossible to soothe his itch other than by returning newsmen's calls. So it was that less than a year after he helped make his first king, John Sears was banished from his court. Under Mitchell's pressure, Sears left the White House staff to go into private law practice.

The god of young king-makers was looking after John Sears. But before his judgment regarding the way to operate in Washington was vindicated by the subsequent fate of the men who expelled him from the throne room, Sears spent a half-dozen difficult years maintaining his reputation as a quotable Republican political expert. From an affluent corporate law office a block from the White House, he worked diligently, first, at cultivating press contacts, despite the disadvantage of lacking a political power base; second, at finding that base in the form of a new Presidential candidate.

The effort had its frustrations. At times even Sears, for all his verbalizing skills and cool self-confidence, must have wondered whether his special god was permanently out to lunch.

From 1970 to 1973, for example, news and column reports mentioned him in connection with an Agnew campaign for the Republican nomination in 1976. Then there were reports Sears would join Nelson Rockefeller's staff. Finally, there was Ronald Reagan.

In the summer of 1975, John Sears found his new base. He flew to California, talked to Reagan, and signed on. He and Nofziger on the East Coast, Mike Deaver and Peter Hannaford on the West Coast, would form the top echelon of a Reagan campaign staff. Sears, as national campaign director, would serve as chief organizer and head-hunter in the contest for convention delegates against Gerald Ford.

Sticklers for constancy might note that, like Stu Spencer and Clif White, John Sears is not a man hung up on ideological or personal attachments. He is a Republican who deals in Republican candidacies; but beyond that categorical definition, politics-as-a-game is his business. No matter that Rockefeller and Reagan are at opposite ends of the ideological spectrum. Like a good lawyer, Sears can represent either side of an argument with equal skill and drive.

Reporters with memories that stretch to August 1968 may

even recall that after Nixon's Miami Beach victory, Sears confided his team's "middle road" tactic for dealing with wavering convention delegates. Depending on the bias of the particular delegate, said Sears, the game plan had been to "threaten the Right with the horror of Rockefeller, and the Left with the catastrophe of Reagan."

But that was another campaign, seven long years ago. Ronald Reagan holds no grudge. He knows he is fortunate to get John Sears's talents as a campaign coordinator and press-spokesman-without-portfolio—talents sought by the opposition. Why, the White House even dispatched one of its Highly Placed Emissaries to Sears's law office not too many months ago to ask him to join the Ford team. Sears refused, choosing instead to go with Reagan.

It was a grim portent for the President's campaign, and was so reported early autumn, 1975, by (who else?) Evans & Novak.

When Lyn Nofziger was Reagan's communications director in Sacramento—the euphemism for chief administration flack that he concocted, then passed along to Herb Klein at the Nixon White House—cartoonist Art Hoppe caricatured him as a porcine Sancho astride a donkey, riding alongside Reagan's Don Quixote. The cartoon was physically precise, but inaccurate in terms of Nofziger's true role in California government from 1967 to 1972. He was not so much the obese, obeisant sidekick as the lance-bearer.

At fifty-one, Nofziger, like his onetime ally and current nemesis, Spencer, belies the stereotypes of his trade. True, he can put down several Tanquerays-on-the-rocks at one luncheon sitting without any noticeable thickening of the tongue or mind. But there is also the quick (if sometimes heavy) wit, and the pronounced déshabillé: an uncombed thatch of hair, a tie twisted beneath an upturned shirt collar.

Nofziger clearly relishes this professional anti-image. In the country club ambiance of Republican political public relations, with its Clif Whites and John Searses, this is his *shtik*. In any case, his No. 1 client hasn't complained—though the client's wife long ago let her husband and others know that she is annoyed by Nofziger's calculated uncouthness.

Regardless of what Nancy may think, however, Nofziger, like all political PR pro's who stay with a single candidate over the years, identifies completely with "Ron." He has been with Reagan long enough to speak of "we" when he means "he," to feel every barb aimed at the candidate personally, even those the candidate aims at himself.

Take Reagan's recent reply to a question about the Republican Vice-Presidential nomination: a week ago the candidate told an interviewer that he might, under certain circumstances, consider accepting the No. 2 place on the Republican national ticket. Nofziger read the report of this exchange in the Washington papers with disbelief. *No* candidate for President ever concedes, at the outset of the campaign, that he might settle for second place.

"The problem is that when Ron travels alone . . ."

Nofziger's voice trails off. He dips into his *cervelles*, which, oddly, he has sprinkled with Tabasco sauce. The Southern California touch.

"Anyway, beginning with the Announcement I'll be on the road with him."

Technically, of course, Ronald Reagan is not yet a candidate. That too is part of the flack's game. For months, since John Sears came on, there has been a continental struggle between Reagan's advisors in California and his Washington staff concerning the timing of the Announcement. The California staff, reflecting the candidate's go-slow instinct, doesn't want him to commit too early. The Washington staff, responding to the pressure of restless supporters eager to go to work, have been needling Reagan to get moving before the White House locks up key party leaders throughout the country.

However, Nofziger confides, the issue has now been resolved. Reagan will declare "before Thanksgiving." The time and place of the Announcement have not been idly chosen. Properly handled, says Nofziger, Reagan should get live coverage stories in both *Time* and *Newsweek*. Total impact—for a week.

From that time on, says Nofziger, media attention will be harder to come by. The White House incumbent will enjoy a clear advantage in publicity. The Announcement, as the first pure media event of the campaign, must be something that will stay in public memory. It should have a rolling rather than one-shot impact. It has to set a tone, provide a lasting image of destiny in the making.

The Retired Flack recalls candidate Barry Goldwater's Announcement in 1964, outside his home in Scottsdale, with the Arizona hills on the horizon as a symbol of free Western man. Goldwater did it New Year's Day. His birthday. That made for a nice news sidebar. But the real PR impact of the chosen date was its promise of a fresh beginning, the promise Americans look for every quadrennial. We must always begin anew—even Presidents going into their second term. They will correct past errors, give the country a fresh start; while would-be first-termers call for a fresh deck, a new deal, a new freedom, a new frontier . . .

John Kennedy announced from the Caucus Room of the Old Senate Office Building. The idea was to highlight his Capitol Hill experience at the very site where he first came to national attention through the televised Senate Labor Racket hearings. Earlier this year Lloyd Bentsen used the same Caucus Room spot for his Announcement. Not because he had distinguished himself through televised hearings, but to remind people—so his image-counselors hoped—of the Kennedy campaign.

Reagan's variation, Nofziger relates, will be to make his Announcement in the manner of a Saturn-cluster rocket. He will make it in not one, not two, but no fewer than *six* locations across the country. First, Washington, at the Madison Hotel, timed midmorning for maximum network coverage. Live. Then a reprise for the evening news. Then Florida. Then New Hampshire . . .

"You know what *they* wanted to do?" Nofziger asks. "*Their* idea was to announce on the Saturday before Thanksgiving. They said we'd catch the Sunday editions. I checked the date. November twenty-second."

He polishes off his brains with capers, shakes his head.

"The anniversary of Kennedy's assassination. Can you believe it? *That* day? Sunday morning front-page pictures all over the country. The Kennedy family at the gravesite, alongside Ron Reagan's smiling face, announcing his candidacy."

"You changed it?"

"What do you think? November *twenty-second?* No way."

Which is why Lyn Nofziger who has been with Ronald Reagan going on ten years, is paid three thousand dollars a month, plus expenses, and, why, regardless of what Nancy Reagan thinks about his soiled ties, rumpled manner, and outrageous punning spasms, he is worth having around. But more to the point—for those interested in how destiny in the making is made—it is why Jerry Ford's opponent for the Republican Presidential nomination made his Announcement on November 20, 1975. Two days before "they" (and the candidate himself) had originally scheduled it.

Meanwhile, Back at the Ranch . . .

Deaver and Hannaford, the Los Angeles-based Reagan aides Nofziger refers to as "they," are known to Stu Spencer as "the Palace Guard." Deaver, thirty-eight, is chief of staff, in charge of campaign logistics, including scheduling. For Reagan, not one for the exhausting campaign regimen made popular in the 1960 Kennedy-Nixon race (the logistical standard by which the press has measured all subsequent Presidential campaign operations), this is a position he would not trust to an aide who did not meet precise specifications. Deaver will not *push* his candidate in the way some members of the Reagan staff think he ought to be extended.

Ron simply isn't comfortable with "pushers" around and Deaver's job is to protect his candidate against them. His success at that assignment over the years has made him aide-closest-to-Reagan. That he also gets along well with Nancy hasn't hindered his rise.

Hannaford, forty-two, is the ideologue responsible for basic position papers and speech drafts. Since January, when Reagan left office, Hannaford has been writing first drafts for the ex-Governor's syndicated newspaper column and radio commentaries. The Deaver-Hannaford firm handles all Reagan's professional media relations, as well as arrangements for the lucrative speaking schedule. They ask, and get, six thousand dollars for a single forty-five-minute rendition of The Speech Ron has been delivering, with minor variations and updates, since his amateur political days on the lecture circuit for General Electric.

When Spencer was in L.A. during the late 1960s, Deaver and Hannaford were in Sacramento, along with Nofziger, as key members of the Reagan inner PR circle. In time, the process encouraged by the First Lady, their influence with the Governor came to exceed Nofziger's. It totally eliminated Spencer's. On the day Reagan left office, the new Deaver-Hannaford agency was already at work, setting up his media franchise, laying groundwork for a Presidential campaign; though, in fact, Reagan had not yet made up his mind whether to run against Jerry Ford . . . Just as he has been reluctant to commit himself in recent months, despite the pleas of his ardent right-wing supporters.

"The office," Reagan kept repeating, "seeks the man."

Stu Spencer thinks that's funny. Reagan says the office seeks the man, says his former flack, because Reagan just doesn't like to *work*. At least, not at political campaigning. Ron doesn't want to be President. All he wants is the President's bully pulpit, a platform for his Speech.

"He's lazy, that's all," is the way Spencer assesses his former client. "I think his energy level is going to be a problem. Low blood sugar. I think that's why he likes those jelly beans."

As Spencer tells it, his fall from grace with Reagan wasn't so much due to Deaver-Hannaford's business competition as his own non-ideological brand of politics. "I never passed their blood test for conservatism," he says, when asked to explain why he is working out of Gerald Ford's campaign office this year instead of Citizens for Reagan headquarters two blocks down L Street. "After the Rockefeller campaign, I was always suspect."

California   May 1964
The final Republican primary shootout: Eastern Liberal Nelson Rockefeller vs. the Conservative champion, Barry Goldwater.

Whitaker-Baxter, out of San Francisco, is handling Goldwater's PR. Their campaign theme is that the Governor of New

York—in addition to being a wild-spending fiscal radical—is a wife-dumper, a dirty old man who lusts after young married women. (Rockefeller's divorce and remarriage are still fresh news.) Spencer-Roberts, out of Los Angeles, counters with the charge that Goldwater, if elected President, would abolish Social Security before lunch, then, before dinner, trigger a nuclear war.

Goldwater wins. Narrowly. On the strength of Whitaker-Baxter's brilliantly timed stratagem of persuading or, possibly through voodoo, inducing "Happy" Rockefeller to go into labor and deliver a few days before the primary vote.

It is not a pleasant campaign. Eleven years later, Orange County still recalls it with an ideological bitterness approaching hydrophobia. At the mention of Stuart Spencer's name, "Duke" Wayne, one of Ron's strongest backers, will cut loose with X-rated, non-family-viewing, expletives.

But Spencer-the-Goldwater-baiter of 1964 becomes Spencer-the-Reagan-flack, of 1966–68, just as Spencer-the-Reagan-flack has now become the director of Reagan-baiting. Rockefeller, Reagan, Ford. Depending on time and place, it's all the same to a pro.

"I can see," Spencer explains, "the positives and negatives of *all* these guys' positions."

It isn't that a professional flack is politically amoral. He's simply a commercial pragmatist. Spencer tells of rejecting the chance to get a piece of the winning Nixon action in 1968. Out of loyalty to Reagan? No. Spencer is candid: he went along with Reagan in '68—against a sure winner—because it would have been "bad business practice" to have done otherwise.

"I had a business in California," he says. Reagan was Governor. *Then.* But *now* Ford is President and Reagan is just another politician looking for a new job.

For professionals like Sears and Spencer, who move back and forth across the ideological spectrum, handling political campaigns is a business. There are limits, however. Money isn't everything. Spencer wouldn't offer his talents to a candidate he considered bad for the System. Someone beyond the "mainstream" of American politics. Say, a Communist, a racist, or a radical Democrat. But moving laterally between one Republican who calls himself a "liberal" and another who calls himself a "conservative"—let's not kid ourselves.

The spectators in the stands, sitting in front of their television sets, cheer, roar, cry, even come to blows at times over the respective virtues of their teams. But to Stu Spencer, Reagan is the Rams, Ford is the Redskins. When George Allen moved from L.A. to Washington, no one except the zealots called him a turncoat for trying to beat his old squad.

Politics is a game. I'll take my candidate and beat yours or, if the coin flip comes up otherwise, your candidate and beat mine. It's X's and O's on a media blackboard, mousetraps and blitzes and crackback blocks and penalties and desire and execution and fumbles and breaks. Putting points on the board during the network evening news show. Adding up delegate counts, like touchdowns and field goals. Entertainment for the masses, America's No. 1 sport.

"I wanted to be a football coach," sighs Stu Spencer. "But I had lots of interest in social problems. Not that I've ever been a bleeding heart . . ."

"Sure, aides can brief him. But if a guy's deep, he's deep. If he's shallow, he's shallow."

STU SPENCER *to Myra MacPherson, re What Lyn Nofziger Can Do for Ronald Reagan*

The professional image-maker, unlike the hot-eyed amateur campaign worker and tunnel-visioned ideologue, assesses the strengths and weaknesses of the opponent and his own candidate with a certain technical detachment.

Spencer concedes that Reagan is one of the best political speakers in America, a powerhouse personality on television. But he also believes that his former client is subject to lapses and is vulnerable to the Big Mistake if caught by questions "when his blood sugar's low." Unless Reagan is kept on a leisurely paced schedule, says Spencer, he will "pull a Goldwater" and self-destruct.

On the other side of the field, Spencer concedes that his own candidate's road-show campaigning poses a major problem.

Somewhere between Reagan's low blood sugar and Ford's political hyperkinesis is a perfect candidate, and someday Stu Spencer may locate him. Maybe build one from the ground floor: a Bionic Candidate. For the moment, it is enough to weigh the strengths and weaknesses of both sides and say: "I work for the President of the United States. That's a fair beginning for any campaign."

True, but Jerry Ford's problem remains: after a year and a half he doesn't project as a PRESIDENT but as an accident who stumbled out of Watergate into the Oval Office. Stu Spencer knows that his client has squandered the Executive presence in sweaty photo opportunities and celluloid-thick media events. Kennerly to the contrary, there is no such thing as a free publicity lunch. Apart from the self-inflicted damage of having issued the Pardon (with its PR rationale of *"Take the public opinion heat now, not later"*), Ford's decline in the polls is the high price of un-Presidential exposure.

After eighteen months of giving the White House press corps the "Hi, guys" treatment, Jerry Ford, who wants to be seen in the image of another accidental President, Harry Truman, has come through only as a Republican Hubert Humphrey. Available, like a friendly puppy. But not a national leader.

For a President, there is a time to mingle at the grass roots and a time to stay in the Oval office; a time to speak and a time to say no comment; a time to ask for network preemption and a time to turn away from the cameras.

ESOTERIC MARGINALIA FROM LOSING CAMPAIGNS PAST

How Richard II Blew It

The skipping King, he ambled up and down . . .
Grew a companion to the common streets,
Enfeoff'd himself to popularity;
That, being daily swallowed by man's eyes
They surfeited with honey and began
To loathe the taste of sweetness, whereof a little

More than a little is much too much.
So, when he had occasion to be seen,
He was but as the cuckoo in June . . .

. . . Or for That Matter, December

Ron Nessen went into a late afternoon tirade yesterday, following adverse coverage of Just Plain Jerry's televised pratfall on skis. Nessen was furious. He told an informal gathering of reporters that "this President is healthy, he is graceful, and he is by far the most athletic President within memory."

Oh, yes, one more item: "He is the best-coordinated President in recent history."

A White House scenario as written by Mel Brooks: There is the echo here of Kenneth Mars as the looney, unreconstructed Nazi in *The Producers*, fulminating that "Hitler was a better *dresser* than Shurshill, Hitler was a better *dancer* than Shurshill . . ."

The President's second press secretary came to the job from television—the first electronic journalist ever named White House spokesman—and up to now has demonstrated a greater gift for the cosmetics than the mechanics of his new assignment.

Nessen's most significant innovation to date has been the Presidential news conference *al fresco*, using the Rose Garden as a backdrop for Ford's meetings with the press. There has also been much consideration given by the White House press office to "new and different formats" as well as increased use of "visuals" to jazz up the dull routine of merely furnishing substantive answers to questions. Ford's wearing that WIN button at the first Rose Garden news conference a year ago is an example of what a "visual" can do to dramatize a Presidential program. (O.K., the program was a dog—but the *button* was a winner . . .)

Appearances, appearances . . . Yet, in this latest flap the Retired Flack has it on good, leaked authority that the press secretary is simply overreacting to his Boss's mood, not unusual for PR men who take their jobs seriously. Even-tempered Jerry, according to my sources, has privately been bitching about the emphasis the news media keeps giving his alleged clumsiness.

Publicly, however, Ford claims he isn't as concerned about the ski-dumping episode as his press spokesman. He tells Frank Cormier of the Associated Press that the television clip and front-page photos of his falling might even be a "plus" (a favorite Fordism), since most skiers take falls.

Ford needs eyeglasses. He carries eyeglasses with him. But the uncosmetic President won't wear glasses in public, for the cameras. Some staff members say that the Boss's stumbling and head-bumping—notably, the missed airplane ramp steps and his helicopter exit-and-entry problem—are the result of his refusal to concede his optical age.

Nixon had the same hang-up. What is contradictory about Ford's vanity, however, is that his two professed Presidential heroes, Harry Truman and Teddy Roosevelt, both wore glasses in public. If Ron Nessen's boss were sufficiently introspective to assess his strengths and weaknesses as a national leader in terms other than the personal vanity of an aging former jock, he might realize that being photographed wearing eyeglasses isn't that bad for the Presidential image. His pollster, Bob Teeter, could even take a survey on the issue: more Americans wear eyeglasses than fall on their prats on the ski slopes of Vail.

Year's end, '75

"Jim's a pure pragmatist. He'll push for major policy positions solely on the basis of how they will play in the media. Under Nixon, he'd come up with entirely new programs overnight, just so they'd make the Sunday papers and the news magazines."

> *Ford staffer describing*
> *administrative skills of James*
> *Cavanaugh, White House holdover*
> *from the Nixon years*

The congenital PR problem of the Ford Presidency is one of historical self-identity. Any effective political image-projection has to proceed from the candidate's sense of his own *persona*. Jerry Ford is at home with the trappings of the Presidency, but when he looks in the mirror he still sees the Congressman from the Fifth District of Michigan. He has spent his entire political career as one of hundreds in the Congressional crowd that stood to applaud and fawn over Truman, Eisenhower, Kennedy, Johnson, Nixon, when they traveled in *Limo One* to Capitol Hill. When he thinks of "the President," he thinks of them, individually and collectively.

For a Presidential PR man, this makes for malleable substance. But malleable substance is not necessarily the stuff of good public relations. When a client is too malleable, given to taking advice from professional and amateur flacks alike, he comes out silly putty. Ford, exhilarated by the wonders of his new PR machinery, is not like his predecessors, Johnson and Nixon, who, while PR motivated, were convinced they were the best PR men on the premises. The incumbent is open to all the in-White House advice he can get, from his photographer, to his press secretary, to the gagwriter, to his son Jack. And so he stumbles from Presidential image to Presidential image, his disparate assortment of flacks one week patterning his incumbency after Truman's, the next week after Eisenhower's—and, during *Mayagüez* week, even reminding reporters of the "parallel to Teddy Roosevelt."

But behind this personal coterie of advisors, there is another public relations apparatus around Jerry Ford—holdovers from the Nixon years, whose PR modus operandi leads him in the direction of the Presidential image he most needs to avoid.

If there was one area in which Richard Nixon succeeded in shaping his desired image as a national leader, both as Vice-President and President, it was in the field of foreign affairs. Whether Nixon was a foreign policy expert in fact as well as reputation—more so, for example, than John Kennedy or Lyndon Johnson or Hubert Humphrey or George McGovern—is neither here nor there. How do you measure the unmeasurable? Nixon simply worked, over the years, to create his public image as a national leader "experienced" in foreign affairs, on first-name terms with foreign leaders; and the news media, whatever scrutiny it gave his qualifications in other areas, did not question his "grasp" of the international situation.

From the mid-1950s, when he determined that his best route to the White House ran through Moscow, Paris, London, and Bonn, Nixon worked to mold that image, to gain that media acceptance.

It was the priority item on his PR agenda during his years as Eisenhower's Vice-President.

And how does the ambitious national office-seeker establish an image and reputation as a foreign policy "expert"? He travels. Armed with briefing books prepared by the State Department, he flits from capital to capital, every mile in motion representing another course credit. Two trips without an unfavorable incident provides any working politician a media-conferred degree in foreign affairs. Graduate degrees come with additional trips. The number of courses required here may vary. It takes only one trip to South America, for example, to qualify as an authority in that area, but three to five trips to earn media recognition for special knowledgeability about Western Europe. The Middle East, as any journeyman flack on Capitol Hill knows, can be had in two lessons: one trip to Tel Aviv and Jerusalem to demonstrate "concern" for the area; a second to Cairo and/or one other Arab country to get a graduate degree. Asia requires a few more fly-ins: Peking, of course; then Tokyo, Jakarta, New Delhi, Singapore, Bangkok; topped off by a layover in Hong Kong to talk to "refugees" and to be photographed shopping.

What the traveling politician actually absorbs by quick-hitting junkets composed of stilted foreign policy "discussions" with foreign leaders is nebulous. But Vice-President Nixon established the PR form and any contemporary Presidential candidate who has *not* traveled overseas is at a terrible disadvantage. (Note: Military service doesn't count in grading foreign policy expertise.) The press will label him "inexperienced"—as distinguished from an opponent who has "conferred" with heads of state and shopped in Hong Kong.

One of Jerry Ford's priority PR concerns on taking over the Presidency is establishing an image as a foreign policy expert equal, if not superior, to his predecessor. There are those still around the White House who are familiar, indeed intimate, with the thinking and logistics that went into Nixon's 1971–72 travels. Nothing can better enhance the "Presidential" look as an election year approaches, they advise their new Chief, than broadening overseas travel. The Presidential seal abroad is a publicity grabber no competitor can hope to match.

"But as I return from this trip, just as been the case on my return from other trips abroad which have taken me to over eighty countries, I come back to America with an even stronger faith in our system of government.

"As I flew across America today, all the way from Alaska, over the Rockies, the Plains, and then on to Washington, I thought of the greatness of our country. And most of all, I thought . . ."

PRESIDENT NIXON *on his return*
from China, 1972

So Jerry Ford travels to China, the first President to take a Congressional publicity junket with no substantive purpose. The news media understand the trip as a PR contrivance, as do the Chinese. Inevitably the trip gets bad reviews.

Piercing the White House flacks' façade, newsmen zero in on bickering among Ford staff members. They are particularly critical of such Barnum & Bailey publicity stunts as Ford's pushing his schedule up to cross the International Dateline to place a wreath both at Corregidor and Pearl Harbor on both December sevenths.

In his frenetic drive to establish himself as "Presidential," Ford succeeds not for the first time in proving the opposite: "Only Jerry Ford," says one exhausted critic en route home, "could make a trip to Peking, China, seem like a trip to Pekin, Illinois."

What the traveling press doesn't see and hear, however, is the running skirmish among the President's flacks regarding the lead line in Ford's Honolulu speech summing up the "achievements" of his journey. Should he announce a "Ford Doctrine"? The President's speechwriter, with support from the press staff, believes that putting your name to a major foreign policy pronunciamento is *de rigueur* for any self-respecting American President in the latter half of the twentieth century. Why, every President since FDR had a "doctrine" of one sort or the other. Why shouldn't Jerry Ford have his own?

Kissinger thinks not. There is nothing really innovative about the President's speech, says the Secretary. Not enough to be called a "doctrine" in the sense that it represents a major departure from previous U.S. policy. In the argument between puff and substance, a compromise is reached. There will be a "doctrine" but not a "Ford Doctrine." Rather, "the New Pacific Doctrine."

Son of CREEP

The PFC. When Jerry Ford was honeymooning the country in the autumn of 1974, he brought an audience of Republican regulars to their feet by promising that "never again" would a political organization independent of Republican national and state committees be permitted to operate a Presidential campaign. Meaning, no more CREEPs. Now the honeymoon is over. There is a President Ford Committee, operating independently of party machinery, responsible only to the White House, running the President's campaigns along the same lines—presumably, minus a dirty tricks department—of the Nixon Committee to Re-elect the President. The old CREEP mailing lists are used to solicit volunteer workers. The same advance men work up crowds, arrange balloon lifts and other visuals for Presidential travels. And the same graphics on brochures, streamers, and buttons merchandise the candidate: the identical bold serif Times Roman typeface, that this year says only PRESIDENT FORD. White letters over dark blue on the buttons, over sky blue on the posters (or, on some buttons and posters, flush red). Strong, but "dignified," says Jack Frost, the fifty-eight-year-old former J. Walter Thompson designer responsible for Ford's campaign graphics.

Frost, like other key advertising personnel with the President Ford Committee, is a holdover from the Nixon campaigns. Four years ago, CREEP's in-house ad team, called the November Group, was headed by Peter Dailey and John Deardourff. This year the same people call themselves Campaign '76 Media Communications, Inc. The organizational name is changed but not the basic advertising approach on huckstering a White House incumbent. Thematically, this is 1972 all over again, but with a sloganeering twist provided by, of all people, George McGovern.

Gearing his work to overall Ford PR strategy, Frost is enveloping his current client's campaign material in Presidential aura. Thus, the slogan without a predicate: PRESIDENT FORD '76. Giving birth to this understated incumbency message, Ford's admen had a problem they didn't face four years ago. RE-ELECT THE PRESIDENT would be a misstatement, since the client had never been elected to office. ELECT THE PRESI-DENT, on the other hand, is less than incumbential. VOTE FOR and SUPPORT are punchless, uninspired.

One offbeat possibility suggested was to dredge up Pierre Salinger's 1964 campaign verb. That year the former JFK press secretary, as an appointee to the U. S. Senate who also sought the aura of incumbency, asked California voters to RETAIN him. For Ford, this idea was heard out and dismissed. Possibly because Salinger lost his race (to an ex-movie actor yet!). More likely because RETAIN THE PRESIDENT comes off like a solicitation for legal business.

Yet, when the PFC's experts finally did come up with their slogan, it was a steal from another Democrat. McGovern admen, trying to counter Nixon's heavy incumbency theme with a political science-fiction projection, produced PRESIDENT MCGOVERN '72. White typeface on a blue background. Strong, but dignified.

So PRESIDENT FORD '76 it is. A variation on graphics by George McGovern, based on an original theme by Richard Nixon.

FAST FORWARD SPEED *August 1976*

Everywhere the Republican Convention delegates travel in Kansas City this week, Their President Is Watching Them. Ford's Group has cornered the local political billboard market. Huge four-color outdoor boards are at key locations to and from the convention hall. Again, the November Group m.o., reminiscent of Miami Beach in '68 and '72, when NIXON'S THE ONE and RE-ELECT THE PRESIDENT were, if not ubiquitous, at least everywhere it counted.

This year, the stark lettering PRESIDENT FORD '76, with its implicit imperative, is accompanied by the candidate's official campaign photo. Not a smiling Jerry looking his neighbor in the eye over the back fence, but a grim-visaged PRESIDENT, photographed close-up, at the angle Kennerly prescribes as his Boss's best. The close-up is taken from below a podium, so that Ford appears to be looking down from Above, exuding command, firmness.

At the convention hall Reagan's flacks try to counter. They

hand out white on deep-blue placards proclaiming PRESIDENT REAGAN '77. It's a cute idea, but Jack Frost's graphics win the day. Republicans love Father symbols, and that face on the billboard is what they see, coming and going. There He is: PRESIDENT FORD, staring down Kosygin, the Cambodians . . .

January 1976 White House Watch

"At the start of 1976, after 18 months of his first full year in the Presidency, Gerald Ford was on the skids . . . Mr. Ford was increasingly perceived to be a loser, a bumbler, a misfit President who for some reason or other, a reason probably unflattering and possibly dangerous in itself, was prone to slip on airplane ramps, bump his head on helicopter entrances, entangle himself in the leashes of his family dogs, and fall from skis in front of television cameras . . ."

JOHN OSBORNE, *The New Republic*

SOCIAL NOTES Happy New Year, Sheila

The Retired Flack celebrates the New Year at Pisces, the Georgetown club where political power and Potomac panache, such as it is, converge. The club is owned by Peter Malatesta, former Agnew aide who came East from Los Angeles, and Wyatt Dickerson, Nancy's entrepreneur husband. It is politically and socially ecumenical, but no open collars or non-Bloomingdale jeans allowed: strictly Establishment ecumenicism.

Two hours into Election Year, Nick Ruwe, the State Department protocol deputy who entered politics as one of Nixon's early advance men, has an elaborate and forgettable political fable to tell, the moral—not terribly original these days, but unique in parable form—being that Jerry Ford is a klutz.

When Nick finishes, the group around the table, Scotch-by-Scotch, begins to expand on the theme, each with his or her own story: a sort of *Canterbury Tales* covering various facets of Fordian klutzery; continuing, a laugh a minute, until Sheila Weidenfeld, who has been with another group across the room, joins the table.

Sheila Weidenfeld, the career wife of a Washington corporation lawyer, is Betty Ford's striking, dark-haired, come-on-

65

strong news secretary, brought into the White House from the local NBC-TV affiliate. She has been the chief flack in changing Betty Ford's image from that of Congressman Ford's loyal little helpmate to a public personality in her own right: a mediamorphosis capped by a year-end *Newsweek* cover showing a sprightly Betty decorating the family tree, with the bannerline *Free Spirit in the White House*.

The Retired Flack is in the middle of his *Canterbury Tale*, one involving the mangling of a Captive Nations Week speech he wrote for Ford in 1966, when Betty Ford's news secretary leans across the table, coming at me like the Great White Shark.

Now the rule of Republican White House feminist PR is *Smile, don't make waves*. But Betty Ford's husband has had a tough year and Sheila Weidenfeld doesn't intend to ring in the new by taking any crap.

"You PEOPLE . . . you underestimate this man! You're writing him off, BUT YOU'RE WRONG! WRONG! YOU'LL SEE!"

Nick Ruwe rescues his glass from the edge of the table. He smiles his Most Favored Nation protocular smile. "Could be," says the Canterbury pilgrim who advanced for Nixon, nodding in the direction of the pilgrim who flacked for Agnew. "We've been known to have our off years."

The Free-for-All
January–March 1976

The Elimination commences. Like Don Meredith in his cherry-picker announcers' booth, the Retired Flack kibitzes the Candidates, their Game Plans and their Teams, Wednesday morning quarterbacking the Thrill of Victory, the Agony of Defeat.

June 1976

Political image-molders divide into three schools when asked when, as distinguished from how, Presidential elections are won. There is an Early Bird school that believes the first two weeks are the key to winning because, they argue, as the campaign moves along voters turn off the rhetoric. And first impressions stay fixed. The Fast Finish school builds toward a "peak" in the final two weeks, working on the theory that voters don't tune in to candidates or issues until Election Day approaches. Finally, there is the Prenatal school composed of political determinists whose experience included work for candidates like Barry Goldwater or George McGovern. This school believes that some Presidential elections aren't won. They're lost—before the campaign even gets under way.

"Why didn't Jackson go into New Hampshire?" I ask Ben Wattenberg.

"You mean this year? Scoop didn't go into New Hampshire this year because he didn't go into New Hampshire four years ago," Wattenberg replies.

"That's a habit, not a reason," I say.

Wattenberg corrects me: "When you're dealing with a United States Senator," he explains, "a habit is the strongest reason there is."

Wattenberg sits across from me at a red-white-and-green-covered table in the main dining room of the Greenbrier. He wears a pleased expression, having just flown in from Democratic platform meetings in Washington, where, presumably, things are going smoothly. The McGovernites have not taken over the platform, and the Wallaceites have not walked out. Wattenberg is too smart to believe a platform can win an election. But he knows it can lose one.

"So what happened, Ben?" I ask Scoop Jackson's demographics expert. "How did Carter do it?"

"Red-neck chic," he shrugs, using the term become popular in Washington during recent months. "What else can I say? They wanted a centrist candidate, not too far to the left. We had a centrist candidate, not too far to the left. They wanted a low-key candidate with a friendly smile. We had a low-key candidate with a friendly smile. They wanted someone who could prove himself in the primaries. We had a candidate who proved himself in the primaries."

"Come again?"

"You win Massachusetts and New York—two of the biggest Democratic states in the country—you've proved yourself in the primaries. Scoop got more actual Democratic votes than any other candidate." Wattenberg's voice expresses irritation not so much at his questioner as the illogic of the paradox he is spelling out. "If you'd told me last January, 'Jackson will win *both* Massachusetts *and* New York,' I'd have said, 'That's it, he's the nominee.'"

At forty-three, looking fifty, Ben Wattenberg is a Happy Days-throwback, a political theorist absorbed in the lore of the Great Roosevelt Coalition. Jim Farley would have loved him. Better than anyone now living, Wattenberg can explain brilliantly, scientifically, in graphs, charts, old bones, and tea leaves, why FDR won and what it takes for any Democratic Presidential candidate to get elected.

We are at the Greenbrier, White Sulphur Springs, West Virginia, a glistening emerald set in the midst of grubby Appalachia. When the Jacobins finally make their move in America, it will begin here, not an inner city ghetto. There will be coal-blighted miners and their sooty broods coming over the hills from four sides, trampling the greens, one through eighteen, plundering the midday buffet by the tennis courts.

Wattenberg and the Retired Flack are visitors passing through, participants in one of those Washington Experts forums held by business associations for their members; the kind of forum that this year finds the Washington Experts explaining how we went wrong. We are in the dining room with our fellow panelists, awaiting our cue to go on stage, soaking up the opulence: Wattenberg and I, Pete Lisagor of the *Chicago Daily News*, Hugh Sidey of *Time*, Senator Jim Buckley. The only person who looks as if he belongs is Buckley.

During the panel discussion the Retired Flack, uninhibited by his poor record as a prognosticator over the past six months, predicts that Carter will pick Ted Kennedy to be his Vice-Presidential nominee and that John Connally will win the Republican nomination after a Ford-Reagan deadlock.

Wattenberg gives me a pitying look.

"If he's smart," Wattenberg tells me after our Expert panel adjourns, "Carter will pick someone slightly to the right of center. Someone from Washington. Someone who knows the Hill . . ."

He is describing Scoop Jackson, of course. Jackson wants the Vice-Presidential nomination. But he will not get it. I know that, and in his private moments, alone with his charts and demographic *gris-gris*, Ben Wattenberg has to know it. He knows but cannot accept it, for the same reason he finds it hard to explain what happened to his candidate in the primaries. Because to accept what really befell Scoop Jackson and the rest of last winter's thundering Democratic herd is to concede that the world of substantive politics he grew up in, the political discipline in which he is expert, is of secondary tactical importance in a Presidential race; that in the making of a coalition, a good image will beat a good theory every time.

Wattenberg details, in the rationale of his special discipline, what went wrong for the Democratic Establishment candidates of 1976: "When Jackson and Wallace didn't go into New Hampshire, that left it Carter-against-the-Liberals. Carter came off as the conservative. Then the Liberals played it cute: they said, 'Let Carter knock off Wallace,' and they stayed out of Florida. That left Jackson and Wallace to split up the conservative vote. So Carter came off as the liberal to beat Wallace. O.K. Then we got to Pennsylvania and Hubert starts playing games, making suggestive speeches around the country. So people started saying, 'Jackson isn't serious, he's a front for Humphrey.'"

Wattenberg bites his lip, then strokes his mustache. "You know," he says, grimacing into a coffee cup as if it were a crystal ball view of what might have been, "we had a shot in Pennsylvania. We really did—until Hubert started playing his games."

"That was the turning point?"

"No," says Wattenberg, "that was the nail in the coffin." He shrugs. "We dug our own grave. We made Carter. We made him with our own mistakes."

And now, because he is rare among the breed, this substantive political expert makes the supreme concession. He concedes, finally, somberly, that there are elements working in the equation which he perceives but cannot quite make fit into his theories.

"Even New Hampshire wasn't the turning point," Wattenberg admits, shaking his head, half-Lee J. Cobb, half-S. J. Perelman, the tough, shrewd political operative up against an uncomputable absurdity. "The turning point was . . . Iowa. We overlooked Iowa. I've been in this business, how long? Until this year, tell me, who gave a good goddamn about *the Iowa caucuses?*"

In the beginning, there was *Des Moines.* The producer said, *Let there be lights,* and there were lights. And he said, *Let there be sound,* and there was sound. On film.

70

The Iowa caucuses were the ultimate political media event. Ultimate—until television creates and produces its *own* event*oid* in 1980: the First Quadrennial Superpol contest. It will be staged on Tuesday nights of December 1979, advancing the 1980 political season by a month. A preseason invitational, on the order of Roone Arledge's ersatz Superstar contest, with a series of specially simulated political obstacles for the Superpols to overcome.

All in a closed studio. Debates, interviews held on simulated landing strips, with the recorded blast of jet engines piped in. Simulated endorsements, switches, campaign crises. An egg-throwing incident for visual action. Even a William Loeb-type figure standing out of camera range, shouting pungent insults at the candidates and their wives.

All a realistic test, the anchormen will assure us between commercials. A test of the nerves, stamina, ability of the candidates to stand up under pressure. Their capacity to make the sort of on-the-spot visceral decisions required of Presidents.

This was the rationale for the multiplicity of primaries in 1976, the election year in which the news media covering the event did not simply carry the message but influenced the course and outcome of succeeding events.

January 1976

In the green room of "Good Morning, America," John Lindsay, the mediagenic politician turned political analyst, is slumped on the couch, looking over his notes with the same woeful, bewildered countenance with which he once regarded Mario Procaccino in televised debate. Lindsay has just come off a plane from Des Moines.

"It's a bloody mess," he tells me. "There are more reporters and cameras than there are voters. When they ran out of Iowans, they kept asking *me* for interviews."

How much is the media affecting the outcome of the event? Self-consciously, on television and in print, correspondents covering the campaign are asking this question as they pack their bags and head for New Hampshire, where the question will be-

71

come: *How much is the media, by asking themselves how much they're affecting the event, affecting the event?*

Jimmy Carter and the Cult of Personality

In New Hampshire, Democratic voters who had never heard of the man suddenly knew him on the morning after the Iowa caucuses. There was the Cheshire cat winner's grin, seen for the first time on national television. The "Today" show that morning was worth fifty thousand handshakes. And confirmed fifty thousand more.

Don't we remember that face? Oh, yeah. He was the fella who had shaken their hands at shopping centers sometime during the year past. And they had nodded when he said he was running for President, but you know, they hadn't really *heard* of the man, in that way voters have to *hear* about a candidate before they'll mark his name on the ballot.

Iowa confirmed Jimmy Carter's political existence to the voters of New Hampshire. Iowa and "Today." If you see him on "Today," he must be Somebody . . .

"In a state with an established political organization ambitious politicians find the surest road to political success via the organization. (In Georgia) the story is different. Cohesive political forces with lasting power usually consist of the personal followings of an individual. There is no room in it for the professional who wants to ascend to the top, for the top place is taken . . . In consequence, the professional who wants top honors must place himself in opposition, must become an 'anti' " . . .

v. o. KEY (1950)

In the year of the "anti" image, the Southerner has the head start. Jimmy Carter won't have to take any cram course in How to Campaign Against an Establishment. For the ambitious national candidate who sharpened his skills in the South, it's only a matter of elevated sights and adjusted geography. Six years ago, Carter was elected Governor of Georgia running against "the Atlanta crowd." Now the target of his scorn is "the Washington crowd."

Modulated scorn. This isn't the year for pulsating rhetoric. The exhortation and electricity that went with the original John F. Kennedy look is out of style. The haircut still goes, and the even-toothed smile. But not the *haute rhétorique*. Shriver, Udall, Bayh, even the down-home populist Fred Harris, don't comprehend this. Or if they do, don't react to it properly. They speak hotly of hot issues. Carter speaks softly of dimly limned Sunday school precepts.

Such is his style. Rather, one of his styles, since he has several in his political clothes-closet. But this is the style that comes to him naturally. A style of modulated intonation, comfortable sermonizing. Carter is projecting himself, not a political program. Shriver, Udall, Bayh, Harris can no more be separated from their programs than can Siamese twins be unlinked at the skull.

To this natural Carter style, his public opinion expert, Patrick Caddell, has now given a label: *thematic campaigning*, yet another fad term in the polling trade, as was "programmatic" in the early 1970s.

Caddell is one of those young, bright, campaign technocrats that the political press finds irresistible. Like John Sears, he loves to talk, converting into jargon things that old, bright campaign managers, the Farleys and Len Halls, knew but did not publicly classify at news conferences. In his mid-twenties, Carter's pollster was certified a genius at his craft four years ago, in the Democratic primaries. His reputation didn't suffer even after his candidate, George McGovern, was annihilated in November. *That* was the candidate's fault, whereas winning the primaries was *Caddell's* doing.

This is the mark of the political professional. It is also the reason their clients sometimes tend to regard them as hired guns, not members of the "team." Credit is all theirs, failure is the candidates'.

Caddell has claimed Jimmy Carter's natural style as his own professional creation. In Georgia they call it a handshakin'-and-smoke-blowin' campaign. Now it is Caddell Thematics. The pollster would lead the news media to believe—and it suits the purpose of key columnists and reporters to report—that Jimmy Carter's every word and gesture is diagrammed on Pat Caddell's blackboard.

73

Carter, for his part, doesn't go out of his way to discourage this image, although it could come back to haunt him. He believes Caddell's reputation with the press gives his campaign credibility. He seeks to project himself as a man who knows where he's headed, a candidate sure of his destiny, like JFK in 1960.

"When I become your President—" Carter tells audiences, risking an impression of arrogance in order to jolt listeners into taking him seriously.

Even Carter's accent, in the political ambiance of these early caucuses and primaries, works to his advantage. The quiet Southern country softness contrasts favorably with his opponents' substantive intensity. Shriver, Udall, Harris, Bayh have the quick, ready answers. But Johnson had answers. Nixon had answers. The best political answer for a candidate this year is that you don't have any answers.

Just as the New Rhetoric is anti-rhetorical and the New Public Relations is anti-public relations, the Politics of 1976 is anti-politician. This, claims Peter Bourne, is where the Carter image has the edge. Bourne says he calculated 1976 would turn into this sort of political year when he wrote that first letter memo to the Governor in 1972, setting out all the reasons why the time would soon be ripe for Jimmy Carter, a Southerner, to run for President.

"I first brought up the subject on a plane ride back to Atlanta from Washington," says Bourne. "Jimmy had just testified before Muskie's intergovernmental committee. I talked and he listened, looking out the plane window and smiling every now and then. When I finished, he shook his head and said, 'No, I'm not interested—but if I were . . .' And he began to tick off the things that would have to be done, what he would do, to put a Presidential campaign together. That was when I decided it wouldn't be a waste of time to put it all down on paper."

Only Jody Powell, of all the members of Carter's inner circle, couldn't see it. *If Jimmy runs*, said Powell at the first of the 1973 meetings where plans were laid for the Presidential campaign, *he'll only embarrass himself. Vice-President, maybe. But not President.*

Odd. Bourne isn't a native Southerner and Jody Powell is. I would have thought that Jimmy Carter's native Georgia press secretary, rather than his English-born house intellectual, would have been the first to grasp the perfect logic of the situation. Which is this: If the trick is to run against a political Establishment, who knows how to do it better than a Southern politician?

Yankees, unless rich and arrogant, like Rockefeller, or rich and hyperactive, like Shapp, are conditioned by political upbringing to start at the bottom and work their way up. But young, upwardly mobile Southern politicians come kicking at the door of power at whatever level they choose. They show little respect for organized political authority and no appreciation whatever for electoral order. Contempt for the "crowd," the "machine," the "gang" in Atlanta, Montgomery, Jackson, Baton Rouge, lack of awe for power-brokers, a refusal to stay in place, are the distinctive political characteristics.

In this anti-Systemic electoral milieu, personal image, not campaign organization, is the single most valuable element in the winning of elections. A Jimmy Carter or George Wallace, no matter how small his home community or political base, can go as far as hubris and image will project him. Unlike his counterparts in the organized two-party North, he does not have to say please or thank you to qualify for top office. Nor does he have to start his career as a go-fer, toting ham-and-cheese sandwiches and coffee to the bosses in the backroom, then becoming an alderman, then a county judge or legislator.

No. In Jimmy Carter's Georgia, an ambitious man does not have to go along to get along. He need only read the history of his state and region to know that if Gene Talmadge, Lester Maddox, Big Jim Folsom, Theo Bilbo, Earl Long can become Governor, anybody can become Governor. It was only a matter of time until one or more such Southerners took the measure of Presidents and arrived at the same conclusion.

SEND THEM A MESSAGE: Conserving his energy, George Wallace is spending his time in Massachusetts and Florida during

75

this early primary phase. But his spirit broods over New Hampshire, the archetypal primary state.

This is the ideal starting point for an irrational process. New Hampshire isn't even a good cross section of New England. It is important, even newsmen admit, only because they say it's important. (NEWS MEDIA MAGNIFY CAMPAIGN is the headline in the *Times*.) That confessed, they continue to say it's important.

In terms of geography alone the process is ass-backward. California first, New Hampshire last, West to East, would make more sense. Politically, because California *is* the American Cross Section State, a good place for a weeding-out process to begin. Climatically, because campaigning the San Fernando Valley in January–February beats Concord by several dozen degrees. Nevertheless, there are no local fears that New Hampshire might one year give a primary and nobody will come. Politicians are creatures of bad habit. However inane, a political process rooted in tradition cannot easily be changed.

Besides, New Hampshire will go to any extreme to remain the First Primary State. When Florida threatened to advance its primary, the legislature in Concord took emergency measures to guarantee that no matter how any other state juggles its schedule, this will remain the first of the Presidential obstacle courses. A logician in Boston has recommended a more meaningful referendum on national leadership: an all-New England primary. But Concord turns a deaf ear trumpet.

We have a good thing going, explain the locals. *Why share it?* Cost media observers trace this parochial view to mercantile greed. The candidates' ad agencies and touring news media are quadrennial boons to the local economy. But talking to New Hampshire pols and businessmen, I get the impression that their hunger is spiritual as much as commercial. They want New Hampshire on the map. Local pride, and more. They like the national recognition and civic excitement that comes with occupying centerplace in the political world, if only for six weeks every four years.

This is why George Wallace's slogan of four years ago (created by his Montgomery flack Joe Azbel) is a model for all

76

political slogan-makers. SEND THEM A MESSAGE exploits the main motivational factor that drives primary voters to the polls in an age of political disenchantment. It goes to the *why* of primary voting: not to elect a President, but to register political dissent. New Hampshire to California, January to June, the process isn't a popularity but an unpopularity contest. Primary voters are out to vent frustrations. Come November, they'll choose a President. For now, they'll cattle-prod the politicians.

SEND "THEM" A MESSAGE: but *whom?* PR strategy in primaries is aimed at avoiding any voter perception of your candidate as one of THEM. This is why front-runners operate under a handicap—apart from the national media's peculiar grading system for registering Wins and Losses: once a candidate is identified as the front-runner, he becomes a target. Primary voters are out to rock the boat, attract national attention to grievances. By the time they reach voting age, they have watched enough TV and read enough newspapers to know that you don't achieve this by doing the predictable. The spirit that broods over the Presidential primary process this year—in any period of popular disenchantment with the system—is one of perversity, not affirmation. The *anti's* have it.

New Hampshire, 1952

ESTES IS THE BESTES' is the soft-spoken Southerner's slogan (and why not the best?). Without entourage, the upstart anti-Establishment populist from Tennessee, opposed by the bosses from the outset of his political career, shuffles through the unfamiliar snows of Manchester, Concord, Laconia. Holding out a hand at shopping centers. Smiling his self-effacing smile. Telling anyone who'll stop to listen: "Hello, my name is Estes Kefauver and I'm running for President."

The political press in this pre-Supermedia era is not yet obsessed with the mechanics of campaigning. There are no in-depth interpretive analyses of Kefauver's "game plan," technical apparatus, or psycho-history. Nevertheless, copy coming out of New Hampshire contains bemused references to the candidate's unusual apolitical style: Estes (he encourages first-name familiarity) doesn't come on strong, preceded by political hacks work-

*ing for local ward leaders. Nor does he have big-name Washing-
ton endorsements. All he has is housewives, middle-class
suburban volunteer workers who discovered their candidate on
television, watching him beard the criminals and corrupters who
came before his Senate crime investigating committee. Estes, they
believe, isn't like those other politicians. He's clean. He owes
nothing to the bosses. He'll straighten out the mess in Washington.*

*Kefauver is the first politician to realize that the old political
process is changing. Mass communications and transportation
have produced a political anomaly: while American society has
become less individualized, new opportunities have opened up for
the individual politician who knows his A.M. and P.M. deadlines.
An ambitious office-seeker who makes contact with the public
through the press rather than a power broker can acquire a personal following distinct from anything a political organization
has to offer.*

*Another decade will pass before anyone outside academe
quotes Marshall McLuhan. The word "cool" is still known only
to progressive jazz musicians and their followers. But the year
before, in 1951, Kefauver's live daytime TV drama, featuring the
Honest Country Boy Senator versus the Big City Mob, gave him
instant national celebrity. Now he is challenging an incumbent
President of his own party in a primary. It is an unheard-of act
of political insolence.*

*When Kefauver wins in New Hampshire, the incumbent Pres-
ident decides he will not be a candidate for re-election. Estes has
deposed the leader of the Washington crowd, but he has under-
estimated the residual power of the political Establishment. In
1952 a maverick can win every primary, but the bucking
stops at the convention. In Chicago, the old crowd rolls over the
Kefauver Phenomenon in full view of tens of millions of Americans who are watching their national conventions on television
for the first time.*

*So much for the New Politics in Grass-roots Harry Truman's
day. But Estes' experience with the politics of direct national
campaigning is not wasted on other ambitious politicians in-a-*

78

hurry. Two decades later an anti-Washington candidate, boning up on the history of modern primaries, takes extensive notes on the Kefauver New Hampshire campaign of 1952. He concludes that Kefauver's campaign style has considerable merit for a country boy candidate from the South. The Tennessean was simply a political John the Baptist for a Georgian to follow.

The New Hampshire locals are not alone in their egocentric desire for national attention, of course. The need for recognition —other than by being declared a federal disaster area—is endemic to states and communities outside the Celebrity Belt of national media concentration. In a sense, the primary is to New Hampshire what that Ozymandian oddity, the Superdome, is to New Orleans. Or what being named to the top ten on the Soviet hit list meant to Birmingham, Alabama, in the mid-fifties.

The Retired Flack recalls a 1957 campaign, during the Dig-a-Shelter era, when what was then called the Office of Civil Defense issued a press release designating Birmingham one of the most likely American cities to be atomized in the event of World War Three. Local political incumbents flaunted this citation as evidence of community industrial progress. Under their administration Birmingham had been *put on the map*—if only one that a Ukrainian navigator could read.

So with New Hampshire. The Granite State hasn't had much to brag about since Daniel Webster. Its primary gives it a place in the sun, by dang, and that's the way folks hereabouts mean to keep it. Let Boston have its own primary if it wants. But not before Manchester's.

In 1968, George Romney was "brainwashed" into political oblivion and Lyndon Johnson's latent hopes for re-election were stillborn in the snows. Four years ago Ed Muskie, impelled by his own PR instincts, was televised speaking from a flatbed truck with snowflakes running down his face. Was it melting flakes or tears? Whichever, the Muskie Presidential campaign was never the same.

As Ohioans once took pride in their state as the Mother of Presidents, so do New Hampshire voters now relish their reputa-

79

tion as the Aborter of Presidential candidacies. Johnson's stand-in actually won the raw vote count in 1968, as did Muskie in 1972. But both "lost" New Hampshire. They failed to beat the spread. Victory here consists of more than winning at the polls on primary day. The news media's High-Low Expectation scoring system requires that a candidate measure up to newsmen's predictions. If a candidate is predicted to do poorly, as were Gene McCarthy and George McGovern, losing by less than the spread becomes a victory.

Jimmy the Greek would understand, but Ed Muskie still doesn't. He fumes, as only Ed Muskie can fume, when the subject of news coverage in New Hampshire comes up in conversation. Aside from being the front-runner, the Senator was expected to win overwhelmingly because he is a "neighbor."

This year's "neighbor" is Sargent Shriver, who, while not strictly a New Englander, has the Kennedy connection. This is reflected in his campaign by the presence of Dick Drayne, Teddy's former press secretary, as media coordinator, and by various members of the family speaking at coffee klatches around the state.

Shriver has taken elaborate precautions to avoid Muskie's fate: *absolutely* nothing is expected of him. *I am running fifth*, he tells reporters, *in a field of five*. He gets no argument. Drayne is among the best of Democratic publicist-speechwriters, a flack who, if handling Ted Kennedy, would be acclaimed by the media as a master PR strategist of this campaign. But something is missing in Sarge Shriver, an indefinable chemical element that political observers recognize only after a candidate catches fire. Drayne's candidate entered this race under the misapprehension that his 1972 Vice-Presidential campaign had established him an attractive candidate in his own image, apart from the Kennedy connection. He meets people well, is pleasant-looking, has a firm handshake, is articulate to a fault (there is the reminder of Humphrey, not a Kennedy, in the way Shriver *spritzes* his ideas at audiences). Sarge even claims—and it checks out—that Carter's "outsider" theme is one he used on the Vice-Presidential campaign circuit four years ago. Still, *something* is missing. The

80

element that no amount of flackery, no PR mastermind, can instill. Candidates either have it or they don't. Dick Drayne in New Hampshire this year is the Casey Stengel of the Brooklyn Dodger period. Give the man the right elements, he could win it all. Ted Kennedy would sweep this field, beat the spread, and big. But Ted's brother-in-law leaves his neighbors cold as a snowbank in Laconia.

Fred Harris is too fat. Either Jim Hightower, his national co-ordinator, or Frank Greer, his media coordinator (Harris is big on "coordinators," not "managers"), should have put the candidate on a protein diet before he came to New Hampshire. Harris needs to lose thirty pounds, for credibility's sake. He has the populist message down pat, but a candidate who rails against hunger with shaking jowls is only making it hard on himself. Add Arlo Guthrie, who plays at Harris rallies, and you come up with a great draw for Southampton and Beverly Hills Gucci Radical fund-raisers. But not much appeal for Nashua, New Hampshire.

Harris represents Hot Populism, the old-fashioned soak-the-rich, tub-thumping kind, straight out of the 1930s. As a spellbinder, he is no match for the old-timers of my Louisiana youth, Huey and Earl Long. But in his own ham-voiced way, Harris remains authentic. An authentic throwback. He pulls no punches, says exactly what he means. Simplistic answers, fierce ideology, but the most honest candidate in the race. What you hear is what you'll get, no fuzz around the edges.

QUESTION AT TOWN HALL RALLY: *What is your position on a constitutional amendment to outlaw abortions?* HARRIS: *I'm against it.*

Three words, that's it. No ifs, ands, buts. It is the trait the people say they most seek in candidates, yet the trait least found, because smart candidates know the *people* don't mean what they say.

Harris makes audiences uneasy. The Gucci Radicals give him money only because they know he won't be elected. He frightens all but True Believers like Jim Hightower, in the way Goldwater frightened everyone but his faithful. Fred will be a folk hero of the left, the candidate-who-would-not-compromise. It is a nice image to paste in his scrapbook, something to show his grandchildren. Except for that, Oklahoma Crude is wasting his time.

Mo Udall, because he is six feet plus, gaunt, and furrows his brows when making a rhetorical point, is being called "Lincolnesque." Bad imagery. The last Lincolnesque figure to run in a New Hampshire primary was Ed Muskie. The Lincoln look, for some reason, doesn't sell well here.

Udall is another unanswered media mystery for PR experts to ponder. By any objective standard, an Arizona Congressman and former basketball jock who plunges into a Presidential race should be embraced by newsmen as good copy. Yet Mo's campaign is getting bad reviews. They say it's his larded liberal rhetoric and monotonal speaking style. But I trace Udall's problem to something else: the jaded perspective of Washington political correspondents covering the primary. To an outside observer, Udall comes through as a grass-roots Western personality, well-informed, quick-witted. But National Capital newsmen see him as the same old Mo they've known for sixteen years, talking about the same programs, cracking the same jokes. Hardly as newsworthy as that new kid on the block from Georgia, about whom they can write reams of fresh copy pondering, in depth, whether he has any programs or sense of humor.

Birch Bayh's problem is *déjà vu*. Audiences leave his meetings with the feeling that they've been there before, seen that boyish grin, heard that let's-get-this-country-moving-again speech. He is ersatz JFK Model 47398, an image whose time has passed. Holding a lemon, his flacks try to make a lemonade. They advertise their candidate's status as a member of the Washington crowd: *"It takes a good politician,"* goes the Bayh campaign theme, *"to run a country."* Also a negative variant: *"There's more to running a country than peanut farming."*

It is all defensive strategy, a loser's theme. The Retired Flack is impressed that Birch Bayh is the sort of superficial whiz candidate that Presidential primaries are intended to weed out.

82

GREAT IDEAS OF MIDWESTERN MAN Senator Birch Bayh

"Those of you who have known me longest know I have never had any burning desire to be President of the United States."

> Announcing his candidacy,
> Shirkieville, Indiana,
> December 29, 1975

"I don't like to be satisfied with third, but I thought from the first that would be the best we could get."

> Assessing a flickering
> desire, Manchester. N.H.,
> February 24, 1976

About all Birch Bayh has going for him here is the opposition of William Loeb and the Manchester *Union-Leader*. Loeb has singled Bayh out for the Treatment, because of his record favoring federal gun control laws. In another primary year, getting singled out for the Treatment by the *Union-Leader*'s publisher-editor could be bad news to a candidate. But this year any distinction that separates a Democrat from the herd can't be all bad. Curley's Law: *As long as they spell the name right* . . .

Besides, Bayh has been spared the full Treatment, the sort of editorial pounding that drove Ed Muskie to that flatbed truck in the snow. Loeb's energies are concentrated on the Republican primary. His *Union-Leader*, taking Gerald Ford at his word that he isn't as paranoid about criticism as his predecessor, is given to front-page description of our Non-Imperial President as "Jerry the Jerk." It could get worse. As an editorialist, Loeb thinks nuance is a four-letter word. Hard as he was on Muskie, there is a special editorial hell-fire the *Union-Leader* reserves for those considered errant Republicans.

Loeb is also being distracted this campaign by coverage of his own influence over New Hampshire politics. At age seventy he has become a media celebrity and, appearing on television ("Meet the Press," Susskind, Tom Snyder), where he can be dissected as a political Loch Ness monster, something out of the Neanderthal Age.

In this case media-covering-media may be justified. Whether he operated the biggest paper in New Hampshire (circulation 65,000) or a box factory in Nashua, Loeb stands out as a unique personality embodying, as De Gaulle did *La Belle France*, the First Angry Man spirit of the New Hampshire primary. Right down to the .38 caliber pistol ("to avoid unpleasant situations") that he cuddles by his armpit.

Loeb is an *Agin*-er, distrustful of power and politicians in Washington. To such a man the Nation's Capital is a contaminated precinct where, if even a good Republican spends too much time, he can only become a disease carrier. The *Union-Leader* once backed Eisenhower and Nixon, later opposed them with the same energy and nuance it now gives Jerry Ford's incumbency. Were Loeb's current favorite, Ronald Reagan, elected President, his day as "Ronnie the Wriggler" wouldn't be long in coming.

Bill Loeb hasn't paid much attention to the candidate from Georgia, but if the *Union-Leader* starts to give the Treatment to Jody Powell's Boss, Loeb might find himself reaching for his .38 to avoid one of those unpleasant situations. Journalists who torment Jody's Boss hear from him instantly, by telephone or letter, a favorite conversational opener being the threat of a heavy lawsuit. That bluff failing, Jody will refute the offending piece, point by frigging point. Like his Boss, he is a deep-fried Southern Baptist who knows how to blaspheme in two languages: south Georgia Holy Roller and West Coast Rolling Stone.

Jody Powell is your loyal, overprotective, combative flack of political legend, wholly dedicated to the exaltation of his client. The client wouldn't have any other kind of press secretary. Not for long. Jimmy Carter doesn't like a critical press, and not just in the way that Hubert Humphrey and most politicians don't like a critical press. Rather, the way Lyndon Johnson and Richard Nixon didn't. Very tough. Hardball. Screw the bastards.

Jimmy can get mean. Jody's blasphemous calls only reflect his Boss's mood of the moment. Carter felt that way about the press in Georgia and he isn't about to change for the Washington crowd. As a state Senator, Carter introduced himself to Reg Murphy of the *Atlanta Constitution* waving a rolled copy of the paper in Murphy's face, telling him that a critical piece carried in his rotten rag was a crock. That was the high point of the Carter-Murphy relationship. After Jimmy became Governor, Murphy, then editor of the *Constitution*, went to the head of Jody's List. Sure, good ol' Reg could see the Guvnah. The day after Second Coming, provided Jimmy's not busy doin' the Lord's work.

To the extent that Powell precisely mirrors his Boss's policies and attitudes, he is a very good press secretary, even if his care for logistical detail in a national campaign isn't what it should be. The prime requisite for a good press secretary is one who takes the heat. The bad press secretary disclaims personal responsibility for carrying out his job, blaming the freeze-out of a reporter on either his Boss or some other staff member. The bad flack looks after his own popularity, not his client's. Still, Jody Powell remains popular with the press, despite his peevishness when provoked. For this he can thank the good Lord for blessing him with a glib Country Boy wit. But if worse came to worst—if Jimmy wanted it that way—Jody could put every frigging member of the press corps on his shit list and live with it, no sweat. Even, if she had press credentials, his own grandmother.

Jody Powell is the advisor closest to Carter, the candidate's alter ego, his other self. The Carter-Powell relationship is tighter than that generally found between politician and flack because of the way Powell came to his position. He didn't become Carter's chief spokesman after the candidate had arrived. He knew him *when*. Before *when*.

Now thirty-two, Powell began his political career as Carter's driver during the 1970 race for Governor. Few professional endeavors are more likely to draw two Americans together in common bond than the boredom and frustration of traveling twisted, concave, one-and-a-half-lane blacktop roads, one Southern town to the next, to arrive for a nighttime speech before twenty members of a Lions Club seated around checkerboard tablecloths in back of a local, GOOD EATS—STEAKS—CHOPS establishment, in a bone-dry county; after which the candidate and his driver-aide lay down their day's burden in a bare bed-and-dresser Mom & Pop motel or, if they're lucky, the town's early-model Holiday Inn; after which, next morning, they put down rubber scrambleds while riffling through the Atlanta/Birmingham/ Tallahassee paper, only to discover that the bastards didn't even run the press release specially hand-delivered the previous afternoon.

That was the beginning of Jody Powell's education as a political flack. He began by carrying his candidate's press releases to editors in small Georgia towns, sweet-talking for space, thinking all the while, *Screw the big 'uns.*

You've met one Establishment press, you've met 'em all. In the campaign, Jody Powell plays favorites. With a few exceptions, such as the Washington Star's *Jack Germond (the only professional observer to contend that Carter won the first debate), Powell finds it more convenient to accommodate correspondents based outside the National Capital. Respected old-line Washington journalists like John Osborne if the* New Republic *travel to Plains on the press secretary's promise of an interview with Jimmy, only to be left standing with the pack gathered 'round the fishpond. Osborne's magazine ran Reg Murphy's unflattering piece on Carter during the primaries. It is on the list, until further notice. Osborne will eventually get his interview. But only after Jody has delivered the Boss's message.*

Jimmy, it develops, has a way with non-Establishment journalists, those who work outside Washington. He converts Hunter Thompson at an early stage, based on repeated references to Bob Dylan and The Allman Bros., and, more importantly, a speech on American justice delivered before a Georgia bar group. The same speech, word for word, delivered by Hubert Humphrey before a Minnesota bar group, would leave Thompson retching. But in dealing with the New Left press, Carter benefits from low prior expectations. This fits into Wattenberg's Red-neck Chic thesis. Disenchanted with the political hero-images and crusades of the 1960s, Thompson and other New Journalists are now strangely drawn to a Southern Baptist who says "Eye-talian" (a slip for which Jerry Ford would be mercilessly ridiculed) and owns a wool-hat brother who explains that pronunciation by telling newsmen, "Shit, it took us eighteen years just to learn to say 'colored.'"

More like Gonzo Chic. To such converts, Carter is one last kinky trip beyond traditional liberalism. To say, "So he's a Southerner, so what? is the ultimate shock to their ideological forebears. Carter becomes an item of political exotica, Hare Krishna on the Campaign Trail.

ENCOMIUM: *"Personally, Carter is a soft-spoken, thoughtful, likable man, an introspective man who enjoys the songs of Bob Dylan, the poems of Dylan Thomas, and the writing of James Agee, William Faulkner, John McPhee, and Reinhold Niebuhr. Yet this slightly built, seemingly shy man is also one of the most driven, relentless, downright stubborn political campaigners who ever came out of the South. He stubbornly defied segregation in his home town of Plains; he stubbornly overcame overwhelming odds to become Governor of Georgia, and now he is just as stubbornly running for President."*

Peanut Farmer for President,
by PATRICK ANDERSON, The New York Times
Magazine, *December 14, 1975*

It was Peter Bourne, not Jody Powell, who made the key contact that led to Jimmy Carter's first major Establishment press breakthrough as a Presidential candidate. Bourne met Patrick Anderson last spring at a wine-tasting party hosted by neighbors Gus and Faye Hewlett in Waterford, Virginia, a small semirural village just beyond Washington's suburban sprawl. Between sips and cheeses, Carter's agent stroked Anderson's ear with sufficient eloquence to inspire the writer—fresh from a successful collaboration on Jeb Magruder's best-selling *mea culpa*—to want to meet and travel with Bourne's candidate.

The result was a panegyric published at a crucial time in the pre-primary campaign phase. *The New York Times Magazine* cover enhanced Carter's credibility as a candidate and Anderson's word portrait couldn't have been better for the boss's image had Jody Powell written it himself. Nevertheless, although Powell and Anderson hit it off while on the road with Carter, the press secretary had misgivings about the way the piece was initiated. A jurisdictional dispute is now stirring between Powell, the Country Boy closest to the candidate, and Bourne, the candidate's emissary to the Washington Establishment. With the campaign under way, Powell intends to curb Bourne's flacking activities. The press secretary resents Bourne's first-name relationship with National Capital publishers, editors, and columnists—contacts that were essential to Carter's pre-campaign strategy.

It is a familiar political story and the outcome is predictable. A proconsul to the outer regions, having served his purpose, will inevitably be cut down to size by those closest to the throne.

CARTER N.H. VICTOR;
FORD TRAILS REAGAN

PRESIDENT'S AIDES
BLAME NIXON TRIP

Headline, *Washington Post*

"We knew where our standing was Sunday night. We were ahead. The only thing that could change it was that event. Look at the papers, look at the TV Monday morning—that toast from Peking. It reopened the pardon issue . . . He knew what he was doing. I think he's for John Connally."

Old Pro STU SPENCER,
coolly assessing early returns
from Manchester circa 11 P.M.,
January 24, 1976

"There were two premature headlines in the primaries," Dave Keene says. "The first, after New Hampshire, screwed Reagan. The second, after Wisconsin, screwed Udall."

An academic response to a straight question: *What happened to Reagan?* It is October: Keene is adapting to his new environment, sitting out the general election campaign on the Harvard campus. He has gone where all lucky losing Presidential campaign aides go to recover equilibrium and contemplate their might-have-beens: the John F. Kennedy Institute for Politics.

This is the Retired Flack's second visit here. My first guest lecture was at the invitation of Mark Shields, the Democratic political handler who suffered through the 1972 primaries with Ed Muskie. Shields recuperated by teaching here for a semester, then went on to renew an apparently incurable habit for primary losers. When last seen, he was suffering through Ohio with Udall.

That Keene, a Reaganite and former president of the right-wing Young Americans for Freedom, should be invited to teach a seminar on Presidential campaigning at Harvard is proof that the political climate has changed for the better since the Retired Flack's active days. Ten years ago the idea of a Goldwaterite instructing an Ivy League class would have been considered material for slapstick. Apparently Harvard students and conservative ideologues have matured over the past decade. That, or somebody has sold out.

Keene looks overweight, but not, he assures me, from a sell-out. Gained it, he says, working early and late for Ron after the failure of John Sears's first game plan.

REAGAN GAME PLAN NO. 1: *To win the first four major Republican primaries, one victory leading to the next. The game is dominoes. When New Hampshire falls, Florida falls, then North Carolina, then Illinois. With that the party hack coalition behind Ford collapses. The right-wing pols with Ford for no other reason than his incumbency move to Reagan, a winner, while the left—Percy, Mathias, possibly even Rockefeller, who still has ambitions—begin to set up their own individual shops. There could be as many as four Stop Reagan entries in the later primaries. Too many, too late. After Ford retires from the race, the job will be mop-up until Kansas City, and Reagan's nomination on the first ballot.*

"I had a friend overseas who first heard the results from New Hampshire in Paris," Keene begins his Tale of Two Headlines. "He didn't get the early report, the one that had Reagan winning. Only the final, that Ford had squeaked through. He remembered how Johnson quit in 1968 when McCarthy got forty percent, so his first impression, before he got the American media's interpretation, was that any sitting President who could carry only fifty percent in a party primary had had it."

What happens to Reagan in New Hampshire later happens to Carter in the first of the Presidential candidate debates: Ford

89

benefits from his inordinate capacity to get himself underes-
timated. Because the public sees him as the stumbling klutz im-
personated by Chevy Chase, the President exceeds popular expec-
tation merely by surviving any adversary confrontation. This
denies Reagan his chief advantage entering a race against an in-
cumbent in the White House. The challenger is the front-runner.
Ford has the Presidential aura that goes with flying into Man-
chester in Air Force One, yet bears the image of an underdog.

HOW THE EAST WAS LOST: Meldrim Thomson is a Republican Governor after Bill Loeb's heart, a granitic right-winger convinced that the country started going to hell when Roosevelt became President. The wild-eyed one, Theodore. To no one's surprise, Thomson enthusiastically prefers Ron Reagan to Jerry Ford, throwing himself into the contest with an abandon that alternately pleases and dismays Reagan's PR strategists.

Thomson knows his state. He comes up with a PR ploy that's a gem. But he hasn't quite got the hang of the Presidential primary publicity game. A second PR ploy, designed to create a bandwagon effect for his candidate, is a bomb.

First, the gem, instantly recognized as such by Reagan's PR staff—a Question-and-Answer format that eliminates the journalistic middleman. What Thomson calls Citizens Press Conferences. Here, perversity is the mother of invention. Thomson, too, has mixed feelings in this campaign. His relate to the national press: reporters from Washington make him either sick or splenetic. He has watched these verbalizing smart-asses operate at news conferences and knows they're no good. No good at all. What they want to do, pure and simple, is stir up trouble for conservatives. Thomson remembers how the press gave Barry Goldwater a hard time in 1964, to the end that Goldwater lost the New Hampshire primary on a write-in, organized in Boston, for that liberal UN nincompoop, Henry Cabbage Lodge.

The Governor will be goddamned if the smart-asses do the same thing to his man Reagan this year. He recommends that instead of holding standard press conferences, Reagan take his Question-and-Answer sessions to the public. He wants Reagan's campaign schedule built around an adaptation of New Hampshire's venerated town hall tradition to modern political format. At Citizens Press Conferences, held throughout the state, the voters themselves will ask the questions. In effect Reagan's answers will be mini-speeches, outlining his position on issues. But the feel of the event will be of "a dialogue instead of a monologue." Rather than COME SEE, HEAR RONALD REAGAN SPEAK, the invitation to the public is COME ASK RONALD REAGAN WHERE HE STANDS.

Participatory public relations. Not without risks, of course. There is predictable adverse reaction on the part of some members of the traveling press, excluded from the CPC questioning process and limited simply to reporting the event. These newsmen consider the CPC format a gimmick.

Gimmick it is. Not, however, a gimmick contrived in the way of Nixon's 1968 televised campaign Q.-and-A. sessions—the ones in which Bud Wilkinson acted as interlocutor and the participating interrogators were shipped in from campaign headquarters central casting. Reagan's citizens are for real. The sessions can get heated. Enough at times to make Lyn Nofziger nervous. Nofziger knows his candidate's testiness under Q.-and-A. pressure.

The CPCs don't preclude the opportunity to plant questions on subjects that Reagan wants to talk about. But in an open, Come One, Come All format, planting can work two ways. Stu Spencer, who also knows about Ron's testiness, can run in ringers to push questions that Reagan doesn't care to be hassled on. Questions such as *Would you provide more details on how you intend to cut the federal budget by ninety billion dollars?*

"The American people," says Nofziger, "aren't interested in details."

This isn't professional cynicism but professional experience talking. Nofziger has worked with candidates hung up on details. He knows there's no faster way to lose a crowd. Political audiences, as Adlai Stevenson once commented, come to cheer. They expect their speaker to act as the cheerleader. Start providing fiscal analyses of the comparative defense capabilities of General Dynamics TFX versus Boeing's model—as Goldwater insisted on doing in '64—and a candidate leaves his followers cold and cheer-less.

Traveling political correspondents, on the other hand, love de-tails. Particularly at the beginning of Presidential campaigns, after they've filed their first run of stories on the candidates' rec-ords and prospects, styles, staffs, families, and medical histories. At that point newsmen are desperate for traction, fresh copy to help them keep their own momentum back at their home offices. The campaign publicist who can imaginatively fill his candidate's stock speech with a novel news lead twice a day, one for A.M.'s, another for P.M.'s, gets high grades. But the candidate who makes the same speech, without innovative inserts, more than four news cycles in a row, becomes a natural enemy to the competitive press. When a Washington bureau correspondent is traveling, salary plus expenses, his editors expect more than copy that says:

> NASHUA, N.H.—Ronald Reagan/George McGovern today re-peated what he said yesterday and the day before—that if elected President he will "bring the federal government closer to the people."

No. At this point the candidate, whether Republican or Demo-cratic, conservative or liberal, must either embellish what he said before or suffer the consequences of a press without traction. This means that the search will be on for speaking fluffs, reports of problems within the campaign organization, crowd estimates—especially low estimates. If the candidate's flack won't supply the imagination, the enterprising political correspondent must do the best he can:

> NASHUA, N.H.—Visibly tired and apparently concerned over rumors of dissension in his campaign organization, Ronald Reagan/George McGovern today stumbled through his standard campaign speech, before a disappointing, listless crowd of . . .

For the flack, speech embellishment in a state or local cam-paign is a relatively simple matter. Promises made by candidates running for state or local offices are taken for what they are: mere campaign rhetoric, something to get the candidate's name in the headlines, his face on the evening news. Something more, however, is expected of candidates for President. Thus, Presidential campaign press-agentry is as it should be—the art at its most sophisticated level. A Presidential speechwriter-flack reaching for a dramatic news lead can only go so far without risk. The flack's trick is to imply solutions while avoiding specifics.

Campaign '52

The polls show that ending the Korean war is the No. 1 issue that concerns voters. Ike's speechwriter Emmet John Hughes, on leave from Tom Dewey's flack corps, turns out the line "I shall go to Korea." An ideal political code line, it leads listeners to infer that which they most want to hear without raising questions as to specifics. Ike does not say, "I shall end the war in Korea," which might lead to problems (At what price?, etc.). This way, the promise to end the war is implied and accepted, no risk involved, no questions asked. Except one from Adlai Stevenson. The Democratic candidate claims he turned down the same line two weeks before and wants to know, in detail, exactly what Ike's going to Korea will accomplish. Stevenson, as Harry Truman by that time is telling everyone around who'll listen, keeps missing the political point of things; which in this case is: the American people aren't interested in details.

But the traveling press *is* interested in detail, not so much for what a candidate's program might reveal as for the questions it might raise. On the national level, a good detailed plan from a candidate is worth anywhere from one to three weeks of news cycles. Beginning (as McGovern learned when he outlined his "Demogrant" program) with the question *How?* Or (as Romney learned in 1968) *Why?*

It was fear of such hot pursuit from the news media that caused Nixon in 1968 to reject the idea of detailing a proposal to end the Vietnam war, drawn up by speechwriter Richard Whalen. Whalen left the Nixon campaign in protest. Romney, under similar pressure, went public with a proposal to "de-Americanize" the fighting. Romney's plan did not, however, satisfy the press. It simply led to more questions as to why the candidate, once a hawk, had shifted his position. And to a memorable answer. After which, Nixon's brainwashed opponent joined his outraged speechwriter along the campaign sidelines.

So Nofziger is right, however cynical he may sound. It's not the American people who are demanding details, it's the press. But that being the case, how did Lyn's candidate come to dig himself into that $90 billion hole?

Beware idealistic speechwriters. They write for a constituency of one, and the one isn't necessarily the candidate. There is no plan-to-end-the-war that has to be spelled out in New Hampshire this year. The No. 1 issue in both primaries seems to be the size and efficiency of federal government. Among the Democrats, Carter is preaching a vague but reassuring sermon on *reorganizing* the bureaucracy, which his New Hampshire listeners interpret to mean *reducing* it. Two different things, but like Ike and Korea, Jimmy is simply promising *I shall go to Washington*. Stevenson-like, his opponents keep asking for details on what he means to do when he gets there. They miss the political point.

Reagan is also running as an anti-Washington candidate who wants to go to Washington. Ron, however, has an idealistic speechwriter, Jeff Bell, a Harvard-educated conservative economist in his early thirties. Bell joined the Reagan campaign in August 1975. From the beginning, he has been leery of the pernicious influence of pragmatic John Sears.

If elected, Bell broods, will Reagan move to the center? Down the primrose path of crypto-liberalism? Or will he take the hardline tack on bloated federal bureaucracy he's promised? By strict conservative standards, Reagan's record as Governor of California was soft in spots. The idealistic researcher-speechwriter, for his own peace of mind, needs to pin his candidate down.

He does just that, in a speech he drafts for Reagan's appearance before the Chicago Executive Club, September 1975. In it, Reagan, not yet an announced candidate, tells his business audience that if he were to run for President and get elected he would return federal taxing authority to state and local governments so that the elected officials closest to the grass roots could handle domestic programs such as welfare, education, housing, medical care. This is standard revenue-sharing rhetoric. Where Bell's proposal is unique is in citing a specific figure. Reagan is pinned down with the line "*Transfer of authority . . . in all these areas would reduce the outlay of the federal government by more than $90 billion.*"

"*Some sapsuckers talk about cutting down taxes. Where are they going to start cutting expenses? On the* spastic *school? They want to cut down on the spastics? On the little children, enjoying the school lunches? Or on those fine old people, white-haired against the sunset of life . . .*"

EARL K. LONG, *quoted by A. J. Liebling, circa 1960*

Stu Spencer knows a contradictory corollary to Nofziger's Rule of Details. It is that if a political candidate chooses to go into specifics on a program that affects a voter's self-interest, the voter *gets* interested. If the proposal involves money, *very* interested. He or she wants to know much more. So Reagan is talking about a $90 billion cut? All right, *whose* programs does he intend to transfer from the federal budget?

Spencer, like Nofziger, practices California jugular PR. When Jeff Bell's September speech surfaces in midwinter, the President Ford Committee blankets New Hampshire with material that charges Reagan with advocating programs that mean increased state property taxes, putting social security on a voluntary basis, doing away with old-age pensions. Everything but cutting down on the spastics and little children enjoying their school lunches.

It is blood-in-the-streets month. Ford is running behind in both New Hampshire and Florida. Spencer sees the $90 billion speech as the specific needed to put Reagan on the defensive. The media is onto the issue. Evans & Novak, the National Capital certifying agency on what constitutes a campaign error, have pronounced the speech a major gaffe, of the magnitude of McGovern's "Demogrant" plan in '72.

Reagan's bottom-line argument when questioned at his Citizens Press Conferences, is that he never said he'd eliminate necessary programs for those fine old voters, white-haired against the sunset of life. The worst that could happen, he says, is that the programs would be turned over to the states. *Look,* insist Ron's flacks, *it's really not that much different from what Ford wants to do with federal-state revenue-sharing.* True. But Ford hasn't said *$90 billion.* That is sapsucker talk.

"It wasn't Bell's fault," says Dave Keene. "It wasn't anybody's fault. Let me put it another way. It was *everybody's* fault. We weren't rushed, and it wasn't a matter of throwing a speech together and putting it into the candidate's hand at the last minute. I looked at it, Sears looked at it, Lyn looked at it, Hannaford looked at it, Deaver looked at it, and Reagan studied it over at the ranch. Right up the line. None of us saw any problems. And the truth is there wasn't any problem. Except the press kept saying we had one. On social security in Florida, maybe. But not the $90 billion in New Hampshire. Our polls said voters generally agreed with the idea, even if they didn't buy the figure. But we still had to spend time trying to answer Stu Spencer's crap. Understand, we were still eight percentage points ahead going into the final week. All that wasted energy, we were still up eight percent."

Complacency. Reagan is fixated on Tom Dewey. He shakes hands with an overweight campaign worker at a fund-raiser.
"You got it made, Governor," says the man.
"That's what President Dewey thought," grins Reagan.
Yet he runs like Dewey. In New Hampshire, he campaigns as if he has it made even as he denies it. He lays into federal bureaucracy and the Washington crowd in general, but not Jerry Ford and his administration in particular. Reagan is adhering to what California Republicans call "the Eleventh Commandment," which grew out of that state's history of acrimonious party division: *Thou shalt not,* it directs, *speak ill of any Republican.*
What bullshit, says Stu Spencer.
"I believe that Jerry Ford, the President, is a fair and honorable man," Reagan tells a crowd at Concord. "I cannot make my-

self believe that he had a hand in some of the things his lieutenants are doing."

What bullshit, says Lyn Nofziger.

But Nofziger is stuck with his client's gut instinct to observe the Commandment, to think only kind thoughts about a fellow Republican. Only in the closing days of the campaign, after Nice Guy Jerry has flown into New Hampshire aboard *Air Force One* to put his official imprimatur on Spencer's tough line, does Reagan react. By then it is too late. Ford, says the news media, has seized the *initiative*, taken the *momentum*.

Reagan is weighed down by the self-administered handicap suffered by all middle-class Republican candidates. He worships at the altar of respectability, conformity. In his case, the handicap is unusually heavy. As a former Democrat, Reagan is exceedingly reluctant to jump on a Republican sitting in the White House. The convert must be more Catholic than the Pope.

Nancy Reagan has no such hang-up. Once, at a state party convention, Keene is explaining a complicated delegate strategy which entails a degree of compromise with Ford forces.

"We have to do it," says Keene, "though, personally, I'd rather sail in and kick the shit out of 'em."

"Now *that*," exclaims Nancy, eyes gleaming, "is the kind of talk I like to hear."

"People are always saying that the Governor should mix more with politicians, but you have to remember that he is a very private person."

MIKE DEAVER, *Ronald Reagan's chief of staff*

We understand, Mike. A very private person. He vants to be alone. Which is why he spent a quarter century in show biz and the past dozen years running for or holding public office.

But let's not be too hard on Deaver. The poor guy's stuck with that anomalous life form: a candidate who likes politics but not *people*. Not, at least, in large numbers. Or not after working hours, nine to five. A shortcoming, you might say, in a man running for public office.

Not necessarily a fatal one, however. With or without a PR man to euphemize their desire to be alone, some private-person politicians have gone on to bigger and better offices. For every flesh-pressing, backslapping mixer like Hubert Humphrey and Nelson Rockefeller there is an Adlai Stevenson (both II and III), or Ronald Reagan, who would as soon campaign by writing monographs or recording TV speeches in sound-and-people-proof studios.

Nevertheless, despite Deaver's euphemizing, the press is onto his antisocial candidate. Reagan has been labeled "aloof." Whenever a candidate is given this tag it means that either he isn't holding enough news conferences to keep the traveling press in fresh leads ("REAGAN CHARGES . . .") or, worse yet, he hasn't gone out of his way to be one of the boys. To be sure, there is a fine line here. Bill Miller, of American Express card fame, was the first Republican Vice-Presidential candidate in history to play bridge with members of his traveling press corps and, as a consequence, got tagged for not doing his homework, goofing off on the campaign trail. Reagan veers to the other extreme. He treats the news media as a necessary nuisance, though his PR men are cordial and cooperative in dealing with all segments of the press.

The problem that Deaver, Nofziger, and Reagan's other flacks are up against is one the Retired Flack recalls from the Goldwater campaign. Newsmen who want to get close to a candidate, but feel put off, transfer their personal resentment. They don't criticize him for shunning *them*, but for shunning his political peers. They become PR experts, criticizing his political work style: *Why doesn't Goldwater,* they used to ask, *spend more time with local politicians? Is he a candidate for President or a political dilettante?*

What these critics ought to know, if in fact they don't, is that nothing can waste a national candidate's time and energy as much as local political hacks with small axes to grind and broad-gauge counsel on how to run a campaign. An effective campaign staff works to spare the candidate's adrenals for bigger audiences. But what do you tell the press when someone asks why Reagan didn't meet with Senator Blank when visiting his city last night? Deaver can't just say, *"He didn't meet with him because the last time they met the old bastard got drunk and kept everybody up to three in the morning."* Yet, watching Reagan operate, the press inevitably comes to endorse Stu Spencer's low appraisal of his ability as a campaigner. Deaver's man, it is reported, is lazy. The Reagan schedule is too soft. He seems to lack that quintessential requisite the American people have a right to expect from the man who presumes to the Presidency. Specifically, *he doesn't have fire in the belly.*

FIRE IN THE BELLY: This is the virtue the campaign press finds most promising in Presidential candidates, an attribute equaled in the estimation of newsmen only by the ability to amuse Gridiron members with snappy one-liners at the club's annual spring dinner. Whenever a consensus of traveling correspondents concludes that a candidate, whether a conservative Goldwater in 1964 or liberal Gene McCarthy in 1968, lacks this quality—once newsmen begin to ask each other over late-night drinks, *"Does he really want it bad enough?"* a campaign is in trouble. Thereafter the candidate is looked on by the press, with a certain condescension, as a flawed leader, unworthy of his mission.

Goldwater, a candidate with a passion for ham radios, got bad reviews because he insisted on maintaining his interest in the hobby during the campaign. Recalling the frenetic Kennedy-Nixon competition four years earlier, when the candidates made eight to ten speaking stops per day, the traveling press criticized Goldwater for averaging a mere five. Again, in 1968, McCarthy could campaign from New Hampshire to the Chicago convention and still be faulted as a man who didn't burn sufficiently for the Presidency because he displayed no hard-panting enthusiasm for TV-covered ghetto walks and other photo opportunity gimmicks.

Even in 1960, reporters found a candidate they could needle for lack of ambition: Nixon's running mate. The thing about Cabot Lodge, you see, was that he took naps on campaign afternoons. An un-Spartan weakness that neither Nixon nor the press could condone in a man who, if elected, would be only one heartbeat and/or one impeachment from the Oval Office.

FIRE IN THE BELLY: Now this new man Carter, he has it. True, he doesn't spend much time shmoosing with other politicians, but, then, that's his bit, you know. He's the candidate who admits he doesn't like politicians. But Jimmy takes that extra step to the back of the plane, tends to his personal relationships with individual reporters. They like him personally, he seems to like them. With a few exceptions. Rowlie Evans and Bob Novak have been on his tail since Iowa, doing columns on what they claim are his inconsistencies on abortion and other issues. But their complaint isn't that Carter lacks fire in the belly. They feel that he has it in too great abundance, on the order of two recent ex-Presidents.

Theirs, however, is a minority view. What's important, says the vast majority of the working press, is that this new man Carter is up earlier than anybody and beds down hundreds, sometimes thousands of miles from the spot he began his campaign day. Even Reg Murphy concedes the point. Jimmy Carter, he writes, is "the best and most tireless campaigner I've ever seen."

Praise from Cassius, smiles Jody Powell, is praise indeed. But I get the decided impression that Reg didn't mean the line as a compliment; that what he meant was that *fire in the belly*, by another name, is megalomania.

"Some bureaucrats tellin' the steelworkers, 'You don't know where to send your child to school so we gonna write some guidelines for you.' Well, when I get to be President, I'm gonna call in a bunch of bureaucrats and take away their briefcases and throw 'em in the Potomac River . . . And if any demonstrator ever lays down in front of my car, it'll be the last car he'll ever lay down in front of . . ."

GEORGE WALLACE, *belly afire and in the prime, Campaign '68*

As the executive jet's engines whined into life on the Orlando tarmac, the pilot's voice crackled over the intercom: "They just cleared us for taxiing calling us Air Force One." *George Corley Wallace, 52, was headed back home to Alabama on the morrow of the greatest victory of his turbulent political life—winning a stunning 42% plurality in the eleven-candidate Florida Democratic primary . . .*

"A Jarring Message from George," Time *cover story,* March 27, 1972

Years ago, when the Retired Flack was working the political fields in George Wallace's home state, there was a legislator from Mobile named John Tyson who lacked fire in the belly.

In its place he was afflicted with that most serious of all political infirmities, a sense of humor. E.g., on a slow legislative day in the mid-1950s he rose in the state House of Representatives to introduce a bill to annex the Florida panhandle to Alabama. The panhandle strip, argued Tyson, cut Alabama off from its "manifest destiny" as a great Gulf Coast power.

"Let me assure our neighbors in Florida," he told the Alabama House, "*that this is positively my last territorial demand.*"

The bill went unreferred to any committee. Its sponsor was soundly defeated in a succeeding election. So much for irreverent humor in George Wallace's fatherland.

Yet there was demographic truth in Tyson's whimsy: the Florida panhandle is Alabama's Sudetenland. It is Alabama in everything but name. Its people are Alabamians. Their cultural and economic ties are infinitely closer to even the northernmost inland section of Alabama than to southernmost Florida, the land of Cuban refugees and condominiums.

Straight east, running along the panhandle strip to the Atlantic, Floridians become Georgians in everything but name. In this area Wallace rolled up nearly sixty percent of the vote in the 1972 Presidential primary. Here in Duval County, as well as the panhandle and farther south in central Florida, with its conservative Disneyland East-cum-orange farming economy, is where Wallace's political wraith hopes to repeat his triumph of four years ago. But George's campaign workers, confident three months ago, are *up-taht.* This is no longer flat-out Wallace

Country, where voters will single-shot their ballots for their Southern neighbor against a field of Yankee intruders. There is another neighbor in the race this year, from Georgia, and he sounds like he might deliver the message to Washington just as well—even better—than Wallace ever did.

"George is spending time in Massachusetts," complains one of his field men, "when he oughta be spending all of it right here. Nothing up there is gonna do him any damn good if he gets his ass whipped in his own backyard."

Pumpin' Gas in Jacksonville

Whether or not they love him in the condos to the south, up here "Scoop" Jackson is a nebbish. He has identification but no image. The Retired Flack learns this by running his own Les Biffle-style survey of gas station attendants in the Florida Sudetenland and the central citrus region.

Biffle was the unscientific hip-pocket pollster of the Roosevelt-Truman years. Between national elections he served as secretary of the Senate. Before each Presidential campaign he would pull on threadbare clothes, get into an old-model car and travel to key areas around the country, chewing the fat with gas station attendants along the way, querying them on their voting preferences. Legend has it that Biffle called every Roosevelt victory margin, then Truman's 1948 upset of Dewey.

There is folk wisdom in a hip-pocket pollster's surveying gas stations rather than, say, hack drivers. In his day on the campaign road, the Retired Flack learned to distrust overcommunicative interview subjects letting off steam. Taking a Biffle-style sampling, you have to work at extracting information. Small-town-rural interview subjects, particularly Deep South, are innately suspicious of strangers asking questions. The hip-pocket pollster's trick is never to ask them what they think. Only what they've heard. What they think is nobody's business. What they've heard is gossip, free for the asking.

"Jackson?" says the old Sunoco gas-pumper, squinting at the gauge as it dings past $4.00. "No, I haven't heard much talk about him." But a good man, he supposes.

The politician who forgets history is condemned to get his

butt kicked repeatedly. It is 1972, all over. On paper, Jackson, a northern Democrat with an anti-school-busing stand pleasing to the white natives, should by all projections register well here. But with Wallace and Carter in the race, what are the odds on a "neighbor" from the state of Washington?

"Mo" Udall is worth a shrug at a Texaco. Milton Shapp is unheard of in a sweep of four Exxon's, two Sunoco's, and a Gulf.
"Say Milton *What?*"
Very bad. Now, if it had been "Milton *Who?*" Shapp might have a future.

"THE MONSTER HAS ESCAPED FROM ELBA" . . . On the morning after Florida, the Ex-SOB Club meets on Capitol Hill. The club—as its name indicates to Washington cognoscenti —is composed of former staff employees at the Senate Office Building: one time top-level aides to Senators, now earning their living as lawyers and lobbyists—a living wholly dependent on their Hill-acquired contacts in federal agencies. Until now, the Democratic members of the club have been divided in their campaign allegiance. Some are for "Scoop." Others are for Bayh. A few for Udall. A scattering are still holding out, waiting for HHH to get into the race.
"Let me tell you, it's not just that I don't know Carter," one Democratic lobbyist is explaining to an unsympathetic Republican, "and it's not just that I don't know *anybody who knows* Carter. What really scares me is I don't even know *anybody Carter knows!*"

A Reagan loss in New Hampshire by the sliver of a percent could have been salvaged as a media-perceived "victory"—except for Meldrim Thomson's second bright idea of the campaign: to create a bandwagon effect for his candidate. Thomson predicts Reagan will carry the primary over Ford, fifty-five to forty-five. On hearing this, John Sears shudders. His surveys show Reagan ahead by eight to ten points. But Thomson has just set High Expectations for the media. It now becomes possible for Reagan to win by two percent, yet lose the spread.

In real political life, Thomson's ploy—to swing undecideds who like to go with a winner—would have been sharp PR strategy. But this isn't real political life. This is a Presidential primary. Thomson may be Governor of the state, but he doesn't understand the rules of the game that put New Hampshire on the map.

At the President Ford Committee, "Bo" Callaway will not play the game. His critics question "Bo's" judgment, but he knows the art of Southern po'-mouth talk. Asked for a projection he says, "Fifty percent plus one is a victory." In real life, a banality; but cutting through the miasma of media speculation, a stunning political insight.

L. E. (Tommy) Thomas, Reagan's Florida campaign manager, is, like Meldrim Thomson, a deep-dyed conservative. Otherwise, he is to Thomson as Florida in midwinter is to New Hampshire. Tommy is overweight, buoyant, and voluble. He talks—always Chamber of Commerce upbeat talk. *This is the greatest state in the greatest county in the greatest cosmos . . . Ronald Reagan is the greatest candidate . . . Come primary day he will have the greatest victory . . .*

Weeks in advance of the primary, Thomas predicts: *Reagan will carry Florida over Ford with sixty-five percent. You heah me? Almost two to one!!!*

"Tommy Thomas lost Florida," says Mike Deaver to a campaign planning committee after enough time has passed to cool intra-staff tensions. "He lost it by the stupid way he handled the social security question on the 'Today' show."

"There was only one asshole who mishandled the social security question," shouts somebody from the back of the room, "and he was from California, not Florida!"

Sandwiched among the media specialists, gagwriters, and other non-Imperial flacks on the White House payroll, Ford has retained a PR expert on Christian evangelicals. He is the Reverend Richard S. Brannon of South Carolina. When a convention of soul-savers arrives in Washington at the crest of New Hampshire-Florida campaigning, Dr. Brannon asks the President's schedulers to set aside an hour for a trip to the Shoreham Hotel.

There, Ford comes down strongly on the side of morality, is given an ovation.

During the President's visit, a moment for prayer. Prayer and photo opportunity. But *who shall lead the assembly in this solemn ceremony?*

Ah . . . the convention chairman knows just the preacher. On the podium, the prayer leader takes the President by the hand. Heads bowed, Caesar and Christ, they stand together. In the name of the Father, the Son, and the Associated Press. Amen. The photo moves. There is front-page coverage in the prayer leader's home state.

What do you know—he is from West Palm Beach.

"What coincidence?" Stu Spencer says.

"That out of four thousand preachers in a hall, the one who's picked to lead the prayer comes from Florida," the Retired Flack replies.

"Very perceptive," says Spencer. It is two days after New Hampshire and the President's chief flack seems to be breathing easier. "You know," he tells me, "there's lots of Baptists in Florida. They're not all Democrats, either."

"The picture," I ask. "How did you set it up?"

"Well, it wasn't coincidence," smiles Spencer. "Call it an act of God."

In May, during a period when the mood at the PFC has changed, Spencer's deputy, Norman (Skip) Watts, a Californian in his mid-thirties who once worked for Reagan, sits in his cramped office, worrying about Michigan. He gazes across the room at a smiling photo of Congressman Lou Frey.

"I keep that picture there," says Watts, "for inspiration. It gives me a lift when things look bad. It gets my adrenals going. It makes me mad. You know, he's a real bastard. When we won, of course, he claimed all the credit . . ."

Lou Frey, Ford's Florida campaign manager, tells newsmen that while he backs the President he likes Reagan too. Bearing out his divided loyalties, Frey runs a half-assed campaign. Finally, Spencer calls in his former agency partner from Los Angeles, Bill

Roberts. The Republican campaign, both sides, is now overquo-
taed with California PR men.

In Florida, Roberts feels at home. Not just the climate but the
potential for media saturation, the diversity of constituencies,
north, central, and south. Roberts, unable to match Tommy
Thomas's organization for Reagan, concentrates his efforts first,
on quick-hitting TV and photo splashes (importing Michi-
ganders with snowballs, a bagpipe band in kilts). These at least
give the appearance of a campaign that's organized. Next, Roberts develops his volunteer phone bank. Smelling blood in
Reagan's social security statements, clarifications and denials, Roberts programs his volunteer callers to zero in on areas populated
by the elderly and the retired. The *momentum* begins to shift. In
Florida, across the country.

Spencer's strategy has been elemental: *Just hang on through
the early primaries. Keep the President looking Presidential.
Push the idea that Reagan is Goldwater II. Wait for a break.*

Now Spencer is beginning to look like a genius. Everything
he's said about his former employer is proving out. Reagan, despite staff efforts to restrain his impulse to overexplain positions
and free-associate ideology (*"Hmmm . . . maybe we oughta put
social security into the stock market"*), is self-destructing on the
same volatile issues that plagued Goldwater.

An image shift has occurred, a change in public perceptions.
Reagan, poised and confident in December, is beginning to appear the political bumbler, a loser. It's not that Ford really looks
any better. It's that his opponent has done everything but fall
down an airplane ramp to even the odds.

The charge that Carter runs a double-image campaign, one for
New Hampshire, another for Florida, underestimates the man's
profound PR skills. He is running that campaign in Florida *alone*.
In the north-central part of the state he is the anti-Washington
linthead conservative. Nothing agin Cousin George, but the pore
fella just can't get around any more, y' know? To red-necks,
Carter's appeal is different from Wallace's—even the vigorous,
gut-burning Wallace of 1968 and 1972—in the way he says, *"I
intend to win."*

George always talked about a Southern Governor's *right to run* for President. Jimmy is telling them he means to be something more than another wasted message to Washington.

THE SEMANTICS OF AMERICAN POLITICS

believability n. also *credibility*, the known trustworthiness of the source of what is proposed for acceptance, e.g., "He's a conservative to conservatives, a moderate to moderates, a liberal to liberals. Jimmy Carter has believability." (Attribution, Midge Costanza, Carter spokeswoman, New York)

In New Hampshire, Carter seems to run the risk of inflicting cultural shock on voters by flying in select teams of Georgia doorbell-ringers on a Cracker Express. The risk is minimized, however, by putting selectees through classes on How to Talk to Yankees as If They Were Real Down-home Folks. The first cadre is composed of Carter relatives, teenage to elderly, reminiscent of the Kennedy family onslaught in 1960 primaries. Then come Carter "neighbors"—pleasant housewives and clean-cut students whose courteous Southern-style "ma'ams" and "sirs" are calculated to convince staid New Englanders that, odd accents aside, there is a common denominator between the small-town America of Jimmy Carter and their own way of life. (No, not *life-style:* a life-style is what they have in big cities; in Laconia, New Hampshire, and Plains, Georgia, there is a *way of life.*)

The Cracker Express also brings a publicity bonus—as Carter PR planners in Atlanta expected—with the news media instinctively drawn to the cutesy-pieism of sho' 'nuff Jaw'juns "invading" Yankeeland.

But when the Cracker Express rolls into Florida it comes by wheels, for another PR purpose. The word is out (spread by Cousin George's folks) that Carter left office an unpopular Governor. Georgians for Jimmy, ringing doorbells, handing out brochures in shopping centers, are walkin', talkin' commercials refuting that charge.

Imitation, as Lyn Nofziger would say, is the sincerest form of flackery. The President Ford Committee has borrowed the

Carter home folks idea, shipping one hundred Grand Rapids friends of Jerry and Betty's to trade Michigan apples for Florida oranges. Also, five thousand snowballs to be pelted at friendly greeters on the runway, a political vaudeville act put on for local and regional TV stations. It is so obvious a publicity stunt that no serious political reporter will pick it up. Of course not . . .

ROY REED, *The New York Times* (excerpt)
The snowballs melted as soon as they hit the runway. The temperature was 83 degrees.

One of Ronald Reagan's campaigners said with a trace of envy, "That's funny. Do they really think that 5,000 snowballs are going to translate into 5,000 votes?"

Maybe not, but they translated into several hundred feet of television film and many inches of newspaper space.

Including, by caliper count, 5¼ inches Fit to Print.

Jimmy Carter and Ronald Reagan both run as anti-Washington candidates, but there is a difference in the way their campaign organizations project this image: Carter has no face card, no campaign manager, no visible physical tie to the Washington scene. There isn't a single Establishment politician, up-front, in Jimmy's organization. Reagan, however, does have a face card: Senator Paul Laxalt of Nevada. Not a member of the Washington power structure, but nevertheless a link to the political world.

A face card is a public official, active or retired (with honorable discharge), whose name on a letterhead or press release gives a national campaign legitimacy with professional politicians and viability with the press. In brief, a chrome-plated pitchman who can be depended on (1) to make gut-cutting statements that the candidate himself can't without losing credibility in some other area of PR operations; and (2) to deliver rousing pep talks to the candidate's followers and lure the undecided, either in person or through the media.

Ideally, for maximum flack value, a face card should be (a) a name politician in his own right; (b) wholly committed to the candidate; (c) bright, up to a point; (d) willing to sign off on any press release or statement without undue nit-picking; or, when a news conference is called for, able to be sufficiently glib to bluff his way through oblique questioning on issues he isn't briefed on.

Most important, however, the face card must be a Professor Pangloss. Upbeat whenever discussing campaign prospects. Always sanguine. Smiling into the teeth of adversity . . . *This is the best of all possible campaigns . . .*

We lost Illinois? Well, don't jump to any hasty conclusions, Scotty. I'll let you in on a secret. We planned it that way. Yessir, that was our strategy. You see, if Ford takes Illinois, that means he's in deep trouble in Mississippi . . .

Or if up against a hostile newsman: *What you mean we LOST Massachusetts and New York, buster? Look at the demographic breakdown. We're actually ahead of where we expected to be . . .*

Unfortunately for Reagan, his national face card, in the manner of Meldrim Thomson and Tommy Thomas, doesn't quite get the hang of the thing.

"Well," sighs Laxalt after his man takes a waxing in the early primaries, "it really hasn't all been a waste of time. Ron's been a good sparring partner for Ford. He's made the President a better candidate for the fall campaign."

(No, dummy, it's before the primary, no matter what the polls say, that you're supposed to be pessimistic. After the primary, no matter what the voters say, you're supposed to be optimistic . . .)

"Bo" Callaway is the ideal campaign face card. Always smilin'. Some smart asses make snide remarks about "Bo's" competence as a campaign manager. But "Bo" answers, *Look at the record: I haven't lost a primary.* Then, too, there was that gut-cutting job he did on Nelson Rockefeller—and carried it off just the way the President wanted. Nice Guy Jerry: Rockefeller would have been a drag down South. He had to go. Somebody had to give him the message. That's what face cards are for. Once Callaway said publicly that the Vice-President would hurt the President's chances down South, and no voice was raised at the White House to rebuke "Bo," Rocky knew it was just a question of whether he chose to walk the plank or be pushed off. Callaway delivered the message and took the heat from Rockefeller's friends and the press.

But now a Senate investigation is under way, triggered by an NBC-TV news report that "Bo," while Secretary of the Army, tried to pressure the Forest Service to acquire two thousand added acres of federal land to build ski runs on his Crested Butte resort in Colorado.

Callaway denies it. Says it's not a thing except "damn Democrat politics, a Democrat Senate Committee tryin' to hurt a Republican President in an election year." But "Bo's" loudest political (as distinguished from legal) detractors of the moment aren't working on Capitol Hill. They're in the White House and the PFC, working for his pal Jerry.

THREE QUICK CUTAWAYS:

MORTON TO BE CAMPAIGN CHIEF

"A lot of people around here breathed a sigh of relief" when Callaway left the President Ford Committee, said one Presidential advisor who regarded Callaway as a drag on the campaign . . .
Washington Star, March 18

"Many of Ford's difficulties can be traced to his White House staff, which is disorganized . . . Another problem is Ford's campaign chairman, Rogers Morton . . . The genial Morton has not been a conspicuous success in organizing Ford's campaign; in general, he remains the glad-handing front man while decisions are made by Political Director Stuart Spencer . . ."
Time, May 24

JAMES BAKER IS NAMED
TO MORTON'S POST

". . . Mr. Morton, a former Commerce Secretary and Maryland Congressman, assumed the campaign post . . . after the abrupt resignation of Howard H. Callaway. Mr. Callaway resigned during an investigation of charges, of which he was subsequently cleared, that he had misused his post as Secretary of the Army to seek advantage from federal agencies for a ski resort that he owned in Colorado.

"The President was said to have been disturbed by occasional free-spirited remarks by Mr. Morton. After a succession of losses in Republican primaries in May, Mr. Morton compared the campaign to the *Titanic*, a passenger ship that hit an iceberg and sank.

"Mr. Morton said today through a spokesman that he had asked the President to relieve him of the obligations of running the campaign and to give him a post in which he could travel as an advocate of Mr. Ford's candidacy . . ."

The New York Times, August 2

A Rose Garden Campaign by Any Other Name

In 1972 the Committee to Re-elect the President coordinated a task force of face-card speakers called Presidential *surrogates*. They traveled the country speaking at Republican fund-raisers, enabling the incumbent to remain in the White House, looking "Presidential," until the closing weeks of the campaign. At the outset of the 1976 campaign the Ford campaign was in the process of lifting this idea intact when mention was made at a staff meeting that the term "surrogate," aside from sounding pretentious, was unpleasingly reminiscent of the Nixon campaign. As a result, what were "surrogates" in 1972 became "advocates" in 1976.

Like organized crime and the Mafia code, the technology of political public relations has in recent years been the subject of a burgeoning mythology. The profession has attracted a cult following of journalists and scholars who conjure up legends of the flack as a technician who, given money and media access, can do wondrous things to the political process, for good or evil. Generally for evil, since that makes for more interesting legends.

To be sure, some few PR techniques are more exact science than art. An experienced speechwriter should be able to predict, within one or two cheers, the number of ovations his speaker will receive; or, conversely, in a case where audience antagonism is desired for TV purposes (e.g., delivering a pro-amnesty speech before an American Legion Convention) the approximate number of grimaces and stony silences the cameras and soundmen will pick up. Given a candidate with M.A. (Media Appeal), a trained publicist knows how to time a press release so that it has a maximum chance to top other political news of the day on the all-important evening shows.

But despite the mythologists, such successes are limited. If massive efforts to manipulate or influence the media could do the job, the Vietnam war would have been the most popular in American history, with Lyndon Johnson completing his second full term in January 1973. If public relations technology and a bankroll were the be-all and end-all of the election process, Nelson Rockefeller would have made it to the Oval Office during the sixties and seventies on something other than a Presidential invitation.

In short, flackery may be a necessary adjunct of modern campaigning, but it is not the omnipotent political force the cultists claim.

Nevertheless, the mythology of political public relations flourishes, probably for the same reason the mythology of the Mafia endures. Evil or not, it apparently comforts many Americans to believe that in a world of screw-ups there are still areas where Something Works, where humans operate with absolute efficiency. The man in the button-down shirt and the button man: two symbols of victories of our species over the environment; living, if sometimes disquieting, proof that our Puritan ethic survives; that discipline, planning, and teamwork always pay off—just the way we tell the kids in the Little League.

In the spring of 1976 three PR myths—two new, one retread—were propagated by campaign flacks of three Presidential candidates and their cultist friends in the news media. The first involved the genesis of Jimmy Carter's campaign. The second, the importance of TV advertising experts in shaping voters' attitudes and the outcome of elections. The third was a variation of an old myth. It had to do with the expertise going into the re-re-re-re-generation of a New New New New Gerald Ford . . .

"I never say or do anything unintentionally. It might seem that way at times, but I never do."

JIMMY CARTER, *omnisciently*,
October 1976

Peter Bourne says that while Jimmy was thinking of running for President it was he, Bourne, who drew up the first actual campaign plan, in a letter-memorandum in late 1972.

Down in Georgia, Hamilton Jordan and Jody Powell have a different version of the Genesis. *That's typical of Bourne*, growls Jordan, Carter's thirty-year-old campaign director, *claiming all the credit. It wasn't HIS letter that started Jimmy movin'. It was MY memorandum. MY game plan. You hot shots in Washington better get your heads on straight about who's who in this organization. WE did it, down heah in Georgia. Just think . . . a little Ol' Country Boy like me writin' seventy pages, outlinin' step by step the Makin' of a Presidential Candidate . . . Whoo-ee!*

Jordan and Powell, now moving front and center as the subjects of media attention, are two of a kind. Of the original Carter campaign nucleus, they represent two thirds of the authentic Ol' Country Boy team that shares visceral as well as political impulses with their candidate. The third sharer is Charles Kirbo, a fifty-one-year-old Atlanta corporation lawyer. Kirbo is the elder-statesman advisor that every national campaign since Woodrow Wilson's has required in order to complete the media's casting of insider stereotypes, e.g., (1) the Loyal Press Secretary Who'd Go Through a Wall for the Man, (2) the Chief of Staff Who Intuitively Knows What the Man Wants, and (3) the Sage Elder. *Kirbo*, Joseph Kraft will surely write should Jimmy Carter ever become President, *is the Colonel House of this administration.*

Since the glamorizing of the Kennedy campaign team in 1960, a new dimension has been added to the media's penchant to reduce Presidential contests to formula melodrama with stock characters. In recent campaigns, staff members themselves have lined up for assigned roles. *Who will be the New Sorensen? The New O'Donnell? The New O'Brien?* The passion for anonymity that once characterized top-level Presidential campaign aides has been replaced by a passion for personal publicity. A winning candidate image these days produces spin-offs like a successful TV series: a corruscation of mini-images all eager to be interviewed by Mike Wallace, to be quoted by *Newsweek*.

The first wave of network correspondents and in-depth newsmen interested not simply in Carter the Candidate but Jimmy the Man (*What Makes Him Tick, The Men Around Him, etc.*) hit Georgia shortly after the first of the year. The crowd has since been quadrupled. And with that growth, the competition for deeper in-depth stories, spin-offs from spin-offs, has become more intense. Since the temptation of national media recognition proved in past campaigns to be too much for city slickers to resist, it was certain to overwhelm Jimmy Carter's Georgia cadre.

This includes not only Powell, Jordan, and Kirbo, but Jerry Rafshoon, the forty-two-year-old Atlanta adman whose own personal puff-piece in *The New York Times Magazine* follows his client's by a mere four months. The article by Joseph Lelyveld should be about as helpful to the Carter image as Joe McGinniss' inside look at political advertising was to Nixon's eight years ago.

With these differences: for one thing, *The Selling of the President* appeared *after* the 1968 campaign was over, not at its outset; and second, Harry Treleaven, the Nixon adman who brought McGinniss behind the scenes for a look at the candidate's TV spot production, had no idea what the writer was up to; whereas Rafshoon, with self-promotion aforethought, has gone out of his way to invite a cynical look at "The Selling of the Candidate" (as the *Times'* piece is indeed titled).

In return for being given such access, Lelyveld, as the unwritten rules of the game require, has done well by his sponsor. Rafshoon is portrayed as the advertising genius of the decade, the man responsible for the Jimmy Carter image that won in Iowa and New Hampshire.

"If there has been any breakthrough in the occult craft of political persuasion in a campaign that's already overextended and overexposed," writes the *Times*man admiringly, "it has come in the media campaign that Jerry Rafshoon fashioned for Carter."

And so forth. The Lelyveld copy, by doing nothing more than quoting Carter's advertising genius, presents the candidate as both calculating politician and flack-manipulated tool. There is even a photo of Jimmy in the snow at Concord bridge, with the cut line "*Rafshoon rehearses Carter.*" Another of Jerry perched Gandhi-like on his mod desk in Atlanta as he "*ponders the candidate's image.*" And a wondrous quote from Ham Jordan, the Ol' Country Boy, explaining that "to really convey something of substance on an issue, you've got to spend at least five minutes on it."

All this on behalf of a candidate whose prime PR message is that of the nonpolitical, natural whole wheat populist choice for President—not like those big city phonies, with their Madison Avenue budgets.

I finish the piece but can't believe I read it. It is marvelous publicity for Jerry Rafshoon, the Atlanta wizard with the $7 million agency, and growing, *growing, GROWING.* But what's the percentage for Jimmy Carter, the candidate? The Retired Flack thinks Rafshoon owes his client a fifteen percent commission. At least.

But for all the *Times'* puffery, and despite his having been with Carter since 1966, Rafshoon, like Peter Bourne, isn't really one of the hoe-down boys. They are instead the exotics of the Carter team: Bourne, a London-born egghead with a liberated wife who won't even give up her maiden name; Rafshoon, a divorced Yankee émigré given in moments of creative stress to using odd, un-Georgian words like *putz* (printed p—z by the prim *Times*).

No, I advise Gus Hewlett, his friend Peter just isn't one of Jimmy Carter's red-clay soulmates. The word I hear is that Bourne is getting, if not castrated, at least vasectomized by the Georgia Brotherhood.

We are at the Class Reunion, an after-hours hangout in the Nixon years for middle-echelon White House staff members. The place also attracts newsmen and flacks, in the way the Press Club bar did in the prehistoric Truman era, when that club included in its membership more men of the pen than the lapel; writers, that is, as opposed to lobbyists.

The CR has the intimate, yet raucous atmosphere of a political rathskeller of the 1950s. Anti-nostalgia: on one wall, a stark black-and-white blow-up of Joe McCarthy in action, before a microphone; on another, Ike and Nixon waving to the crowd at the 1952 Republican Convention. Then there is Charles Van Doren, enclosed in his TV booth, presumably answering a fixed $64,000 Question. The good old days.

To help those over forty forget them, the drinks at the CR are murderous. Three times the whiskey served at any other bar at half the price. With hard ice. Thirty minutes in the place after a day of shuffling papers and shouting into telephones at the Executive Office Building, the White House aide begins to unwind. In an hour he is loose. In ninety minutes, destroyed. The CR is the best bar within a 250-mile blackout radius of McSorley's. If H. R. Haldeman had dropped by only occasionally, Richard Nixon might have finished a full second term. In fact, Haldeman's college-age son spent evenings there in that summer of '72: a pleasant, long-haired kid who dropped by after volunteer work at the Committee to Re-elect the President.

Hewlett, the executive director of the Alcohol and Drug Problem Association is sipping dry white wine and peripherally watching future business prospects. The Retired Flack is on his second Chivas on hard rocks, moving into contentious gear. I have just given Hewlett, a devoted Carterite, a professional estimate of his candidate's Country Boy staff, with a few added barbs for the self-promotive p——z who handles his advertising.

"You couldn't be more wrong," insists Hewlett after I tell him that his friend Bourne is moving to Carter outer perimeter after being worked over by the Country Boys. "You forget, Peter is a Georgian too."

I reply that while Bourne went to school in Georgia and lived in Atlanta, he isn't a Georgian. Not in Jimmy Carter's eyes.

"I know these Southern country pols. Wallace is the same way. If you grew up with him in the Black Belt, you're in. If you come from Birmingham, you're a Yankee."

The comparison of Carter with Wallace makes Hewlett wince. He doesn't appreciate it, not at all. Neither did Jack Nelson, the Washington bureau chief of the *Los Angeles Times*, when I drew a parallel between the careers of the two country-boy Presidential candidates a little while earlier.

"That's bullshit," snapped Nelson. "There isn't any such comparison. George Wallace was standing in the schoolhouse door in Alabama when Jimmy Carter was turning down the White Citizens Council in Georgia. You're straining."

Nelson is a Pulitzer Prize-winning Washington investigative reporter, trained to a fine skepticism about politicians. Yet there is a special vehemence about his defense of Carter. So I explain my point, only a little less contentiously. What I mean to say, Jack, isn't that Jimmy is a racist. Only that he reminds me of the George Wallace I remember from twenty years back, when I was a young flack in Alabama working for one of his opponents. In those days, George was an all-day-all-night campaigner with a unique talent for drawing support from both liberal and conservative Alabama Democrats, business interests and labor. All belly fire, yet coldly oleaginous on the surface. Something you couldn't quite get ahold of.

To my surprise, Nelson takes only slightly less umbrage even at this mild comparison. Obviously, the anti-Washington candidate has made a convert in the heart of the enemy camp. And a tough convert. I have always thought of Nelson as a journalist who, more than any other (except Bob Novak), held to the credo laid down by the *Baltimore Sun*'s Frank Kent many quadrennials ago: "*The only way a reporter should look at a politician,*" wrote Kent, "*is down.*"

"I'm from your part of the country, you know," Nelson reminds me. "Talladega. I've worked out of Atlanta, I covered Montgomery in the Martin Luther King years. So don't try to tell me anything about Wallace and Carter. It won't stand up."

I had forgotten. Nelson is a Southerner. So is Tom Wicker. So is Scotty Reston. So is Jim Wooten. So is Howard K. Smith. So is . . .

"*Stories in* The New York Times *and* Washington Post *don't just happen, but have to be carefully planned and planted . . . Fortunately, a disproportionate number of these opinion-makers are Southerners by birth and tradition . . .*"

> The Jordan Memorandum,
> origin disputed, circa post-
> McGovern, 1972

Sixteen years ago there was another How-to memorandum on campaign techniques, written by a Boston flack: Larry O'Brien's *How to Elect Kennedy to Anything.* It was a handbook of political detail, down to the last logistic of opening a neighborhood headquarters, arranging a coffee klatch, mobilizing a stamp-licking squad. The nuts and bolts of modern campaign organization.

The Jordan Memorandum is a more ambitious document. It includes, for example, the bracing perception that to be elected President of the United States, Jimmy Carter will have to "convince the press, the public, and the politicians that he knows how to run a government." For openers, not a bad idea. In addition, the candidate must buy a subscription to *The New York Times* and, what's more, read it every day. He must also write a book, like successful Presidential candidates in past years. And, oh yes, be sure to study up on those rules covering state primaries because (this is the point obviously overlooked by Jackson, Wallace, and Udall in their game plans), "*It is here that the nomination will be won or lost.*"

It could all be a *National Lampoon* parody of some imaginary Cracker scenario on *How to Seize Power from the Eastern Liberal Establishment.* Or, if taken seriously, a possible forgery disseminated by Carter's political opponents to bear out their contention that Jimmy is too calculating to be believed. On the order of a phony *Protocol of the Wise Men of Georgia.* I mean, take that point about there being "a disproportionate number" of Southerners in the opinion-making business. With only a change in ethnic reference, it might have come straight from the mouth of the Retired Flack's old Boss, Spiro Agnew.

But no: this is neither a put-on nor a dirty trick. Incredibly, it is Carter's own staff—the Georgia Country Boys themselves—leaking the glad news that Jimmy is everything his opponents charge: a contrived, wind-him-up-like-Nixon-and-watch-him-run campaigner.

This, then, is the myth going the rounds: that what we are witnessing in the Carter Phenomenon isn't a wholesome grassroots response to a genuine man-of-the-people, a popular reaction to the political flackery of recent years. No, that would be too simple. Too heartening. What we are being let in on is that the Carter campaign is the result of a failsafe Plan, drawn up by a Country Boy wonder years ago, and followed, to the letter, by his manipulated and manipulating candidate.

In midsummer it is Kirbo who supplies his variation of the myth, one that runs counter to Bourne's and Jordan's. By the younger men's accounts, Carter, while relying on his aides, never hesitated for a moment in pushing his presidential campaign plans forward. But Kirbo, falling into his media-assigned role as the candidate's *grits éminence*, tells David Broder that in the beginning Jimmy was actually shy and tentative about "the Presidential thing."

Carter, claims Charley, was afraid he would be a laughingstock if he ran. As, indeed, did everyone around him. Except for one advisor. One man alone, Charley Kirbo would have us know, had the political vision to see that the time was ripe. Not the candidate, not Peter Bourne, not Jerry Rafshoon, not Hamilton Jordan, not Jody Powell . . .

Guess who?

. . . *Would You Believe, Greg Allman?*
Success has a Thousand Fathers, etc.

"If you are wondering what Presidential politics has to do with rock and roll music, the answer, in the case of Jimmy Carter is everything. Had it not been for rock and roll, especially the unique, hard-driving sound of Greg Allman, Jimmy Carter might well be down in Plains today, worrying about nothing so much as this fall's peanut crop. To understand how this happened— how it all happened . . ."

Jimmy's Friends in Rock
ROBERT SAM ANSON, *New Times*
September 3, 1976

There is the myth that given a big enough budget, the clever, manipulative use of television can of and by itself win elections.

The chief propagators of this myth, of course, are professionals who produce clever, manipulative political television spots. But while well-produced material can persuade voters to consider the merits of a candidate (or the shortcomings of his opponent), TV spots are overrated as a factor in determining the outcome of all but a few elections. You can take Nancy Reagan's word for it.

For a while, Harry Treleaven had it all going for him, just like Jerry Rafshoon. He was the media-acclaimed advertising genius, on the Republican side; another pioneer in the 1976 television art of *politique vérité:* producing TV spots that look like news reports, not political advertisements.

Treleaven is an old PR pro who, like John Sears, worked for Nixon in 1968 and moved to Reagan, not Ford, this year. He has been around and about Republican campaigns, coast-to-coast, at every level, local, state, national. The Retired Flack worked with him once, in 1969, when John Marchi was running against John Lindsay and Mario Procaccino for Mayor of New York City.

I remember that campaign well, especially the day that the two of us spent eight hours in a Manhattan television production studio trying to get Marchi to read his teleprompter speech, and getting consistently overruled by a schlock pol from Albany who kept telling the candidate to forget the prompter, just "speak from the heart." Unfortunately, Marchi's left ventricle kept fluffing lines. Production costs ran to $15,000 for the day, and we didn't get an inch of usable footage. In the end, however, it was just as well. We wouldn't have had the money to run it outside the 2 to 3 A.M. late-late-late time period anyway. The period, that is, when old Ron Reagan movies are shown.

Which is where Harry Treleaven's problems commenced this year. He began with the idea, generally accepted by most campaign specialists, that for any candidate the worst of political television consists of sitting or standing in a studio, talking into a camera. In Reagan's case, Treleaven had a special reason to avoid that format. He felt that Ron's very *professionalism* in front of a camera could prove counterproductive; that Reagan, in a slickly produced television spot, speaking "from the heart" (but a heart with a teleprompter), would reinforce the impression that he was simply an aging movie actor, a man who could deliver speech lines but didn't have any business running for President of the United States.

It is an old problem for Reagan, the backlash from the legend of Ronnie the Gipper, all the old stale jokes about "Death Valley Days." In 1966, Stu Spencer helped him solve it, working out ways to convince Californians that Ronald Reagan wasn't just another pretty, wrinkled face. But now Spencer is on the other side, spreading the jokes.

In the late, late going for the Republican nomination, a Los Angeles TV film distribution company purchases rights to two old Reagan films, Tennessee Partner *and* Cattle Queen of the Montana. *The Company wants to sell the films to stations in California and elsewhere. But the equal time law inhibits showing any old Reagan movies on television. So the company writes the White House, asking for a waiver of equal time rights by President Ford for any station running the two Reagan films. Why certainly, Jerry Ford replies magnanimously. Consider my rights waived. Run the movies. Enjoy, enjoy.*

The timing of the request is, to say the least, serendipitous to the Ford cause. The President's flacks want the Reagan films shown. They'd run them as Ford spots, if budget allowed. What better way to keep those jokes about Reagan-the-actor going the rounds than by actually putting his old shows back on late night and matinee TV? Truth is, it is Reagan who should be demanding equal time when Cattle Queen of the Montana *is shown.*

Treleaven's counter to the negative image of Reagan-the-actor was to feature the candidate in television spots that weren't slick studio productions. In New Hampshire, advertising film crews were at all Reagan Citizens' Press Conferences, working out rough footage—deliberately rough footage, to simulate the visual texture of actual TV news film. Select interchanges were then broken down into sixty-second spots. Audio reels for radio covered the same material. There was Reagan responding to citizens of all ages and groups asking him where he stood on national defense, social security, taxes. The spots were then put into television-radio time periods when regular news programs were scheduled. This led viewers to believe—unless they caught the tag line (*"Paid political announcement by . . ."*)—that what they had just seen was not a political plug but an actual news segment, thereby adding to its credibility.

It was clever, manipulative, ingenious, but . . .

By all standards of creative TV advertising—originality, concept, technique, placement—Treleaven's spots were the best political commercials run in New Hampshire and Florida. Better than Jerry Rafshoon's. But Rafshoon's candidate won in those primaries. Treleaven's didn't. The professional image-maker is only as good as yesterday's returns; Nancy Reagan decided, after New Hampshire and Florida, that genius was fine but winning was better. Forget *politique vérité*. Go for audience appeal the way we used to back in the good old days when films were films. They want to talk about aging movie stars? We'll give 'em aging movie stars, all right.

Bring in Jimmy and the Duke.

Tom Malatesta, the effervescent nephew of Bob Hope, and younger brother of Peter of Washington's Pisces Club, is John Sears's top PR troubleshooter for non-press-related problems. Now, with Harry Treleaven's genius in question, a new TV-radio package must be put together for the final weeks in North Carolina; but more important, for Texas. Texas could be Reagan's Alamo. If he loses there, it's back to the California ranch.

A thirty-one-year-old Los Angeles businessman (who, for an obscure reason, is known as "Tommy Tux" to his friends Tina Sinatra and Eva Gabor), Malatesta knows the Hollywood scene better than anyone in the Reagan camp. Excepting, of course, Ron and Nancy. *Go West, young flack*, Sears tells his assistant, *come back with a new package.*

"Actually, it didn't seem like that hard an assignment," Malatesta tells me several primaries later, after the trauma has subsided. "They just said, 'Go to Warner's, hand John Wayne and Jimmy Stewart these scripts, let them take it from there.' Mrs. R.

had talked to the Warner's PR people and everybody at the studio wanted to cooperate. That was good to know. Especially after we lost Glenn Ford."

"What do you mean, 'lost Glenn Ford'?" I ask.

"He was supposed to do some spots, some personal appearances. Then Betty Ford called him and he folded, went over to the other side. He ended up working for Ford."

Malatesta sounds like a Bear Bryant recruiter trying to explain the loss of a top quarterback prospect to Oklahoma.

"Glenn had told Ron he'd campaign for us in Texas," says Tommy Tux. "He'd have been a helluva draw for that area."

"You mean the image," I say. "The Ford cowboy pictures and all."

"*Glenn* Ford, yes," Malatesta nods after a fleeting expression has passed over his face that bespeaks misunderstanding: the conjuration, obviously, of Jerry or Betty Ford in saddle chaps. "Frankly, we were disappointed. But what the hell—the aura of the White House and all."

The aura of the White House brings in Glenn Ford as a prize, the spoils of Presidential power. In the flacks' recruiting struggle for show biz celebrities, Democrats and Republicans work with different casts of characters—Glenn Ford, Wayne, Stewart, for the Republicans; Redford, Newman, MacLaine, for the Democrats; among scores of other political cameo actors and actresses on both sides. The purpose of using these big name celebrities is generally the same: fund raising. Reagan's plans for Wayne and Stewart, however, go beyond luring campaign contributions. They will be projected as real-life images of the movie characters they play, with the aim of attracting particular constituencies: Wayne for North Carolina and Texas, to boost Reagan's stock among voters who might be swayed by a straight red-white-and-blue-blooded appeal; Stewart, now an elderly, graying Mr. Smith, to reassure senior citizens of his old pal Ron's concern for their social security income.

"It was supposed to be a snap," Malatesta is explaining, "but I ran into trouble no sooner than I got to the studio. Wayne had seen the copy written by Tom Ellis' people [Ellis was the

123

Reagan campaign director in North Carolina]. They geared it, precisely, to North Carolina voters. A straight All-American national defense pitch. The country was in trouble, we need a strong national defense—good solid copy. Who could do that better than the Duke, right? Wayne didn't like it. He had something else he wanted to say."

Wayne was filming a scene from *The Shootist*, with Stewart, Lauren Bacall, and Hugh O'Brian, when Malatesta arrived. The schedule called for filming the spots on the film set. First Wayne, then Stewart, would read his copy, in costume, with the Western saloon backdrop. Simple as that. Except for the fact, as Malatesta says, that the Duke thought his copy was "a piece of shit."

"He strolls off the set, you know, with that patented pigeon-toe walk, and first thing he says is, 'I can't read the words in this copy.' Very amicable and all, and in his defense, if he needs one, he had a helluva cold. The flu or something," Malatesta continues. "But he wasn't going with the copy and that was that. He had his own ideas about what he wanted to say, and when John Wayne has a political idea of his own, who's to argue?"

Chicago, summer of '52

John Wayne makes his maiden television appearance on behalf of a Presidential candidate. The 1952 national conventions are the first to be televised coast-to-coast and the networks are experimenting with the technique, later to develop into a news media art form, of filling dead convention floor time with celebrity interviews. A network interviewer approaches Wayne in the outer lobby of the convention hall to ask his opinion about the upcoming Eisenhower-Taft race.

"Taft!" booms a swaying Wayne. Then, again: "Taft, TAFT, TAFT! MR. INTEGRITY!"

"Thank you, John Wayne. And now, back to . . ."

"MR. INTEGRITY, BUDDY, MR. INTEGRITY . . ."

Miami Beach, summer of '68

The Retired Flack arrives unduly early at a convention eve dinner, one thousand dollars a head, his ticket purchased by his political client for that year, Mrs. Frances Bolton, the mul-

124

timillionaire Congresswoman from Cleveland. Surveying the gold-plated Fontainebleau banquet hall, I note that only one other person seems to have misread his ticket regarding the dinner's starting time.

"Jesus!" exclaims the Duke, "what the hell's goin' on here? Am I in the right place?"

We compare tickets. Then watches. Then notes concerning the Presidential nomination.

"Well, hell, I'm for Nixon this year," he explains. "I lost with Goldwater 'n' I figure it's time for a winner."

"What about Reagan?" I ask.

"Reagan? Good man. But Ron got into the goddamn thing too late," John Wayne tells me. I discern the same swaying ebullience that marked his 1952 TV interview. "No, we gotta go with Nixon this time. He's the one."

"What about Nixon and Reagan?"

"NIXON-REAGAN!" he exclaims. "Now there, dammit, is a ticket! I'll buy that . . . NIXON-REAGAN'll sweep the country . . ."

"Well, if he didn't like your copy," I ask Tom Malatesta, "what did he want to say?"

"His idea was to blast Stu Spencer," replies Malatesta. "He thought the single most important contribution he had to make at the moment was to blast Stu Spencer."

"What did he have against Spencer?"

"To hear him talk, what *didn't* he have against him? Spencer foreclosed the mortgage on the family homestead. Something like that. Spencer and another PR guy whose name he couldn't remember. That's all he was steamed about. He thought they double-crossed Reagan because they once worked for him and now they were working for Ford."

"Who was the other PR guy?" I ask Malatesta. "Bill Roberts?"

"No, he didn't like Roberts either. But it wasn't Roberts."

"Clif White?"

"No," says Malatesta shaking his head. "Not Roberts, not

White. Somebody else. Mr. X. We stood there fifteen minutes trying to figure out who 'the other sonofabitch' was. And it wasn't just a matter of all these guys, including Mr. X, switching on Reagan either. What really pissed Wayne off was that Spencer and Ford's other people had worked for *Rockefeller against Goldwater* in the California primary of 1964. That was what he wanted to talk about."

"Not national defense, just Stu Spencer," I say sympathetically.

"Well, later he would talk on national defense, but first he was gonna cut Stu Spencer and Roberts and this other SOB, whoever he was—he was gonna cut 'em a new one. They'd demeaned Goldwater—'insinuated the lie' about Barry was the way he put it. Wayne thought it was terrible, the country was in one helluva shape, when people like that could be working for the President."

"Oh, it would've been great stuff," Tom Malatesta reflects. "Going into North Carolina and Texas in 1976, you know, raising hell about some PR men who dumped on Goldwater in 1964."

"Did you talk him out of it?" I ask.

"Talk *him* out of it? I'd still be there. No, I let that go for the moment. You don't argue with a superstar you're asking for a favor. So Wayne got into his limo and drove off into the sunset and I went to work with Jimmy Stewart. A peach of a guy. And we got a lot out of Wayne, too, later. He was a real asset in Texas and out West. But it took patience, believe me. Sometimes I thought I was dealing with the Aga Khan in diamonds."

"He forgot about Stu Spencer and the rest?"

"Oh, hell no," says Malatesta. "He wrote out some copy himself and did a radio tape, then turned it over to us to use. We never got around to it. But Wayne got it off his chest. I guess it made him feel better."

"What about Lauren Bacall?" I ask Malatesta. "You said she was there on the set. Needless to say, you didn't approach her to do a spot."

"No, I muffed that chance. I just didn't feel up to walking

over to say, 'Hello, my name is Thomas Aquinas Malatesta, and I know you're a liberal Democrat, but if you play your cards right I can put you into Republican TV spots . . .'"

Tape, unused sixty-second Reagan campaign spot on "President Ford's Manipulators"

Folks, John Wayne . . . California had a Governor who in eight years took it from a bankrupt state to a four-billion-dollar surplus: Ronald Reagan. His proven administrative abilities are certainly now needed in our country.

Not that I don't think the President is trying. What I worry about is his political camp. It's not a team. They're not his followers. They're manipulators. They have forced him into a position of vacillation many times.

Two of the men in high places and prominent on his team are the same who allowed their names to be used to insinuate the lie against Goldwater in 1964.

The prejudiced press has been forced to admit the lie about Goldwater, and these men, in his own party, knew that to be a fact, but still allowed ads in the *Los Angeles Times,* in the California primary, to insinuate the lie as a truth.

What we need in this country is common sense and mutual respect. Ronald Reagan can inspire this kind of leadership.

In October, John Wayne travels with Ford through Southern California, introduces him at a rally. Reagan is absent—campaigning elsewhere, he says, due to a prior commitment.

I call Tom Malatesta. He has been frozen out of the Ford general election operation by Stu Spencer. Of the Reagan PR heavies, only two—Nofziger and Jim Lake, the traveling press secretary—are put to work for the Republican ticket. Lake heads up Farmers for Ford. Nofziger is called in to handle Bob Dole's touch-and-go press relations.

"Did you ever find out who Mr. X, the other sonofabitch, was?" I ask Malatesta.

"Never did," he says. "The way these things go, he was probably the same guy who wrote Wayne's introduction of Ford for the Orange County rally."

But the aging Hollywood personality whose television efforts finally turned the campaign around for Malatesta's candidate was neither John Wayne nor Jimmy Stewart. It was Reagan himself who, in the process of rescuing his fortunes, put a dent in a modern PR myth concerning what viewers will and won't buy in the way of political commercials.

In the *Times'* paean to Jerry Rafshoon's masterworks on behalf of Jimmy Carter, much was made of the Atlantan's defying the old Madison Avenue shibboleth about the length of political spots. Rafshoon, the *Times* reported, has dared challenge the notion that any political message longer than sixty seconds loses the viewer. He has stretched Carter spots, featuring the candidate talking into a camera, to a risky five minutes—and made it work successfully.

That being the case, the biggest PR genius working in the '76 primaries has to be the grass-roots political clod in North Carolina who kept insisting to Ronald Reagan's staff that what they wanted in commercials for their candidate wasn't five, or even fifteen, but a full *thirty*-minute television speech! The Stone Age 1950 model: just the candidate standing in front of or sitting behind a desk, *talking*.

The pressure for this kind of TV presentation fit the candidate's own ideas (and, needless to add, those of his wife) about how he could best invest his advertising dollar. Ronald Reagan, after all, is a ham. By definition, a person who likes talking *at* an audience, preferably for lengthy periods, without sharing the spotlight.

What's more, this antediluvian television format—thirty minutes of talking generalities about public issues—propelled Reagan onto the national scene in 1964. To tell him that he shouldn't go on television one-on-one—that is, Ron-and-the-camera, alone in a studio—is to take away the man's biggest edge.

That was the way the candidate felt. It was the way Nancy Reagan felt. In the end, they had their way, and to hell with the experts.

Dave Keene reflects on the success of his candidate's half-hour TV tour de force, credited by the news media as a key factor in

Reagan's victory in North Carolina: "Treleaven's spots would have been ideal for ninety-nine out of a hundred clients—but not for Ronald Reagan. You tailor your program to your strength. With Reagan we had a candidate who could sustain thirty minutes on the tube. Nobody else could."

Even discounting partisan bias, Keene is right: for technique and projection, Reagan is the most formidable TV campaigner around, a candidate perfectly at ease with the medium and his message.

Jerry Rafshoon's client, on the other hand, is one of those TV speakers good only for short takes. As a live speaker, Carter does well extemporizing before small groups but is less than spectacular when addressing large crowds. Jimmy simply doesn't read well from a text. The words issuing from his mouth don't always jibe with his expression or the rhythm of his voice; what a PR speech therapist would term lack of projective coordination.

Given time and exposure to various speaking formats, Carter will probably improve his text-reading. But there are limits. Speechmaking is like any other physical activity: you can teach a runner to get off the blocks more quickly, but not to run the hundred-yard dash in 9.1. There is no substitute for natural talent. The idea that any journeyman speaker can become a master public or TV verbalist as a result of expert help is the most persistent—and discredited—PR myth of all.

His name was Leonard Reinsch and he was the progenitor of a long, unillustrious line of expert failures. He was hired to improve an American President's delivery in making speeches to the country via the electronic media, the first TV-radio speech coach ever put on the White House payroll.

The President, a public speaker with a grating nasal Midwestern accent and naturally stilted hand gestures, felt the need to master the new media, especially television, and was a willing pupil at first. But he could not, for all his teacher's efforts, change the speaking habits of a lifetime. So Leonard Reinsch failed and Harry Truman, on the day he left the White House, was as uninspiring a TV-radio speaker as the day he entered it. But from the back of trains on a whistlestop—that was something else again.

"I say—and I say it with emphasis and conviction—that homemaking is good for America. I say that homemaking is not out of date and I reject strongly such accusations."

> Profile in Courage: GERALD R. FORD
> before the North Carolina chapter
> of the Future Homemakers of America,
> Charlotte, March 20, 1976

"The trouble with the President," the latest in the long line of Oval Office speech therapists was telling Gordon Chaplin of the *Washington Post* in early May 1976, is that "half the time he sounds like a Florsheim shoe salesman."

Ah, the Middle American White House . . . so much for the Florsheim shoe salesmen vote. But Don Penny, who is David Kennerly's latest gift to the Ford PR staff, has only begun his critique. Jerry's problem as a Florsheim-style public speaker, says Penny, is that he uses phrases like "the private sector."

"Now what's he talking about?" Penny asks Chaplin. "Somebody's unmentionables or what? What I'd like to do is help him get rid of all that jargon, all that political rhetoric, until he's *completely naked*, until you see the real man."

Take, for example, Jerry the Joke-teller. A dud. He puts a joke to sleep.

"What he needs to do," explains Penny, "is to get more of a feel for one-liners: BANG!"

Dig, Big Daddy? Like it used to be when Don Penny was doing his *shtik* a few seasons back on "The Wackiest Ship in the Army" and "Hennessey"—the television shows that gave him the credentials necessary to be a speech consultant to the President of the United States.

That Jerry Ford would hire a stand-up comic (first at $150 a day, later at $40,000 a year) to upgrade his speechmaking isn't too surprising. The Retired Flack, who once hacked speeches for

Ford during his days as House Minority Leader, is acquainted with the man's fondness for crowd-warming one-liners. Bob Orben—whose nose is now out of joint because Penny has usurped his role as chief White House BANG!-maker—went on the Ford speechwriting payroll chiefly because of his experience as a Bob Hope gagwriter. And working with Orben for the past year and a half has been yet another media expert, a former CBS news film producer named Bob Mead who, while not intending to be funny often comes off that way when discussing Presidential speaking techniques.

"A speech," says Mead, "has to be written in fairly short sentences that can be read without getting lost when looking up from the page and read before losing the thought before finishing the sentence."

Jerry Ford's own Aristotle on the Art of Rhetoric. Then, of course, there is Bob Hartmann, Ford's chief speechwriter, and Ron Nessen whose network TV experience is also available to our uncosmetized, PR-shunning President whenever he goes before the cameras.

And yet, despite all this expert help, Jerry Ford has been persuaded that he needs still more, and different, expertise to improve his act as a public speaker. Kennerly discovered Don Penny, and brought him to the Oval Office in early 1976, after concluding that what the Boss has needed all along is someone to relax him before he goes on camera. Somebody like Don Penny who, Kennerly informs Chaplin of the *Post*, can put life into Ford's wooden speech habits.

"Kennedy had Billy Wilder, Frank Sinatra, and Peter Lawford helping him in those areas," says Kennerly. Jerry Ford has been cramped in his effort to emerge the charismatic leader for the seventies because, claims his photographer, "there are no talent scouts in this administration."

Ever the frustrated Camelotian, Kennerly strains for some parallel between the White House he works for and the romantic White House of his youth. His suggestion that John F. Kennedy looked to Wilder, Sinatra, and Lawford to help him as a public speaker is absurd. True, JFK did tap Hollywood for one-liners. But whatever other "scouts" he had working on the West Coast were scouring there for talent other than that which a Don Penny can bring to Jerry Ford.

So in late spring 1976, Don Penny is mouthing lines about the shortcomings of his new Boss's speaking style that sound very much like those Bob Mead was delivering in the fall of 1974. Except, of course, with more BANG!

"The President," Gerald Ford's latest flack-in-residence informs Fred Barnes of the *Washington Star*, "does more speaking than any other major film star or stand-up comic in America."

Luminous company indeed for Jerry Ford. And yet—Penny has determined during his brief time on the job—the man just doesn't seem to grasp the first thing about speechmaking. Not the first. For example: At one point recently, when Ford was rehearsing a speech, Penny sighs, he was impelled to interrupt to explain: "*Mr. President, these are words. They mean something.*"

With *some* students an Expert has to start on the most basic level. Nevertheless, Penny informs his interviewers, he has high hopes for his new pupil's future as a public orator. Jerry Ford's latest speech expert even has a standard in mind, an image into which he hopes to transform the President. Up against the Gipper, Mr. Smith, and Hondo, what would you say to Mr. Deeds?

"Gary Cooper," says Don Penny, now in a philosophical mood, "was a very unusual person, a sincere, honest guy. You could understand his silences better than his words."

The better to Cooperize his new client, the Ford administration's answer to Billy Wilder has been given broad authority to go beyond sharpening the President's joke-telling in light speeches before the Gridiron Club. He is intruding into Bob Hartmann's domain, editing and rewriting Presidential speeches of all kinds. Paring down a seventeen-minute address on one recent occasion in Alabama to six minutes of speaking (and, presumably, eleven of meaningful Cooper-like silences). Of even greater importance in terms of assessing his impact on the White House staff structure, Don Penny the comic has been given priority access to the President not only in the Oval Office but traveling abroad *Air Force One:* the Wackiest Plane in the . . .

"Everyone should understand that I have no interest in Washington, except on a basis as a consultant to the President."

> DON PENNY, *after a few weeks on the job, disclaiming inordinate political ambition.*

HE'S COOKING UP A
NEW PRESIDENTIAL IMAGE

Headline, *Washington Star,*
May 9, 1976

DON PENNY: THE WOODY ALLEN
OF THE OVAL OFFICE

Headline, *Washington Post,*
May 9, 1976

Once again the President's own flacks have generated publicity that reinforces the widespread view that he is an affable oaf who needs help to thread his way through a sentence. In any prior administration, Don Penny would have been headed back to the Catskills within an hour after the *Star* and *Post* stories appeared on National Capital newsstands. But then again, no other administration would hire a Don Penny to join its speechwriting staff.

Why then the administration of Just Plain Jerry Ford, the earnest journeyman from Grand Rapids? The answer is as obvious as that official credit beneath the four-column picture accompanying the *Post* story: the President of the United States, behind his Oval Office desk, being briefed by a second banana TV comic on the rudiments of communicating to the American people. The credit lines reads: *White House Photo.*

It is *Mayagüez* black-tie publicity—the sort of "humanizing" copy that the President's swinging photographer believes is great for the Boss's image. The camera pro as a PR amateur. Bearing out with a BANG! what the Retired Flack has long suspected: not Ron Nessen, not even Stu Spencer, but David Hume Kennerly is the flack who has the last word when it comes to the shaping of Jerry Ford's image, both as President and as Presidential candidate.

PRES. FORD STAFF RIFT
DEEPENS AS NEWEST
ADS AIR IN CALIFORNIA

Headline, *Ad Age,*
June 7, 1976

BY BOB DONATH

"New York—President Ford's controversial new slice-of-life commercials . . . seem to be getting mixed reviews in California, but they have gouged a serious rift between the President's Oval Office intimates and his professional advertising advisers in the final days of the primary vote drive . . .

". . . In Washington, copies of memoranda from Mr. Ford's ad advisers obtained by *ADVERTISING AGE* indicate strong disagreement with the ads, which use professional actors portraying citizens discussing Mr. Ford's accomplishments in office . . .

"A long memo from the Campaign '76 advisory group, headed by Peter Dailey until he quit in protest, expressed 'deep concern' with the new ads, calling them counterproductive and the techniques 'very popular for selling soap, but highly questionable for "selling" a man.' Another said the format 'runs the risk of insulting the intelligence of the viewer.'

"Apparently, national campaign director Rogers C. B. Morton had nothing to do with recruiting BBDO domestic president James Jordan, who actually wrote the new commercials. Instead, Mr. Jordan had been brought directly to the President by Don Penny, a New York film production sales representative who, reporting to White House staff coordinator Richard Cheney, has been editing Mr. Ford's speeches and coaching the President's delivery for the last six weeks.

"As Mr. Penny and Ford family confidant *cum* White House photographer David Kennerly told AA, Mr. Ford's advertising failed to humanize the man . . .

"Knocking a commercial recently completed by Campaign '76

134

in which President Ford speaks of his accomplishments directly to the camera, Mr. Kennerly asked, 'How can you get on TV and just say what a great job you've been doing? That turns people off and goes against the President's nature. He's not a boastful man.'"

Associated Press photo cutline, *Washington Post*, October 16, 1976: *Mary Louise Peterson, president of the Iowa State Board of Regents, looks skyward as Ford mistakenly refers to Ohio State instead of Iowa State to a crowd he was addressing . . .*

Outside the Kennedy apparat, the first working politician who ever talked to the Retired Flack in terms of "position papers" happened to be Congressman Gillis Long of Louisiana. I was stunned. Hearing the nephew of Huey and Earl talk about the "position papers" he intended to develop before he ran for Guvnah of Loozyana, I knew the old populist days were gone forever.

In 1976 the think tank approach to defining issues is integral to every Presidential campaign. Stung by charges that he doesn't speak out on the issues, Grass-roots Jimmy Carter flaunts a published List of Position Papers, numbering ninety Positions, from A (Abortion) to W (Women's Rights), each available on request. Carter also has what he calls his "issues group," willing to talk to any Democratic convention delegate who needs clarification on any of the candidate's Position Papers.

Where campaign technocracy comes up short, however, is in its failure to spot the sleeper issue that can rear up and bite the candidate when and where he least expects it. Thus, for all their cerebrations, Carter's staff didn't adequately prepare him to deal with Abortion. Jimmy is surprised by the heat the subject generates. He had no idea it would develop in a way that would take so much time and energy away from what research had indicated would be the Important Issues of the campaign.

In Reagan's case, a sleeper—at least in the short, primary run—has been the biggest boon to his campaign: "The Issue," according to one of his field men, "that turned it around in North Carolina." And Ron didn't even go into it with a Position Paper. Only a snappy slogan.

135

"We built it, we paid for it, it's ours, and we intend to keep it."

> *The Shade of Teddy Roosevelt,*
> *re The Big Ditch, 1976*

Better than any think tank, the polished political speaker can pick up the vibrations of an issue by the way his audiences are responding to his standard speech. Sometimes, however, even a pro like Ron Reagan can be surprised by a sleeper.

He had been using the line since the beginning of the campaign, with hardly a ripple of response from either his New Hampshire audiences or the media. He kept it in because his chief speechwriter, Pete Hannaford, had this hang-up about the Zone.

Then, suddenly, it hit paydirt. In, of all places, Tampa. Before, of all audiences, a crowd of senior citizens pre-advertised by the advance man as being interested in Reagan's stand on social security.

"He was making the standard speech, with a lot more material on social security than usual," says Dave Keene. The audience was listening quietly, not really too responsive. But when he came to the line about the Zone—'we built it, etc.'—out of the blue, the crowd was on its feet, cheering, clapping. Reagan couldn't figure out what was happening. Neither could we. Why Tampa? Why that audience?"

Whatever the reasons Reagan didn't wait for any think tank to confirm his findings. Carrying the line to North Carolina, he began to pace it better. The cheers got louder. By some unknown chemistry, post-Tampa, it had become his Issue. Why? Keene had an answer, but Reagan couldn't have cared less. The polished political speaker takes what his audiences give him: Never look a gift ovation in the mouth.

"The Canal," Keene tells me, "was a litmus, important for what it symbolized. Reagan was articulating an inchoate popular feeling, particularly among Republicans, in terms they could appreciate. The Zone issue tapped a nerve in Americans tired of seeing their country retreat from Vietnam and lose ground against the Communists in Angola."

"That's pretty heavy," I reply. "It seems I read that explanation somewhere."

"You should have," Keene says. "I fed it to enough columnists."

The Zone issue is good for North Carolina, Texas, and the South. It helps Reagan carry Indiana and Nebraska, putting Ford on the defensive. Instead of Reagan denying he intends to sack the social security system, Ford is now denying he intends to give the Canal away. But John Sears recognizes those ovations for what they are: primary gains and general election headaches. To turn things around, Reagan has adopted the '64 Goldwater image of War Hawk. Now even Goldwater himself, dragooned into the argument by the White House, is warning against the danger of a hardline Canal Zone stand. It could lead, says Barry, to another Vietnam—a guerrilla war right in our own backyard. And the press, too, is picking up the theme.

Bob Novak to Dave Keene, March 1968: "*Are you going to defoliate the Canal Zone or does Reagan just plan to give commanders in the field the option to use nuclear weapons?*"

A candidate makes his standard road speech, five, six times a day. Traveling correspondents grow tired of hearing it all. Why doesn't that character up there change his lines? That the audience the candidate is addressing hasn't heard the lines is beside the point. The press has, and is bored, bored, BORED.

In North Carolina, Ford repeats his line—once too often—that "any government big enough to give you everything is big enough to take it away." He will be punished for his failure to keep the press entertained.

A claque of traveling correspondents agrees that at the next stop, when the President gets to that part of his speech, they will all chant the words with him. When they follow through, Ford becomes rattled. Like Reagan at Tampa, he doesn't quite know what's going on. He hurries through his speech and escapes to his cabin aboard *Air Force One*. Worried, Ford's staff eliminates the line from his next speech, since a traveling press big enough to give a candidate good coverage is big enough to take it away.

But what does a bored press cover? The news behind the words. Sidebars, nuance, EntertaiNews. Rona Barrett, meet Joseph Kraft.

POLITICAL SCIENCE-FICTION FEATURE:
FLASHBACK: *The Retired Flack Fantasizes the 1976 New Hampshire Primary Press Covering an 1863 Address*

GETTYSBURG, Pa., Nov. 19—President Lincoln, in what White House aides billed as a "nonpolitical" speech, dedicated a military cemetery here today before a sparse, unresponsive crowd estimated by local authorities at fewer than 300 people.

In a tactical move clearly designed to get the political jump on Gen. George B. McClellan, his probably Democratic opponent, Mr. Lincoln made one of his rare trips outside Washington to visit this vote-rich keystone state. Judging by early reaction to his appearance, however, the White House strategy appears to have backfired.

Not only was the President's address sharply criticized by political experts for being too brief, but he was upstaged by the main speaker of the day, the brilliant public orator, Everett Hale. Moreover, Mr. Lincoln's glaring failure even to mention McClellan or Gen. George G. Meade, the victorious Union commander of the battle fought here in July, cast doubt on White House staff claims that the trip was "purely nonpolitical."

One veteran political observer, noting recent charges that the Lincoln Administration has created a "credibility gap" between itself and the public, termed the President's omission of McClellan's and Meade's names from his speech text "a serious blunder that will come back to haunt him in next year's election."

"This is another example of the sloppy White House staff work that has plagued the Administration since the day Lincoln took office," commented another observer on receiving news that the President's speech had been hurriedly scribbled on the back of an envelope en route to the speech site.

White House spokesmen vehemently denied this rumor, claiming that Mr. Lincoln had "worked over two drafts of the speech before he left Washington."

While debate went on regarding the manner in which the speech was drafted, there was general agreement with the opinion rendered by a visiting professor of oratory from the University of Pennsylvania that the President's address was "a dud."

Mr. Lincoln delivered his remarks in the same high-pitched, vaguely irritating Middle Western nasal inflection that has characterized his past public addresses. Another criticism was that the speech, in the words of one Gettysburg resident, "didn't say anything we haven't already heard."

"My family and I came out here to see and listen to the President of the United States and all we got was a puny two minutes," said one outraged localite.

Mr. Lincoln remained unsmiling throughout his visit to this small eastern Pennsylvania village. Aides claimed the President's solemn demeanor was simply "appropriate to the occasion," but knowledgeable Washington sources have indicated that serious problems in Mr. Lincoln's home life more likely account for his grim public visage in recent months.

In support of this view, it was noted that Mrs. Lincoln did not accompany the President here.

Another significant absentee from the speaker's platform was Vice-President Hannibal Hamlin. Rumors persist that Mr. Lincoln plans to dump Mr. Hamlin as a running mate next year in favor of a Border State Democrat who would be more helpful in pursuing his Administration's "Southern strategy."

The President, who has not held a major news conference in two years, refused reporters' requests that he answer questions following his address. In the speech itself, Mr. Lincoln said that the men who died in the battle here gave their lives in order "that this nation, under God, shall have a new birth of freedom—and that government of the people, by the people, for the people, shall not perish from the earth."

However, the President, who was elected three years ago on a pledge to preserve the Union, once again failed to provide details on any fresh Administration initiative to achieve this objective.

Pictures don't lie but picture editors can, well, bend it a little. Television gets pounded by the print medium for shallow, quick-hitting reportage. But the print medium has its own image games:

Hundreds of photos are taken of the candidates each week, close-ups that reflect the spectrum of human emotion. The imaginative photo editor is offered unlimited choice. A split instant's expression on a candidate's face, isolated from the flow of moving events, can hype whatever campaign story is selling that week. It cuts off the ragged edges, eliminates the fuzziness, the complexity of the process.

For those who don't watch television, but get their campaign news from the dailies and weeklies, the process comes in image packages no less neat and convenient than those purveyed on the tube. Even more so. Print freezes and makes permanent record of what, in fact, may be only an extraneous expression or motion. A single photo is worth a thousand words out of context:

A candidate is captured full-face by the camera, his brow furrowed in mild distress. What he's actually saying is: *"Would you mind repeating that? I didn't get the question."* But what the camera tells us is, *There is a harried candidate whose campaign is in deep trouble.*

No need, really, to read the copy. A grinning Ford across the page from a purse-lipped Reagan one week, a grinning Reagan across the page from a grim Ford the next. Jackson mopping his brow. Carter grinning. Udall sacked out in his campaign plane, the used-up candidate. Carter grinning. Wallace looking perplexed (not close-up, full-length—with Wallace it's always full-length, wheels and all). Carter grinning. Just look at the pitchers. That's all ye know and all ye need to know about Who's Up, Who's Down, Who's Up, Who's Down. In a PR game in which one week's impression can shape next week's results, the picture editor's "endorsement" can be more important than a Governor's.

The Play-offs
April–August 1976

Jimmy the Front-runner takes on Jerry the Latecomer, Don Quixote de la Boise, and Hubert's Uncommitted. Ford is up, Reagan is down. Reagan is up, Ford is down. On to New York, land of the K. C. Steak. On to Kansas City, land of the New York Strip. The Retired Flack watches the Process in Convulsion.

"*Jimmy Carter*," reads the *Times'* advertisement, quoting a mid-March Gallup poll finding, "*is the only Democrat who can stop George Wallace.*" Two months ago New Yorkers for Carter were only claiming "he is the only Democrat who can stop George Wallace." But Jimmy Who has become Carter the Front-runner. The question now asked by the news media isn't *How did he do it (in New Hampshire/Florida)?* but *Will he stumble before he gets to the finish line?*

An old pol would see Pennsylvania and Ohio as the pivotal primaries, the states that clinched it for Jimmy. But to the Retired Flack, the pivot—for both party nominations—was North Carolina . . .

BIG CARTER WIN
CRUSHES HOPES
FOR WALLACE

Headline, *Washington Star*,
after North Carolina,
March 24, 1976

Before North Carolina, the strategy for Jackson, Udall, and the Democratic Establishment had been to Stop Wallace. Post-North Carolina, the man who had stopped Wallace became the man to stop. Whoever the opponent, from Pennsylvania to Ohio, the game would be ABC: Anybody But Carter.

"I am not part of any Stop Carter movement."

SCOOP JACKSON/MORRIS UDALL/
HUBERT HUMPHREY/JERRY BROWN/
FRANK CHURCH, solo and in
harmony, April–June 1976

"Well, at least it's a change from all those victories in a row."

GRACE MARIE PRATHER, *deputy press secretary, the President Ford Committee, reacting to North Carolina returns*

For the Republicans, too, North Carolina, where Reagan might have been finished, but wasn't, set the pattern for the months that lay ahead: that there would be no pattern. The game would be media leapfrog, a montage of Reagan the winner-loser and Ford the loser-winner, to the end that by mid-August, in the Kansas City heat, it would not be the New Politics of Imagery but the Old Politics of Brokerage that decided the contest between the Celebrated Leaping Frog of California and the Bulltoad of the Oval Office . . .

The Washington Babbitt and the Washington Bromide meet in Lafayette Park, April 1976:

142

"What do you make of Carter?" asks Bob Boyd, Knight Newspapers.

"Don't know," says the Retired Flack. "Bill Moyers thinks he's either a straight arrow, a con man, or a combination of both."

We stand there, across from the White House, pondering Moyers' Paradox. Boyd doesn't get it any more than I do. But since it came from Bill Moyers over educational television it must mean something. Yes: Jimmy Carter is either a straight man or a conned arrow.

"Well, anyway," shrugs Boyd, "our bureau is beginning to think in terms of a Carter Presidency come January. I understand he's lining all the old Kennedy crowd up. Sorensen did his Gridiron script."

"Sorensen's back and Jimmy's got him," the Babbitt nods.

"Not necessarily," replies the Bromide. "It could be the other way around."

Jimmy Carter, the anti-Washington candidate, at the Gridiron annual dinner. O.K., he didn't exactly wow 'em. But the consensus of the drunks sitting in judgment, the cream of the National Capital press Establishment, was that the Newcomer passed the ultimate Test of Self-Deprecating Humor. Jimmy can laugh at himself. At least, he can laugh at himself with the help of Theodore Sorensen.

Thus, the Gridiron Tradition: any candidate who wants to get along with the press Establishment must pay it homage by showing up at an annual spring dinner and doing a self-deprecating bit. In Carter's case, a passing grade at the Gridiron was especially important.

Jimmy grins a lot, is the line that's been going the press corps rounds, *but does he have a sense of humor?* Several serious columns have been written on the subject in recent weeks. Enough to impel Carter's flacks to stick a few prepared jokes into his standard campaign speech (*"A funny thing happened to me on the way to the peanut warehouse . . ."*).

Twenty years ago another Democratic Presidential candidate was criticized for exposing his sense of humor in public. Now Jimmy Carter must prove his worth as a candidate by yukking it up. Political styles change. But although the Retired Flack can appreciate the value of a candidate's proving he has a sense of humor, it remains a mystery what a politician's ability to deliver prefab punchlines tells us about his character and personality. Is it that the candidate who hires a lousy gagwriter or mangles ready-made jokes might also appoint an incompetent Secretary of State?

But, of course, I almost forgot one of the Lessons of the Sixties. The absence of the ability to laugh at one's self, in a Presidential candidate, could also mean the absence of any self-restraint in exercising Executive power. That's it. Nixon had no sense of humor, which absence reflected his megalomania, inevitably leading to *Watergate*. Johnson couldn't laugh at himself. Again, megalomania. Inevitably, *Vietnam*.

Something like that. Whatever, it becomes essential that Jimmy Carter demonstrate to the Gridiron crowd that he can laugh at himself. If he hadn't, there would be more columns and commentaries describing him as an ice-blooded technocratic zealot who might lead us back into the dark, megalomaniacal night of the sixties. An image to be avoided, at all costs. So for this he calls in *Ted Sorensen?*

Jerry Ford, flanked by full-time gagwriters Orben and Penny, has no trouble coming up with stand-up one-liners on a moment's notice. By Gridiron standards—taking into account the amount of time and salary this President expends on his public joke-telling—Ford has to be graded the funniest Chief Executive in American history. And, indeed, there are those who consider him just that.

Ford's problem, precisely. As in the beginning, or at least since the Pardon, there are those Americans who seem to laugh at rather than with Jerry Ford. It started with *National Lampoon's* ice-cream-cone-in-the-forehead cover a few months after he took office, was fueled by publicity given the ramp and ski-falling incidents, and has now taken monstrous audiovideo shape in what, among concerned White House flacks, is whispered about as "the Chevy Chase image."

Chevy Chase's weekly impersonations of Ford-the-lummox on

NBC's "Saturday Night Live" inspire laughs among a select young urban group with a low threshold of tolerance for Presidents and other Establishment institutions.

By Nielsen demographics alone, the White House response to Chase's weekly Jerry the Klutz routine should have been one of benign neglect. Ignore it: by that hour on Saturday night, Ford voters are either sleeping, smashed at the country club, or watching Duke Wayne on another channel. But there are some middle-class suburban Republican politicians (along with their wives and offspring) who are possessed by visions of showing they're really With-It. Even Nixon, trying to soften his image for the 1968 campaign, went that route. On the advice of friend-gagwriter-TV producer Paul Keyes, he did a three-second "Sock-it-to-me" bit for "Laugh-in," the "Saturday Night Live" of a decade ago. Ford is therefore persuaded that he should demonstrate what a reg'lar feller-swinger he is by joining in the laughs. The White House strategy devised by image-groping amateurs, who operate on instincts more in sync with Chevy's fan club than Jerry's constituency, is to meet the Chase Threat by *coopting it.*

A little over a quarter century ago, Bob Hope and Fred Allen, the smart-ass comics of their day, were lampooning an unelected President as obtuse, crude, and wooden. It fazed Harry Truman not at all. At least, not publicly. As a professional with his own sense of PR priorities, he could separate the significant from the extraneous in calculating the elements of political survival. Truman was also a student of Presidential history. He had never read or heard of any President having been laughed out of office. Not even Millard Fillmore.

Jerry Ford, however—a point that cannot suffer from repetition this election year since it lies at the heart of his image problem—is *not* Harry Truman. He may charter a whistlestop train through Michigan. He may make speeches from the rear platform in a Rich Little impersonation of Give 'em Hell Harry. But the difference between the two men lies in the fact that Truman was secure in his own personality, while Ford, by invidious, self-inflicted comparison, has this need to be some *other* President. At times, it seems, some other Jerry Ford.

Cooption (Phase I)

For a Ford speech to the Radio and Television Correspondents Association, Penny provides the Boss with material based on the comic's misconception of an old Harry Truman routine. Truman, following his 1948 upset of Dewey, mimicked H. V. Kaltenborn's election night coverage, in a speech before a Democratic Party audience in Washington. *Now Jerry Ford will do a take-off on Chevy Chase's take-off on Jerry Ford.* BANG! The idea, you see, is that a man can't be a klutz if he doesn't mind doing an imitation of someone doing an imitation of him as a klutz. Dig? So the President opens his speech with a sight gag: knocking silverware off the table, fumbling his text, scattering pages across the floor. The whole "Saturday Night Live" bit, except for Chevy's climactic pratfall.

This President, as his flacks keep telling us, is one fierce political competitor. When he sees a threat on the horizon, Jerry Ford clears his desk for action: first things first. He spends two hours working with staff on the crisis at hand. Not the Ronald Reagan crisis: the Chevy Chase crisis. With the help of his professional speech therapists he gets the timing of his routine down pat. And in the media event, it pays off. Network coverage of the President's hilarious bit, the papers flying off the podium, the whole *shtik*. Great PR, absolutely the best. For Chevy Chase, of course.

Cooption (Phase II)

Ron Nessen is then invited to play the President's press secretary on "SNL"; that is, to guest-host the show and be Chevy's straight man during his fumbling, head-bumping routine. At the last minute, Ford himself agrees to do a taped intro for the show, the entire script of which includes the usual Not Ready for Prime Time quota of gags covering Francisco Franco, abortion, menopause, the gay life . . .

Watching at Camp David, the President is not amused. Kennerly says it was Nessen's idea, not his. Penny agrees with Kennerly. The show stunk. (*Now if HE had been asked to be guest host, it might have turned out differently. Like, first, we have the President coming on as Gary Cooper in a* High Noon *bit . . .*)

146

Get me to His Church on Time

"I don't want any publicity on my going to church tomorrow morning," Jimmy Carter tells Peter Bourne in the hotel coffee shop after the Gridiron appearance. "I may not even go to church."

Bourne has been contacted early in the week by Rosalynn Carter's scheduler and asked to locate a church for the Carters to attend Sunday morning. His choice is a black-Latino Baptist church in the heart of urban Washington, not bad thinking for a PR non-pro. But Jimmy vetoes the idea. Instead, he, Rosalynn and daughter Amy will attend services at a Lutheran church not far from the hotel.

The hotel is the one where Broderick Crawford and Judy Holliday were scripted to stay in the film *Born Yesterday*: the Statler Hilton. It is two blocks and a public square from the White House. While his Democratic opponents take off to Wisconsin and New York for campaigning, the Washington outsider now shows "Mo" Udall and "Scoop" Jackson that he knows more about the way of the National Capital press corps than they've learned in all their years here.

When it comes to Washington, Jimmy may claim to be an innocent but he was not reborn yesterday. He may not want any publicity on *his* going to church, but after checking out his gut instinct on the idea with Jody Powell, the candidate decides there's nothing wrong with taking a ride on *Jerry Ford's* prayer schedule.

At midmorning the usual Sabbath congregation of White House correspondents, photographers, and TV cameramen is gathered outside St. John's, "the Church of Presidents," walking distance away from the hotel, directly across Lafayette Square from the White House. Jimmy and the family decide to stroll past the church. *Why all the commotion?* Jimmy grins. *Oh, the President goes to church here? Well, Lawdee . . . we're just your ordinary run-of-the-town country folk tourists, come to see our Nation's Capital. And look over there, Amy honey, that's the WHITE HOUSE. That's where the President lives . . .*

Across the street the Secret Service gets word that the Carters are by the church, talking to newsmen. The First Family schedule is momentarily delayed until the publicity interlopers move

147

on. Going to church for the cameras is the President's act. He doesn't intend to share a Jimmy-meets-Jerry billing on the Sunday evening news.

But Jimmy gets his television play and Monday morning photo spread anyway. He and Rosalynn and Amy (being hugged by Daddy), with the big white mansion as a backdrop. "Mo" Udall gets a short Sunday evening news bit un-Presidentially sipping suds in Milwaukee, looking like a candidate for alderman, simpering at the cameras, "Well, I guess this oughta get the *beer* vote." And poor Scoop, eating knockwurst in the Bronx, draws a publicity blank.

Jesus, who ever thought it would come to pass? Campaigning on Sunday was a PR no-no in the Retired Flack's active days. No decent candidate ever campaigned on the Lord's Day. It would offend the sensibilities of religious voters. But now that religion, capital R, has come out of the closet as a sacred publicity bovine to be milked, a candidate has to campaign on Sundays just to break even with the competition.

Sunday was once considered Dead Day for publicity. Nothing ever happened on Sunday. Nobody ever expected anything to happen on Sunday. Lawrence Spivak created his "Meet the Press" format around that idea. A guest was assured of making Monday morning's headlines since no other politician would be doing or saying anything significant. It was a blessed day off for Presidential campaigners. Then came the Sunday evening network news, and it's been seven days a week ever since, no time off for good behavior . . .

"What time will he be going to services tomorrow?" the *newly arrived correspondent on the Goldwater campaign plane asked one Saturday night as we flew into Phoenix after a long week's campaigning.*

"He doesn't," I replied.

"He doesn't *go to church on Sunday? But he has to go to church on Sunday. Every politician has to go to church on Sunday."*

148

That was the old PR shibboleth: the candidate didn't campaign, he went to church on Sunday morning. Now he does both. Simultaneously.

Goodbye, "Mo"

It is the perception that might have been. While "Scoop" Jackson is winning New York, Udall comes within a hair of upsetting Carter in Wisconsin. Who can tell (other than two hundred political correspondents) what impact two beatings in one day might have had on Jimmy's *momentum* in Pennsylvania? But no: the Great Flack in the Sky takes care of his Favorite Son Candidates.

"Mo" Udall, the Unblessed, has been running second, second, second, so he gets a new campaign song, to the tune of "Second Hand Rose" (*Ol' Second Place "Mo," they call him Second Place "Mo"* . . .). Why Not Second Best? It is good for laughs and troop morale, but little else.

If there is any railing to be done about the way the news media has *perceived* the race, it is Udall, more than Jackson, who's entitled. If Carter's strong Wisconsin precincts had reported in ahead of Udall's; if "Mo" had been closing the gap through the long night, narrowly losing a state he was supposed to lose big—then what? Instead, there is Carter, grinning. Again. The Great Flack has set up this photo opportunity in Milwaukee, giving Jimmy the opportunity to ham it up for the cameras, the way Harry Truman did the night the *Chicago Tribune* "elected" Tom Dewey . . .

CARTER UPSET BY UDALL: FORD EASILY BEATS REAGAN

Headline, *Milwaukee Sentinel*,
first edition, April 7, 1976

October 1976

"You know, funny thing about the second deck of that headline," Dave Keene says. "Reagan didn't even go into Wisconsin but still got over forty percent of the vote against an incumbent President. Nobody in the press picked that up. I guess they weren't looking for Republican perceptions that night."

When you're cold you're cold. God Almighty does his bit of flackery, but isn't talking to the press about it. "Scoop" Jackson must work with mere flesh, bones, and hyperactive staff egos.

"Scoop" has this minor league Rafshoon-Penny-type self-promoter in Philadelphia, a flack-advance man ready, eager, and slobbering to tell the news media how his candidate is exploiting the news media. His name is William Lalli and he gives the *Wall Street Journal*'s Ron Shafer an ear-and-eyeful on his technique in setting up a media event at the Liberty Bell featuring the candidate and his ten-year-old son, Peter.

"Unknown to the newspaper reader, of course," writes Shafer on the day preceding the Pennsylvania primary, *"was that Mr. Lalli and his associates had arranged for this intimate little family moment to occur in full view of about thirty journalists . . ."*

Unknown to the newspaper readers who saw the photo, but now known to the newspaper readers who saw the photo. In future campaigns candidates will swear their flacks to a code of *omerta.* Mr. Lalli is so tickled with his series of minipublicity triumphs (*getting on the six o'clock TV news, y' see is the name of this game, etc.*) that he blows the cover on the comprehensive Jackson image strategy of portraying himself to the country as the only candidate who won't stoop to publicity gimmickry to get his name in the newspapers and his face on the screen.

Yet Jackson's Washington flacks are bitter about press coverage of the campaign, claiming that reporters are bird-dogging fluffy little publicity rabbits while ignoring the substantive issues. True, all too true. But then, they weren't complaining when the press got after the fluffy little all-white rabbit a few weeks back . . .

"I think most of the problem has been caused by my ill-chosen agreement to use the word ethnic purity. I think that was a very serious mistake on my part. I think I should have used the word 'ethnic character' or 'ethnic heritage' . . . I do want to apologize to all those who have been concerned about the unfortunate use of the 'ethnic purity.'"

JIMMY CARTER, *in Philadelphia, calling off the dogs*

150

It had to happen. The only question was when and how. Jimmy the Front-runner was bound to put his foot in his mouth. Not because he is a boob, but because anybody who must talk, talk, talk, answer, answer, answer, 366 days a year (no Sundays off) is going to blow one. The difference between Jimmy the Front-runner and Jimmy Who is that now people are paying attention.

Political Talk-and-Answer is a game of shading, pure ebony through murky gray to pure white. Avoid the extremes. If caught on the outer limits, leap into the murky gray. And quickly.

Jimmy Who began by saying he would not lie to us, a lie for openers, unless you pare your definition of "lying" to fine marrow. All men running for political office *lie* by shading. In verbal impurity lies safety. A candidate tells a reporter, "*It is night.*" It is in fact day. The reporter has caught him in a bald-face lie, right? Of course not. He checks back to find that the politician has recollected himself, having talked the problem over with his PR man: *Oh, you meant HERE! I thought you were talking about MOSCOW!* Besides, it'll be night in a few hours anyway, so, ha-ha, the subject is really irrelevant. Say, let's get on to the really *substantive* issues of this here campaign . . .

Carter was heading for trouble with the press, either through a misstatement to an individual reporter or a snarl-up at a news conference. The man overexplains. Everybody says he is vague on issues, but it isn't Nixonian vagueness (as on Vietnam) born of a campaign PR strategy of simply not addressing an issue. Carter talks to reporters constantly, explaining why he isn't vague. The man simply cannot say, "No comment." At times, when worn after a long week's campaigning, he will even overexplain testily.

Other candidates say you're not specific as they are on the issues, he is asked/told by one reporter.

Well, snaps Jimmy, *they're the candidates who are losing, aren't they?*

He must always answer the question, even if the answer isn't a good one. It is a compulsive verbal tic, one he recognizes but can't control. All he can do is complain privately afterward to

151

Jody about how the press (are you ready for this, Scoop?) is more interested in his over-explanations about fluff than his over-explanations concerning substance.

What particularly upsets Jimmy is the mandatory tongue exercise he is required to take at every airport after his plane lands. The crush of microphones and cameras, the soundmen sticking their padded cattle-prods in his face, and the same damned reporters asking the same damned dumb questions, nine out of ten having to do with strategy and tactics, the tenth designed not so much to elicit information on a substantive issue as to catch him in a goof.

All they're interested in, he tells Jody and the staff, *is the sensational, the offbeat. I work a week on a speech to set out a position on an issue, then all I see of myself on the evening news is thirty seconds' answering questions about the latest polls.*

One PR response would be for Jimmy to smile away questions about strategy and tactics. Let Jordon and Powell handle those, while the candidate sticks to substantive issues. Train the press. Let them know you don't intend to play their game. If they want Jimmy Carter on camera, it will be Jimmy Carter on Jimmy Carter's terms, talking about issues that Jimmy Carter wants to talk about. That was the way Franklin Roosevelt did it (*"No iffy questions, gentlemen"*). And Truman. And, to a lesser extent, Kennedy. But that style is out this year. Post-Watergate morality includes post-Nixon political PR. God help the candidate who won't answer questions at a news conference, about anything. Even on Sundays.

What most impresses the Retired Flack about the "ethnic purity" flap—initiated at a one-on-one with the *New York Daily News*'s Sam Roberts, then developed into a major story by CBS's Ed Rabel at an Indianapolis news conference—isn't, therefore, that Jimmy Carter finally blew one. I was waiting for him to blow one. What I was interested in was how he would react to a major media problem now that he's the front-runner.

The measure of a candidate's talent for survival (not instinct, *talent*) isn't how well his campaign is planned, but how well he reacts to the unplanned. Particularly a self-created media monster. After the false start of trying to shovel dirt over his mistake, hoping it will disappear (Charley Kirbo's Country Boy lawyer counsel), Carter listens to the advice of his younger flacks and moves quickly to destroy the monster. He doesn't want to admit that he said anything wrong; but it's being *perceived* that way. His choice is either to spend the next three months explaining, "*I am not a racist,*" or to retract by apology.

Simple enough. Yet it also happens to be the most unpalatable advice a political flack can offer since it goes against the fundamental tenet of a candidate's religion: his belief in the infallibility of his own instincts.

Politicians as a genre dread the act of public apology. They are afraid it will be interpreted as a sign of weakness. To most candidates, apology is something that creates, not destroys, ogres. But Jimmy Carter, at least in this case, is different. He decides that if Paris was worth a mass, Washington is worth an apology, admits his error, and leaps back into the murky semantic gray. Then, and only then, can he put the problem to rest with a symbolic ceremony in Atlanta: "Daddy" King's embrace before the cameras driving a stake through the monster's pure white heart.

THE SEMANTICS OF AMERICAN POLITICS   *Spring 1976*
Trigger Words, Labels & Names Division

"America's ethnic heritage is a great treasure. I don't think that federal actions should be used to destroy that ethnic treasure."

PRESIDENT FORD, before the
American Society of Newspaper
Editors, April 13

"Well, the point I made originally was that the Government ought not to deliberately take a posture on a goal of destroying the ethnic character of a neighborhood. I said ethnic purity. I should have said ethnic character, heritage or background."

JIMMY CARTER, "Issues and
Answers," April 25

"The policy hasn't changed, it's only that we're dropping the word."

RON NESSEN, explaining the
expurgation of *détente* from
Ford administration's official
family thesaurus, post-North
Carolina

Q.: Congressman, a few weeks ago you began calling yourself a "progressive centrist" instead of a liberal . . . (W)hat is the difference between a progressive centrist and a liberal?

MR. UDALL: Oh, not a heck of a lot really in substance . . . I am a liberal. You know I don't run away from it. What I am saying is that "liberal" is a worry word. You stop a fellow on the street and say, "I am a great liberal; I want to tell you about my program." He tunes you out before you even get started . . . It is simply a question of getting people's attention. A liberal is kind of a barrier to communicate with people . . . I didn't change anything I had advocated. I simply said: "This is a barrier to communication. Let's not use this word."

Representative MORRIS K. UDALL
"Meet the Press," pre-Wisconsin

FORD IS AVOIDING
MENTIONING NIXON

Headline, *The New York Times*,
April 30

President Ford said today that he would rather not mention the name of former President Richard M. Nixon in public because "it is better for all of us to just not remind ourselves of the Watergate era."

Governor, asks *The New York Times*'s Jim Wooten, traveling with Carter in March, *you know that part of your speech where you mention all those great Americans out of the past? Washington, Lincoln, Roosevelt, and Martin Luther King?*

Yes, says Jimmy, *what about it?*

154

Well, it's just that I noticed, says Wooten, *in one of your talks last week before the all-white audiences in Florida, you didn't mention King. Did you forget?*

(Pause) *No,* says Jimmy, *I didn't forget.* (Pause) *And* (Pause) *I won't ever do it again.*

Next stop, Marion, Illinois, a town, says Wooten, *as racially conservative as any town in Georgia,* where Jimmy Carter was true to his word. He did not leave out Dr. King's name. He omitted the entire list.

The Vice-President, talking privately to a group of Republicans in Atlanta, says "Scoop" Jackson's staff has been "infiltrated" by two employees with Communist connections. Word leaks out. No Vice-President of the United States is going to scatter-shoot into a covey of Georgia politicians without some reporter (in this case, David Nordan of the *Atlanta Journal*) picking it up.

Rocky of late has been . . . well, *rocky.* Uninhibited. Free-spirited. Flaky. Something happened when he was forced off the team last winter. Since then it's been a case of to hell with it, I'll say whatever I please. But when the story breaks it develops that the Vice-President, although he's named names, hasn't got anything to back up his charge. He must apologize. Publicly. So he does, in the Senate Chamber, "To the Senate of the United States, to its members, and particularly to Senator Jackson."

Afterward, Jackson and Rockefeller are pictured on the front page of the *Times.* Scoop says that as far as he's concerned the matter's closed. He does *not* say, "What are you apologizing to *me* for? It's my staff members you ought to be talking to." The Washington Seigneur System: Could this be what Jimmy and Ron are talking about?

"Now, I'm not saying that all of them are on it, but many of these rock 'n' roll people are hawking drugs and want liberalized marijuana and free love."

> *Unidentified Wallace spokesman,*
> *suggesting a difference*
> *between his candidate's musical*
> *tastes and Jimmy Carter's*

In Wisconsin, the Republican flacks have a Battle of the Bands. Much as anything, it points up the cultural gap between America's two major party constituencies. Reagan's team imports a Scottish bagpipe group to draw crowds. Ford's swingers, with Milwaukee's Polish vote in mind, hire a polka band.

Meanwhile, the With-It Democrats are enlisting country and rock stars for more than audience-warming or *Nashville*-style voter lure. In a year when contributions are hard to come by, rock concerts are soft-touch fund-raisers. Even before the formal campaign got under way, three groups—in only three appearances—raised over $100,000 for Jimmy Carter. Working free of charge, Marshall Tucker's pulled in $25,000 in an October 1975 concert; the Allman Brothers, $64,000 in November; Charlie Daniels, $12,000 in January.

More recently, Linda Ronstadt, the biggest draw on the political fund-raising circuit, has gone over to Jerry Brown (now that her first choice, Fred Harris, has dropped out). Under the old rules, entertainers were used for fatcat fund-raisers: Come see Paul Newman and Gregory Peck at a cocktail party, $1,000 to $5,000 an engraved invitation. The format still draws. But the real gold this populist year can be dug in them vibes, at $5 to $25 a ticket. And here, as elsewhere, Country Boy Jimmy is doing a better mining job than his competitors.

Goodbye, "Scoop"

Michael Novak grieves the passing of Henry Jackson's candidacy. Jackson is a man, claims Novak, who has all the qualifications to be President except the ability to win at the Supermedia image game. An odd criticism of the System coming from a self-styled anti-elitist, since it assumes the desirability of an immaculately conceived national leader: a President who can govern but who, just incidentally, can't get elected.

Jackson's inability to sell his candidacy goes deeper than media coverage, however. He rouses within the left segments of his own party the same antagonism that Rockefeller does among right-wing Republicans. There is a flesh-and-blood political chemistry at work here, an element more potent even than Cronkite. "Scoop" Jackson is simply the William McAdoo/John

Nance Garner of our day. There's a place in the System for such leaders. But not, obviously, at the top.

"Meet the Don Quixote of this campaign."

FRANK CHURCH, March 1976

Hello, Frank

Robert Vaughn's *pragmatic* choice for the Democratic nomination (pragmatism on the West Coast being surrealism east of Denver), has lost weight, but not where it counts, i.e., in his tonsils. Frank Church needs no speaking coaches. His problem is that he knows it. Church is the Great Enunciator of the United States Senate, the man who, since the departure of Everett McKinley Dirksen, has no peer among his colleagues for oleaginous diction and oratorial narcissism.

In 1960, there were experts who speculated that this talent at the podium might bring Frank Church the Democratic Vice-Presidential nomination on a Kennedy ticket. He was assigned the keynote at the Los Angeles convention. But following in the tradition of his keynote predecessors at the two previous Democratic conventions—the unforgettable Paul Devers and the Preacher Man ("How long, O Lord, how long . . . ?") Frank Clements, Church blew his chance. He was neither mechanical like Devers nor bombastic like Clements. Just mellifluously dull. The joke afterward concerned the disgruntled delegate leaving the convention hall that first night, being reminded that, after all, Church once won first prize in an oratorical contest: *"Jesus,"* he said, *"suppose we'd had to listen to the* second-*place winner?"*

But that is all past rhetoric. The Senator from Boise, as Chairman of the Foreign Relations Committee, is no longer in the image of Boy Wonder, but Mature Statesman. He has skillfully put himself into the forefront of Presidential politics during the post-Watergate era through exposing clandestine CIA activities overseas. It is a Washington headline issue, but viewed from a strict PR perspective there is this oddity: through the early and middle primaries, New Hampshire to Pennsylvania, it has *not* been an issue heavily used, by any of the Democratic candidates. It could be an incipient Watergate, a sleeper issue that will in time catch fire in the hinterlands. But then, Watergate didn't win for McGovern, despite the headlines it was making in Washington.

Church opens his grass-roots campaign in Idaho City, his ancestral community. Population: 200. Four hundred fewer than Plains, Georgia, if anybody's counting. But Frank Church, whatever down-home backdrop he might choose, just won't project as an Idaho Country Boy. Nor as a Don Quixote.

For one thing, Don Quixote didn't spend a year casing his chances against the windmill: the length of time Church has been laying in lances and staff for a charge into the late primaries. He has played the game safe, grooming for the right moment of entry: when everyone else would be battered and bloodied from the early going.

To be sure, Church did not foresee the rise of Jimmy Carter. But even this development fits into his strategy. The anti-Establishment mood of the 1976 primary electorate is predictable only in its unpredictability. For Jimmy, in the bizarre mediascopic time warp of this election year, is now *expected* to win. Therefore, by voting for Carter the individual Agin-er does nothing to shake anybody up, put his state *on the map*. The way to get on the map, as always, from New Hampshire to Maryland to Nebraska, is by voting *opposite* the pattern predicted by the national media. Jimmy Who was a message-sender. But Jimmy the Front-runner is one of those to whom messages are sent. In 1976, underdoggery, like fame, is fleeting.

So Frank Church is hardly the uncalculating, quixotic political entry he pretends to be. There is no madness to his method. In any case, there is another candidate, less mellifluous and less pragmatic, laying claim to the Don Quixote image this year.

"He was very perceptive in seeing a situation in which people were looking for a new personality cult the time he developed one."

SENATOR HENRY JACKSON,
Manhattan, July 1976,
contemplating Jimmy Carter's
political style

"I have no idea what his positions are on the issues."

JIMMY CARTER, Baltimore,
May 1976, contemplating
Jerry Brown's political style

REVERSE REEL   *July 1975   Chicago*

The Retired Flack is here to participate in a four-man panel on
Irv Kupcinet's show. Senator Charles Percy, just returned from
the Soviet Union, will tell us about Russia Today. Actor-activist
Robert Vaughn will explain why he and Allard Lowenstein think
the Robert Kennedy assassination case should be reopened. Hugh
Sidey of *Time* has just done a photo-essay book on the Ford
White House. He and I will give our worn impersonations of
Washington Experts.

All goes well for the ninety minutes. Percy puts in his plug for
Jerry Ford; Sidey plugs his book; I don't call Vaughn a left-wing
flake; Vaughn doesn't call me a right-wing kook. No major confrontation or fireworks. So-so television, but good group ther-
apy.

"Kup's Show," I recall from the Goldwater campaign, is one
of those "must" local TV appearances for a national candidate.
One-on-one with a good interviewer, such shows offer a candidate an opportunity to expand on a campaign theme without the
clamor of three separate reporters trying to break into the same
act with different lines of questioning. The format does, of
course, have pitfalls. Barry, I also recall, dropped and expanded a
small bomb during his appearance with Kup; though at that stage
of the campaign such explosions were all in a day's work.

After the show, Vaughn and his wife offer to drop my daughter Jamie and me off at our hotel. Inexorably, the conversation
moves to politics. The Washington Expert is in a bind, since I
haven't the least desire to argue, first, with a man giving me a lift
in his limo; second, with an image forever riveted in my sixteen-
year-old daughter's psyche as the Man from U.N.C.L.E. Fortunately, Vaughn provides an opening, the chance to be both tact-

ful and true to self. He asks whether I think Reagan will take on Ford, a subject touched on briefly during the show.

"Probably," I reply. "But the California politician who can really shake things up next year is Jerry Brown."

Vaughn appears nonplussed. He is, as I had assumed, a Jerry Brown fan. "Could Brown run for President next year?" he wonders. "I'd like to think so, but—"

This isn't the first time the Retired Flack-*cum*-Washington Expert has suggested the possibility of Jerry Brown being a candidate for President in 1976. Only the first time the suggestion has elicited anything approaching a favorable response from a Democrat. Always before there has been the same disbelieving reaction, but with a lemon twist. I have tried this conversational gambit on Frank Mankiewicz, who smirked; on a California Democratic Congressman, who gagged; and on a Democratic state chairman from the South (no, not Georgia), who reproved me sharply: "*Jerry*," he said, "*is a weirdo*."

Nevertheless, as of July 1975, I have an Expert's gut instinct that the first post-Vietnam-Watergate election will feature a new face, a fresh mode. That I have in fact already seen this new face, met its owner eight months before in Jerry Brown's home state, does not occur to me. An Expert's gut instinct, even that of a former flack, can carry suspension of disbelief only so far. A young Governor of the largest state in the Union is conceivable. Or a Hugh Carey, or a Lloyd Bentsen (old oil, perhaps, but a new flask). As a Southerner, however, I reflexively dismiss the possibility that Jimmy Carter could be the new face. If driven to naming one Southerner (as distinguished from *Texan*) who might make the national Democratic ticket, I would answer Reubin Askew, ensconced in his mansion in Tallahassee. An antipolitical politician, yes. But one who recognizes his regional limitations. Just as Jerry Brown, an antipolitical politician, is ensconced in his *apartment* in Sacramento, knowing that no thirty-eight-year-old Governor, halfway through his first term, could make a serious run for the Presidency.

For all things political, there is a season. The lucky flack is hired by the right candidate during the right season. The less fortunate prays for unseasonable weather election day. Winter candidates do not do well in summer seasons, and vice versa. In 1960, Nixon, the candidate of retrenchment, could not handle Kennedy. But eight years later, after the excessive heat of the Johnson years, the same Nixon outimaged the Last of the Sunshine Boys.

Post-Vietnam-Watergate, the fresh wind blowing in American politics isn't one of substance but style. The Great Society could not cure warts, as its Leader had promised. Nixon could not keep office buildings, much less streets, safe: What the hell, they're all phonies. You can't believe 'em, can't trust 'em. The only thing you *can* do is knock them off their pedestals.

Visceral populism. Long before Arthur Schlesinger, Jr., concocted the phrase "imperial Presidency," something was stirring at the grass roots, a wind that cut across the left-right ideological flow: a popular reaction against the embellishment of government. Gene McCarthy summed it up in imagery worthy of a rustic Earl Long. If elected President, McCarthy said, his first official act would be to rip down the fence surrounding the White House.

His Excellency Edmund G. Brown, Jr., who sleeps on a floor mattress across the way from the Mansion that Ron Built, has apparently caught the spirit of the times. He rides in a car straight from the state car pool. He spurns the perqs. He is the son of an ex-Governor, has spent his adult life running for and serving in public office, yet takes every opportunity to deride politics and politicians. In short, a weirdo. But even if Brown doesn't see opportunity beckoning, the Retired Flack's instinct says that 1976 could well be a season for weirdos.

To be sure, before 1975 runs out, I will revert to homogenized expertise and, with the blandness of a safe-betting Washingtonian, predict that when the Democrats get to the Garden their nominee will be Mr. Old Face Himself, Hubert Humphrey. But in Chicago that July, I foresaw something else. Enough of a vision that, had I been asked to conjure up from the green grass the image of a Presidential candidate who would capture the country's mood in 1976, I would have begun with a young Governor from the West who spurns mansions, limos, and the perqs of executive power. And who, incidentally, speaks in parables. Indeed, I did. You doubt it? Just ask the Man from U.N.C.L.E.

"I have no goals. They will evolve as I go along."

JERRY BROWN, somewhere
in space, under Aries, 1976

Post-evolutionary analysis

It is over now, the Silky Sullivan run, Maryland to California. Jerry Brown made his move too late, but closed with a rush. Like Silky twenty years ago, another West Coast flash, Brown kept the race interesting for a while, stirred brief hope in the bosom of grandstand rooter Hubert Humphrey, and did sufficiently well to sustain betting interest in his own future. But late foot and lip were not enough. Not this year.

Nevertheless, the Retired Flack, having a lingering crystal ball interest in what-might-have-been, pursues the matter with a genuine Brownologist, one of Washington's sharpest reportorial minds.

Lou Cannon of the *Washington Post* is on deadline, but the invitation to speculate on the Campaign That Might Have Been tempts a reporter whose professional roots trace back to covering the Great State of Oz: California, America's land beyond the rainbow, where straw men of the left, tin men of the right, cowardly lions of the center, contend under skies littered with witch's graffiti: SURRENDER DOROTHY. VOTE YES ON PROPOSITION . . .

To the extent it is possible to understand the Stanislavsky method applied to politics, Cannon knows the current Governor of California, his motivation and technique, better than most of the members of the Washington press corps. The *Post* reporter can remember Jerry as a boy weirdo, back in the days when he lived in the Governor's mansion—presumably under duress—with his father, Edmund the First.

"What *would* have happened if Brown had qualified in time to enter Ohio and New Jersey?" Lou Cannon repeats my question. "Well, that's paradox, you see. What you're asking is what would have happened if Jerry Brown were somebody else."

But who is he? This Jerry also has an identity crisis, though different from the other Jerry's. Edmund G. Brown, Jr., knows exactly who he is but keeps the secret well concealed. He is an impersonator of various political styles, deftly combining George Wallace and Bobby Kennedy with a tandem appeal to Baltimore blue-collar audiences: *"Send them a message,"* he says. *"Give me your hand."*

An impersonator. Some say a stand-in. Yet that last charge, which so upset Jackson—that he was only a front for Humphrey —bothers Jerry Brown not at all. In fact, he welcomes the chance to stage a major media event on Capitol Hill, with HHH beaming at his side and Carl Albert announcing that "this is the only man who can beat Jimmy Carter."

PARADOX: the anti-Establishmentarian who embraces and is embraced by the Washington Establishment; the pure political celibate who launches his Presidential campaign with the support of Marvin Mandel and Tommy D'Alesandro, Jr., in Baltimore, Maryland; with Boston and New Orleans, one of America's three major political brothels.

"I don't call it a machine," says the candidate from Oz of his Maryland backers, *"I call it a new generation of politics."*

And he does indeed excite the young generation on campuses, in Maryland and elsewhere. He reminds them of what they've *heard* about the Kennedys. But more vividly, Brown's undeniable, non-machine-made appeal to youth traces to his having given up the Governor's mansion. Not a PR move but a *non*-move may be the most pervasive word-of-mouth appeal any candidate has going for him this year. Jimmy Carter's smile has its symbolic drawbacks. But Jerry Brown's rejecting the opulent life—*that* impresses the kids.

From college, my oldest daughter, Paige, writes that in a Tulane straw poll Jerry Brown led the field, after only a month's campaigning. Why? He is "young, new" and *"he gave up that mansion."* The PR power of a single gesture—something more lasting, obviously, than mere toasted English muffins—can outdo millions spent in political advertising and promotion.

Brown's advertising program, budgeted at $150,000 for openers, is put together by his "creative chief," Mike Kaye. It is heavy on one-minute TV spots, the candidate giving brief, ostensibly spontaneous answers to questions from an Anonymous Interrogator. This year's vogue: Make it look like anything but a political commercial. Get in, get out, look natural, unrehearsed. Treleaven's technique . . . or is it Rafshoon's?

Brown's are different, however. Not in style but degree. Specifically, he is so *unspecific* as to make Jimmy Carter project like Martin Luther hammering his sixteen points on the church door. With Brown, everything is left to the imagination. It's not a case of: Don't listen to what I say, watch what I do. Rather: Don't listen to what I say but *how* I say it.

Professor Irwin Corey, meet the Governor of California.

We are being put on. Jerry Brown is crying on the outside, laughing on the inside.

I am watching a Brown commercial. One, I assume, designed to appeal to voters concerned about national defense. How do I know? Only by the fact that the intro *tells* me this is Jerry Brown's position on national defense. Slowly the camera closes on the Governor, seated behind his desk. The screen is filled with that earnest new face. This young man, with just a fleck of gray in the sideburns, obviously has something very important, very intense to say about national defense; which is:

"The best strength we have abroad (so far so good) *is the one we have at home* (huh?). *And that's an equal, open ecologically sound and sane society."* (Play that back on the recorder, just to make sure I've heard it right . . .)

But Jerry Brown isn't meant to be heard. Only *perceived,* osmotically. It is something for everybody, with a comic vengeance. Equal. Open. Ecological. Sound. Sane: Civil rights, the environment—*national defense?*

When Jerry Brown is off-camera, say his flacks in Sacramento, he is not so much Don Quixote as Scaramouche, laughing all the way to the polls. "Buzz words," he says. "They're nothing but buzz words." Which is why he disdains politics and politicians. It is all a meaningless game. He grew up with it, learned from living room and dinner talk just how phony it is. And learned, too, how to manipulate it for "a new generation of politics."

HOW BROWN DID IT

ALMOST FLAWLESS CAMPAIGN . . .
SOMETHING SERIOUSLY AMISS IN CARTER CAMPAIGN

> Headlines, *Washington
> Star*, post-Maryland

DISTANT REPLAY *Campaign '60*

The way Lyndon Johnson had it figured, the upstart could run
in all the primaries while he, the old Establishment master, tended
to his business on Capitol Hill. Hubert would be the cat's-paw.
Somewhere along the way—certainly West Virginia, if not
before—Hubert would win a big one, and that would be the end
of the Kennedy threat. Then the old Establishment master would
just move in, brush Hubert aside, and . . .

DRAFT HHH
UNIT FORMED

> Headline, *Washington Post*,
> late-late-late spring 1976

*With front-runner Jimmy Carter showing some weakness in
recent primaries, Rep. Paul Simon (D-Ill.) and New York Democratic leader Joseph F. Crangle announced a "low key" effort
that will continue "all the way to the convention" even if the
Minnesota Democrat asks them to stop.*

*"A lot of people feel Senator Humphrey fills the needs as no
one else does, and we can't just stand idly by," Simon told a news
conference . . .*

"Jerry Brown is the real Jimmy Carter."

> ALLARD LOWENSTEIN, playing
> Sancho Panza on the Don Quixote
> trail, May 1976

"The difference between Jerry Brown and Jimmy Carter?"
Lou Cannon approaches the question with the assurance of a

handicapper who knows the smell both of the political stables and of the winner's circle. "What Brown had going for him was his talent for working the media. Carter had that, and more. If the race had depended on media alone, Brown might've made it. He runs that course better than anyone."

"Better than Carter?" I ask, surprised to hear that Jimmy, who has made himself a household question mark in less than six months, runs behind anyone as a political media manipulator.

"Much better," replies Cannon. "Brown is more at ease with the national press. He knows exactly what we're looking for. He grew up with it, remember—the son of a Governor of a mass media state. Brown's younger. He even fits the Kennedy image better. But that wasn't enough."

"Some other year then," I say. "Maybe 1980?"

"Only if he does his homework ahead of time," Cannon replies. "You know, this theory that Jimmy Carter is some sort of pure media freak is bunk. Unlike Jerry Brown—and the fact, you know, that Brown *wasn't* qualified in time for Ohio tells us something—Carter had planned ahead, studied the new delegate rules, state by state, district by district."

"So what you're saying is, when it came down to the wire, what won it this year wasn't new imagery but old organization."

"No, I didn't say that," Cannon corrects me. "It took both. But the only candidate who had both, from start to finish, was Jimmy Carter. Hey, look, pardon me, you want to know more about Jerry Brown? Consult the zodiac, read Kierkegaard. I'm on deadline . . ."

"There are cycles in life when things flow right. Others not. Whatever happens, happens."

JERRY BROWN, to Sally Quinn
somewhere under Taurus, 1976

"The primaries are over and Governor Carter has a commanding lead. He is virtually certain to be our party's nominee."

HHH, on the ballot in New Jersey
as Uncommitted; final concession
statement, June 9, 1976

He Who Forgets History, etc.

The way Hubert Humphrey had it figured, the upstart could run in all the primaries while he, the old Establishment master, tended to his business on Capitol Hill. Scoop/Mo/Frank/Jerry would be the cat's-paw. Somewhere along the way—certainly Ohio, if not before—Scoop/Mo/Frank/Jerry would win a big one, and that would be the end of the Carter Phenomenon. Then the old Establishment master would just move in, brush . . .

Bonaparte at Grenoble

"For most of the time, the ambitions of the self-styled peanut farmer from Plains seemed ludicrous to most of the Democratic power brokers.

"But no one was laughing when Carter completed his string of Presidential primary successes by finishing first in Ohio and second in both New Jersey and California—gaining more delegates than he had won in any other single day of the 31-primary campaign.

"The first to react yesterday was Chicago Mayor Richard J. Daley, who endorsed Carter and said . . ."

Excerpt, *Washington Post*,
June 10, 1976

FORD AND REAGAN
FACING A SIX-WEEK FIGHT

Second deck, headline,
The New York Times, June 10, 1976

Voices (and Notes) amid the din

"The only answer to Ford's whistlestop in Michigan would have been a Reagan wagon train. I told them that, but they wouldn't listen. We could have had Duke riding shotgun . . ." (*Tom Malatesta, back from two weeks in the field, needing sleep badly*) . . . "I guess he's going after the effluent vote." (*Lyn Nofziger, responding to news that the President has met with the chairman of the Suffolk County, New York, county commission, an "undecided" delegate who switched to Ford after a meeting in the Oval Office, where a pending federal grant to the Suffolk sewer district was discussed*) . . . NOT MIDDLETON, IT'S MIDDLETOWN. MIDDLE*TOWN*. (*Urgent platform note from Governor James Rhodes to Jerry Ford, speaking in Ohio, early June 1976*.)

Sacramento, June 1976

Because Lou Cannon is both a Californian and a reporter with a reputation for balanced coverage, left and right, Ron Reagan takes his follow-up question covering the Rhodesian crisis with his guard down. The candidate has just criticized Kissinger in a speech before the local press club. Reagan says the Ford administration plan for Rhodesia will lead to bloodshed; though the United States and Britain might work out some different Rhodesian solution, one that would guarantee a "peaceful transition."

"How would we do that?" asks Cannon. "With an occupation force, with military troops, with observers, or what?" The question is fair, but hypothetical. It can be skirted on that basis alone. But Reagan expands. He rambles on about "whether" it would be "enough to have simply a show of strength, a promise that we would supply troops, or whether you'd have to go in with occupation forces or not, I don't know . . . But I believe, in the interest of peace and avoiding bloodshed, and to achieve a democratic majority rule . . . I think it would be worth this, for us to do it . . ."

REAGAN WOULD SEND
U.S. TROOPS TO RHODESIA

Consensus headline,
June 3, 1976

Audio, Ford TV-radio spot *California, June 1976*

"When you vote Tuesday, remember, Governor Reagan couldn't start a war. President Reagan could."

Flashback *Campaign '64*

Audiovideo, Johnson TV spot, early autumn: A small girl is picking a daisy, counting to ten—backward . . . 10-9-8-7-6 . . . The screen then dissolves to a mushroom cloud with a voice-over mention of "*President . . . Goldwater . . .*" The spot is run only once, during a Monday night movie, then pulled off the air. It is the creation of TV ad man Tony Schwartz.

BACK TO LIVE ACTION *Campaign '76*

In mid-October, Jerry Rafshoon is uptight about a series of TV spots John Deardourff and Malcolm MacDougall have put together for the Ford Committee. The commercials, picking up the negative advertising theme currently used in product advertising (*Scope tastes better than Listerine, but Listermint is yummier than Scope*), feature non-actors, several from Atlanta, who criticize Carter for vagueness, not having been a good Governor, etc.

O.K., Rafshoon decides, if that's the kind of spots the bastards want to run, no more Mr. Nice Peanut. He counts to ten—then hires Tony Schwartz.

"I think I'm the one who had the lapse back there. I was fishing around trying to answer a hypothetical question and gave him what he wanted. But it was not what I had in mind or what my position has been . . . Much too much has been made of it. But . . . maybe it's because it's late in the campaign and I had a little lapse there."

RONALD REAGAN, explaining
U.S.-troups-to-Rhodesia gaffe,
Sacramento, June 1976

Dog Days, 1976

A little lapse here, a little lapse there . . . *it adds up.*

"Ron takes the position that if he's asked a question, he has to answer it," Lyn Nofziger is explaining. There has been a shift in Reagan PR operations, with Jim Lake taking over day-to-day press relations, and Nofziger coordinating the overall propaganda-for-delegates brawl, first in California, then in Kansas City.

"But I thought you told me—back at the beginning—that you were going to take care of that problem."

"Did I?" says Nofziger, walking shirt-sleeved through the asphalt heat of downtown Washington in late July. "Did I really? Well, let me tell you one more thing, if you promise to take my word for it."

"Go."

"I don't know what'll happen in Kansas City. We're being nickeled-and-dimed at the White House, a delegate here, a delegate there, this one for an afternoon drink with the President, another one for an invitation to a state dinner, a third for a small business loan. Nickeled-and-dimed, and I don't know what'll happen, though I still think we'll win. But—BUT—regardless of what happens, I can tell you this . . ."

Nofziger smiles and waves at a White House staff aide who passes us on K Street. He mutters an incomprehensible oath under his breath, then continues: "Regardless of what happens, I'll guarantee this much . . ."

"So tell me, already."

". . . that this is the LAST GODDAMN CAMPAIGN I ever get into where I don't have complete control, and where I HAVE TO LISTEN TO SONSOFBITCHES LIKE VIC GOLD TELL ME WHAT'S GOING WRONG."

I believe him.

Jimmy Carter isn't alone in his dislike of runway interviews. Jerry Ford's staff dreads them as a press relations hangover from the Boss's days as a traveling Congressional Minority Leader, when being met at the airport by the cameras and microphones meant the trip would get local coverage. Something a Congressman has to worry about, never a President.

For a President, this sort of *al fresco* news conference can be especially dangerous in terms of its possible impact in sensitive policy areas. Better to wait until he gets downtown, to a hotel or hall, where the conference for local press can be held in an atmosphere other than . . .

Q.: *Mr. President . . . (RORRRRR) . . . your position on . . . (BRRTTT) . . . latest developments in . . . Mid-East . . . (FFTTT) . . .*

A.: *Well, there's always the possibili . . . (KAFFOOMKA-FOOM) . . . hostilities . . . ready for any eventual . . . (BRRATT).*

Ford's PR team, to the vast disgruntlement of local TV-radio media, stops the airport runway practice during the late primaries. All part of the newest New Ford press strategy.

Reagan's final thirty-minute TV speech in July is a bomb. Well delivered, but nothing new or specific. Some staff members were pushing for a debate challenge to Carter (to point up Reagan's forensic edge over Ford as a lure for undecided delegates). But the idea was rejected and the final draft was simply a rehash of the standard Reagan campaign speech, with a special pitch for the "ethnic," i.e., Catholic, vote; the strategy being to cut at Carter, who still polls poorly in traditional Democratic Catholic wards.

This explains the emphasis Reagan put on the abortion issue, a major segment of the speech. "I've tried to tell them that Ron doesn't have to keep hitting abortion, abortion, abortion," says Nofziger. "The Right-to-Lifers know where he stands. All we're doing is inciting the other side to work that much harder against us."

By nickel-and-diming, Nofziger refers to Ford's adapting a Presidential press relations technique to his hunt for delegates. When Ford first came to the Oval Office, Margita White—now White House communications director—set up a series of Meet the New President sessions for publishers and editors, not only on the road but at 1600 Pennsylvania.

Ford did well in these sessions, helped in large part by the inflationary effect of a White House invitation on the human ego. Hard-bitten editors from the outer provinces have been known to become plantain-spined sycophants once within the House Where Lincoln Dwelled. And when the editorial Q. and A. session with the President is accompanied by an invitation to a White House social function the same evening . . .

In the case of publishers and editors, the debilitating effect of White House Aura can wear off. But with delegates from the boondocks, invitations for afternoon refreshments—wives and kids included, a photograph with the President (and sometimes Betty) as part of the PR package—have produced permanent switches, from Undecided to Ford—even from Reagan to Ford.

These events originally began on a single delegate or small group basis. More recently, entire delegations-and-families (*Bring the Kids! Free Refreshments! Free Rides!*) have been brought in by the busload. In these final preconvention days, with the race close, the wholesale purveyance of White House Aura is Ford's most effective PR device.

Donkey Days   July 1976
The Perception of Being Perceived

Jerry Rafshoon and Pat Caddell are interviewed by CBS for a Saturday night news feature on manipulative techniques during the primaries. No, they have not defected; though if a pollster and ad man were to sit still for such a feature ten years ago, that would have been the logical inference.

Rafshoon is all smiles as he discusses how shrewd he was when he learned in Pennsylvania that voters were cool toward Jimmy because they thought he was vague on issues: So, *we just used the same spots but put a tag line up front, JIMMY CARTER ON THE ISSUE OF . . .*

The camera's eye then cuts to an actual Carter TV commercial, demonstrating that technique; it is—to drive home the contrast between what viewers see and the operation behind the screen—a spot in which Carter speaks of "honesty, integrity." Then follows an interview with Caddell, emphasizing how closely his polling is tied to Rafshoon's productions. Populism in a new, disposable plastic wrapper. And they keep wondering why voters are turned off about politics and politicians.

The booming sound system rolls into one more rendition of "Oh! Susanna," while Miz Bella eases through the crush of Alabama delegates, their wives and guests. It is convention eve at the Semi-Centennial-plus-Two Oscar W. Underwood for President party.

Miz Bella's trademark, that wide flop-brim hat, suddenly looks, to one sober observer, like one of those classic Sunbelt chapeaux that Miz Scarlett used to wear, back in the days when Atlanta, not Plains, was the center of all the action south of the New York-Washington axis.

"I'll be damned," says a guest with a green Carter button stuck onto his crimson Alabama ribbon. "The South has riz. I never thought I'd see the day Bella Abzug dropped by a party for the Alabama delegation, did you?"

The Retired Flack, a self-certified expert on Deep Southern political vagaries—a dime-a-truckload breed in Manhattan this week—reckons as how he sure didn't either. But there she is, smiling, cordial, Bella Abzug with a politicalobotomy.

"This is my district, so have a wonderful, wonderful time," she importunes a circle of assorted young lints, red-necks, and country boy gawkers and their Harper Valley P.T.A.-type wives. The sound now kicks up on "Sweet Georgia Brown" as the Congressperson from Manhattan shakes hands with an Alabama state Senator, then poses for a photo with Robert S. Vance, chairman of the Alabama Democratic Executive Committee.

"This," Miz Bella allows, stretching tippytoes to pat the six-foot-four Gray Fox of the Alabama political wars on the shoulder, "is a fine man. A *great* man."

With that, the Abzugian entourage begins moving, prodding its way through the mob at The Library bar-and-restaurant, headed past the giveaway tray of instant grits, back to real life on the corner of Broadway and Ninety-second.

Inside, the Retired Flack commiserates with his old buddy Vance.

"You want the negative?" I ask. "That picture, it'll ruin *you* in Alabama and *Bella* in New York."

Vance shakes his head, no. "Four years ago, maybe," he says, "but not this year. Times have changed. Man, we haven't come to New York to fight anybody. There's nothing to fight about. The press keeps asking, 'When is the Alabama delegation gonna caucus?' and I keep telling 'em, 'Hell, we're not here to caucus, just to party' . . ."

"What would poor old 'Handy' Ellis think?" I ask, invoking the name of the Alabama delegation chairman who led the Dixiecrat walkout at the 1948 Democratic Convention in Philadelphia.

"The times," smiles the Gray Fox, an Alabama moderate who has walked the tight rope of George Wallace's sixties and survived, "the times they are a'changin'."

Political scripture, according to St. Dylan-Zimmerman. One of Jimmy Carter's favorites, as he tells reporters under thirty-five. For those over, he mentions "Amazin' Grace."

"I wish the Governor could have made it," muses Ned McDavid, the Alabama-born Manhattan advertising man-entrepreneur who is hosting the Underwood party, as he watches Wallace's press secretary, Bill Joe Camp, walk through the crush. "It would have made a great shot, you know? Bella Abzug, Wallace . . ."

Political imagery-in-flux. That Vance could pose for a news shot with Bella Abzug and she with him, that McDavid, a sophisticated imagectomist with roots in both cultures could mention an Abzug-Wallace two-shot without breaking up bespeaks drastic flux. The full impact of the Carter Phenomenon, pulsing, reverberating through the party structure.

Grits and blintzes. Hominy and harmony. The old Democratic recipe for autumn victories in Presidential election years; that Roosevelt Coalition that the old-timers keep talking about. Oh, not the *old*-timers, the pre-FDR partisans who were here in New York fifty-two years ago for those interminable 103 ballots. That was the summer of '24, when Bill Brandon, the Alabamian who held Bob Vance's job, boomed out again and again and again— 103 times—*"Mistah Chaihman, Ah-la-bah-ma casts twenty-foah votes foah Oscah Double-Yew Undah-woooad."*

It was the progenitor electronic convention, the first national party assembly broadcast to the country by radio. To that extent, Alabama's native son candidate, who had no chance for nomination, became the progenitor political media freak, a name whose impact on the public consciousness vastly exceeded its owner's importance as a candidate. He was a serious man, Oscar Underwood. A Senate leader. But to this day he is best remembered because of those 103 choruses, rather than for anything he achieved on Capitol Hill. From inception, electronic journalism had a way of providing mixed performances. Without radio, the American people might never have heard of Oscar Underwood. With radio they did. But for the wrong reason.

McDavid has arranged to have on hand a scratchy, sentimental recording of Brandon sounding the charge at the Old Madison

Square Garden. As the voice from the Southern past booms across the crowded room, the unsentimental voice of the New South speaks.

"The delegation should go thirty-five to zip for Carter by the end of the first ballot," Vance tells me.

And what about George, the native son? The Man Who, some of the down-home folks here claim, cleared the way for a Deep Southerner to win primaries up North, to capture the nomination of the Party of their Fathers.

"George fought his fight," says Vance, who has managed to maintain his position of leadership in the Alabama party despite Wallace's efforts to unseat him. "You know, one thing they forget about George, he's a loyalist. He was at that 1948 convention but didn't walk out. Didn't go for Thurmond-Wright and the Dixiecrats. No, George is a Democrat, always has been . . ."

"*Mistah Chaihman,*" the record blares, "*Ah-la-bah-ma casts twenty-foah votes foah . . .*"

"But Johnson *wasn't* a Southerner!" A Mutt-size college-age Alabamian with an alternate delegate pin is explaining to a Jeff-size guest with newsman's credentials. "Johnson was a *Texan.* Carter will be the first *Southerner.* You want to know the difference between a *Texan* and a *Southerner? Texans* don't refight the Civil War. The bastards think they *won* it . . ."

"I told my sons before I came up here," Bob Vance is saying, "that when I was fifteen years old, no matter what the textbooks said, I knew I could never be President of the United States. I was disqualified, you see, because I was a Southerner. Well, I brought then up here to the big city with Helen and me so they could see it all for themselves."

"See what?"

"The convention where all that was changed."

"*Mistah Chaihman, Ah-la-bah-ma casts twenty-foah votes foah Oscah Double-Yew Undah-woooad . . .*"

"In *my* neighborhood, it's *Mondale* who has the accent," complains Harry Mabry, general manager of WHMA-TV, Anniston, Alabama. We are in the lobby of the Summit, headquarters hotel for both the Alabama and Massachusetts delegations. It is the dark side of the morning. "Tip" O'Neill has just passed through, emitting cigar smoke through his pores, and for some reason—probably the eccentric hour, combined with free-associating the Irish political contribution—I am reminded that Bill Buckley says Jimmy Carter has been taking Yankee accent lessons for appearances on national talk shows. As evidence, Buckley cites a recent "Firing Line," during which the Democratic nominee went through violent lip contortions to get his "g's" up to speed.

"Generally speaking, I don't mind Midwestern accents," says Mabry, a former local television newscaster. "But Minnesota—that flat, roto-rooter sound Humphrey and Mondale have—it *grates.*"

"Will Mondale have any problem campaigning in the South?" I ask.

"I doubt we'll see very much of Walter Mondale in Alabama and Mississippi during the campaign," Mabry replies. "I think somebody like Glenn would have gone down easier in the South."

"Because of what he says or how he says it?"

"Both," says Mabry. He shrugs: "But you can't win 'em all. Maybe they'll send Mondale to accent school. I have a feelin' dropped 'g's' might be In with Yankees this time next year. Even with William Buckley."

"No," I assure him. "With 'Tip' O'Neill maybe, but not Bill Buckley."

This has been Glory Week for Rafshoon, Caddell, and, now, Pat Anderson, ready and willing interview subjects for wandering TV newsmen at the convention. On the night of Carter's acceptance speech, while the networks are filling until real action begins, Anderson is introduced by TV interviewers as "Jimmy Carter's chief speechwriter," the draftsman of what we're about to hear from the candidate's own lips. Modestly, the writer declines full credit. He explains that the speech will be "all Jimmy Carter."

The Retired Flack contemplates the impact on the 1960 Presidential race if Kennedy's chief advertising man, pollster, and speechwriter had been seen and heard in convention floor interviews, discussing techniques of mass manipulation.

POLITICAL SCIENCE-FICTION FEATURE: FLASHBACK

The Retired Flack Fantasizes Arthur Schlesinger, Jr.'s Final Public Appearance as a Kennedy Speechwriter.

Q.: Arthur, about tonight's acceptance speech—

A.: Well, basically, it's all John Kennedy. But I did lift a slogan from the 1948 Progressive Party acceptance speech at Philadelphia.

Q.: By slogan, you mean—

A.: The New Frontier. That was, of course, the title of Henry Wallace's speech that year. I thought—or rather (heh-heh) *we* thought—it would adapt perfectly . . .

"Mother was a very special woman in Jimmy Carter's life. She was more than the woman who bore him, nursed him, raised him, and loved him. She was the woman who shaped his soul and molded his mind . . . Amy is an enterprising young lady. She has the makings of a tycoon, as she recently revealed when she set up a lemonade stand . . ."

> Excerpted insights from
> *Jimmy Carter: From Farm Boy to Destiny. His Winning Philosophy. His Faith: The Night That Changed His Life,*
> ad treacle, Ideal Publishing Co.

Superstars we create instantly. Political cult heroes take a little longer. The difference? With political cult heroes it isn't just what *he* eats for breakfast, there's his family to consider. The question isn't simply, *Will Success Spoil Jimmy Carter?* It's, *Will Success Spoil His Wife, His Mother, His Daughter* . . .

The buck starts here:

For one dollar you can buy, all in all, seventy-three pages of gushing text and HUNDREDS OF PHOTOS covering the Carter saga. On any newsstand in Manhattan this week. We have a new family to take into our hearts. Teddy, you're Yesterday's Convention Hero. Jackie, you're Old Cult.

Whatever the degree of cooperation between the Carter staff and Ideal Publishing Co.—the quickie magazine is loaded with early, personal family photos—it is all too easy to blame this New Adulation on the candidate and his flacks. Could Jimmy Carter, if he wanted to, turn off the spout? Tell the magazines and the networks, the daily feature writers and that large, important segment of American journalism that now thrives on People and Personalities to cool it?

No. If he tried to maintain some semblance of family privacy (not that he's shown any inclination) the media outcry would be the loudest since Nixon refused to release the transcripts. Today's political family is public property. More accurately, media property. So it's just as well that Jimmy has a colorful old lady and a precocious little eight-year-old blonde who, separately and together, eat publicity like pecan ice cream. And a six-pack brother, something for the Bunker vote. And, of course . . .

THIS IS MY VERY SPECIAL LOVE

> She is still his bride although they've been wed over 30 years. He is still the shy, smiling young man she fell in love with . . . Theirs is a continuing love story; one that grows deeper and richer as the years go by. It is a story that can inspire the lives of all who hear it and take its timeless message of devotion . . .

(Great copy, Jody, but speaking of devotion: where's the *dog?* The motorcycling and faith-healing sister bits are great, but—you forgot *the Fala Symbol.* Kennedy had a dog, Johnson had a dog, even *Nixon* had a dog. The First Canine of the Realm. I mean, do you know how many people subscribe to *Dog World?*)

Pachyderm Days   Kansas City   August 1976

The Retired Flack has deplaned at the wrong airport. This can't be the place. I have witnessed enough Republican Conventions to know that whatever these people are here for, it is not a Republican Convention.

Advanced mediascopia

There is the apparition of Elizabeth Ray in a tight sweater, walking through the Muehlebach Hotel lobby, being stopped by middle-aged men to compare notes.

"*Liz, I'm . . .*"

"*Please to meetcha . . .*"

I fantasize the power-breakers, not the power-brokers. Liz Ray, in a tight sweater—a very tight sweater—and John Dean. Ridiculous. If this were a Republican Convention, what would John Dean be doing here? All I need to confirm the terminality of my condition is the vision of Spiro Agnew . . .

President Agnew, relaxed in tennis shorts, watches the opening ceremonies of the convention on television. On the screen, Sinatra sings the national anthem, then the band picks up "Maryland! My Maryland!" Youth for Agnew chant, "Spiro is Our Hero," while temporary Convention Chairman Ford raps vainly for order . . . Asked whether the President intends to mention his fallen predecessor, Richard Nixon, in his acceptance speech, a White House spokesman says No, because "Your President is not a schnook . . ."

Where is Agnew, where is *Nixon?* Gone to the shadows, Nonpersons. Could it be possible—if this were a Republican Convention—that the party nominees of only four years ago would be expunged from elephant memory? No. This can't be the place.

Where is the Rockefeller-for-President headquarters? I don't even see a Rockefeller for *Vice*-President headquarters. Impossible: a Republican Convention without a Rockefeller-for-Something headquarters is like a Democratic Convention without a Shirley MacLaine convention floor interview.

Another example: Why is there only one candidate grappling with what his press secretary calls a "negative" press. I've been to enough Republican Conventions to know that by this time— twenty-four hours before the keynote—*everybody* is bitching about the press.

Instead, there are entirely too many news conferences going on, too many flacks fraternizing with the Enemy. The operative word here, as opposed to four years ago at Miami Beach, is access. At the Crown Center—not the name for a headquarters hotel for a non-Imperial President I would have chosen, but room service is good—Nessen, Bill Greener, Peter Kaye, and other Ford press aides move around, talking to anybody with a pad, pencil, or camera. In addition, there is the accessible Ford family, Betty and the boys (Susan does her own thing), all flacking for Big Daddy.

At the Alameda Plaza, the Reagan staff is doing the same. Smiling and talking. Sears, Nofziger, Charles Black, Tom Malatesta, are scrounging for loose delegates and talking up a media storm. Access: Jim Lake, Reagan's personable and popular traveling press secretary, even fraternizes with the Eastern Liberal likes of Mary McGrory. What's happened to right-wing paranoia about the media? This is reaction to the old Nixon press strategy. When Jim Buckley's top aide Len Saffir floats a balloon on a possible Buckley Presidential bid, who does he leak to? *National Review?* Wrong: Ken Auletta of *The Village Voice*.

Any minute, or thirty-second intercut thereof, somebody's press secretary is going to work up a softball or, God help us, touch football game between his boss's Secret Service contingent and the traveling press. Everything is out of sync. In my heart, I know from past Republican Conventions that left is left, right is right, never the twain shall meet; which is what Troy Gustavson, a young flack whose candidate is at the right convention at the wrong time—or vice versa, the kid can't figure out which—is learning, the hardball way.

"Oh, we're not *complaining* about press bias," says Gustavson, Dick Schweiker's thirty-year-old press secretary. "It's just that our coverage has always been positive and in the last three weeks we've caught criticism, left and right. I figured we would. The Senator figured we would. Anybody willing to take a political risk has to undergo fire, and it's healthy in the long run . . . *Still* . . ."

This was John Sears's idea: one big gamble for a breakthrough, something to counter the delegate attrition of the White House nickel-and-dime campaign. It would be a surprise raid, the taking of a major Ford delegate from a major, perhaps crucial, state, following long days of maneuver, coast-to-coast flights, and conversations between Reagan the Western Tory and Schweiker the Eastern Liberal.

To say that this was the best-kept tactical secret of the 1976 presidential campaign isn't to say much, really, since there were few such secrets this year. Carter, only by telling no one on his staff until the last moment, succeeded in keeping news of his choice of Mondale embargoed (though the parade of Democratic

Veep hopefuls through Plains preceding the choice kept media speculation going the way Jimmy intended). Aside from that, however, there have been few campaign secrets on strategy and tactics, anywhere. Overexposure and premature disclosure have been the rule in every camp.

The irony in the case of the Schweiker Announcement is that premature leakage and speculation, in this one instance, might have benefited the overall plan. That is, Sears's surprise raid could have come off better had it not been a bombshell.

Such is Troy Gustavson's appraisal, as he forlornly looks at the adverse press clips that have come in the wake of news that his Boss had agreed to run as Vice-Presidential nominee on a Reagan ticket. I tend to agree.

The Retired Flack recalls that in 1960 Kennedy went through some rough media days immediately following his shocker choice of LBJ as his running mate, the choice being heavily criticized by the interpretive press until the surprise news was finally digested. In 1968, Spiro Agnew's problems with the press began from the moment he was picked by Nixon, as much for the fact that the choice surprised the convention press corps as for anything Agnew stood for at the time.

Simply stated, a prime rule of political PR is that the Experts do not like surprises. It makes them look bad at the home office, back at the news room where their editors expect them to be *competitive;* which in such cases as the Schweiker Announcement means, don't just give us the news when everybody else has it, get it *first.*

A leak here, a hint there—some advance information planted in certain areas of media influence, to inspire speculation, make a few prophets—might have cooled at least part of the media firestorm that flared after the announcement. A few columnists and commentators with a vested interest in their own prophetic powers might have written favorable copy on the maneuver. This could have helped.

Helped, somewhat. But not, I tell Troy Gustavson, as much as he thinks. The fact that Sears's stroke surprised the news media and the politicians, left and right, is only part of Schweiker's new image problem. More crucial is the fact that the Pennsylvania

Senator is trying to undergo radical imagectomy under pressure cooker conditions.

Ideological image transitions aren't unusual in American politics. But they take slow months and years. Not quick hours and days.

Bob Kennedy, the tough kid brother, the Senate Committee investigator and hard-nosed political pragmatist of the late 1950s, distrusted by the Democratic left, emerged in the sixties as the New York Liberal who quoted Camus. Lyndon Johnson, *perceived* as a right-wing Texas oil Senator, became the father of the Great Society. Conservative Congressmen representing narrow constituencies often transform into Liberal Senators as, indeed, happened in Schweiker's own case.

The key element in the success of such transformations, however, is time. Given the resources of modern technology, you *can* turn a sow's ear into the chemical equivalent of a silk purse. But when you do it as a rush job, it's difficult to persuade buyers they aren't being conned by some sleight of hand, or tongue.

In future Presidential election years the pre-convention selection of running mates—Presidential and Vice-Presidential candidates going as a ticket—may become a standard part of the American process of choosing national leaders. If so, John Sears's desperation maneuver, the Reagan-Schweiker merger, will be credited as forerunner to the trend. But being ahead of one's time is not, generally speaking, considered a strong suit in seeking a Republican Presidential nomination.

Troy Gustavson's boss can't even sell the idea that he's a right-left coalition package that can unite the party and have a broad appeal to the general electorate, to his own Pennsylvania delegation. Meanwhile, Reagan is getting it, from both far right and left, for sacrificing conservative purity in the interest of political expediency (the implication being that political expediency is the exclusive preserve of Liberals . . .).

"But all Reagan did," Troy Gustavson says, reaching for some handle to his Boss's image problem, "is what they criticized Goldwater for *not* doing in 1964, isn't it? I mean, isn't the idea to broaden the party base . . ."

Not exactly. There is a missing element in the equation. If Ron had first *won* the nomination, his selecting Schweiker—and Schweiker's acceptance of the No. 2 spot on a Reagan-led ticket —might have been hailed as a master stroke. Sears's and Nofziger's only headache then would have been to keep the far right in the fold.

Timing, Troy, it's all in the timing: the fourth and most important dimension of successful image-making.

John Sears's advanced theory about national ticket selection will go to the convention floor for a crucial test vote. A proposed amendment to Rule 16-c of the Republican Convention Bible, which Reagan's protestant faction would alter to read: *"Thou shalt name thy Vice-Presidential choice preceding the Presidential nomination process."*

"Reagan blew it by naming Schweiker ahead of time, now he wants Ford to make the same mistake," fumes a Ford delegate from Mississippi a few hours before the vote.

Mississippi delegates at this convention are in bad humor, bitterly divided. Rogers Morton, who seems determined to head for the lifeboats even if the ship isn't the *Titanic*, has taken another shot from the lip. He tells a *Birmingham News* reporter that if Ford wins the nomination, the President will write off the "Cotton South." This further upsets Clarke Reed, the Mississippi state party chairman, whom the Reaganites are now calling "Lon Chaney"—the Man of a Thousand Faces.

I recall that a month ago, in New York City, the Mississippi delegation was united and placid. Now in Kansas City—at a *Republican* Convention—there is a Mississippi delegation divided, feuding.

Shifting images, everywhere, changed patterns; I feel for Gustavson, would like to give him the benefit of a Retired Flack's experience. But if the name of this game is delegates, I am a single-wing quarterback in a T-formation age.

There is nothing so resistible as an idea whose time has not yet come.

When Reagan loses the test vote on 16-c, the actual Presidential nomination vote becomes anticlimax. An hour before the final vote, while seconding speeches drone on, Nofziger is discovered wandering the lobby just off the convention gallery, holding a Ford frisbee. He is puffy-faced, working on instinct, not quite the jaunty Nofziger of press lore.

There is a network report that Reagan will accept a Vice-Presidential offer from Ford. Lyn dismisses it as a rumor spawned by Stu Spencer's agents provocateurs. An exasperated supporter comes up to complain that two of the three nets failed to camera-cover the speech of Dr. Gloria Toote, the black woman delegate from New York the Reaganites sent to the podium to second Jesse Helms's nominating address. Nofziger dismisses the complaint as water over the dam. What bugs him is the goddamned Ford frisbee.

"I'm gonna to file a *protest*," he says, waggling the frisbee in my face. "Some sonofabitch threw this and hit one of my delegates in the eye. Here, feel the hard edge . . ."

Somehow I feel it is over, the long march that began a year ago. And none too soon.

SEMANTICS OF AMERICAN POLITICS 1976

The Case of the Missing "IC"

In 1952, House Speaker Sam Rayburn, furious over Tom Dewey's repeated references to "the Democrat Party," retaliated in a public speech by dropping the first two letters of "Republican." The syllabic dispute has simmered over the years. It is the contention of hard-nosed, right-wing Republicans that their opposition is *not* "democratic." The ideological purists who make up a majority of the GOP platform committee just won't concede the "ic." Their party platform, from preamble to conclusion, refers only to "the Democrat Party."

The missing suffix draws editorial comment beyond its importance, inasmuch as the Publican nominee is soft on the issue. Ford invariably says "Democratic." What is far more significant in assessing Ford's campaign strategy is his calculated appeal to Democrat(ic) voters in his acceptance speech.

In past years, both Eisenhower and Nixon took pains not to try to *convert* Democrats to Republican ranks, but to appeal to them to cross over at the polls. You can diddle this one time, they implied, without dissolving the marriage. As a President-above-the-fray, Ike was perfect for the role of seducer-without-party portfolio. In '68 and '72, Nixon could take advantage of violent break-ups within the Democratic family to lure voters. The fright word "Republicans" was never to appear in his campaign literature or utterances.

Eisenhower had a pet phrase, created by Emmet John Hughes: "*discerning* Democrats." It also drove Rayburn into a gum-grinding frenzy. *I welcome the support,* Ike would say, *of all discerning Democrats.* By this, he set his kind of *Democrat* voters apart from *undiscerning* Democrats, i.e., the fuzzy minded thinkers and party hacks supporting Adlai Stevenson.

This was defensive political PR. Neither Ike nor Nixon nor Ford could/can attack the opposition party without some qualifying adjective or euphemism. There has been a tacit admission in public pronouncements by discerning Republican Presidential candidates, going on thirty years, that their party is irretrievably the minority party. Republican speechwriters go about their hackwork knowing that the label "Republican" is a loser. They write around the problem, either euphemizing or altogether avoiding specific references to party in their speeches. In Ford's acceptance, his speechwriter, Robert Hartmann, first has his candidate hit the semantic obstacle straight-on, like a good football center, then roll off it.

"I speak not of a Republican victory," the President assures his listeners early on (not addressing the live audience), "but a victory for the American people." He goes on to mention, among former Presidents, Lincoln and Eisenhower. But there are also references to Franklin Roosevelt and Harry Truman in the speech, and not the unfavorable sort that Democratic Convention speakers make of former Republican Presidents. Even Al Smith is quoted by name—the old trite-and-true "Let's look at the record"—Hartmann's idea being to flatter urban Catholic Democrats who, according to Ford's polls, are soft in support of their party's Southern Baptist nominee.

Altogether an ecumenical political appeal, one which dramatizes, for PR students of the rhetoric of omission, the differences between Ford's problem in 1976 and Truman's in 1948. Like Truman, Ford intends to run full force against a Congress dominated by the opposition party. But whereas the Democrat relished his name-branding of the good-for-nothing Republicans, Ford in his speech alludes only to "majority misrule" on Capitol Hill, the "free-spending Congressional majority," the "other party's platform," and "their Congress."

"As I try, in my imagination, to look into all the homes where families are watching at the end of this convention," says the Republican nominee, "I can't tell which faces are Republican, which are Democrats, and which are independents."

Great, high-minded nonpartisanship. A virtue that any candidate whose party claims only eighteen percent of the electorate must hope will be reciprocated by the unseen audience beyond the camera.

Doug Blaser, a young, baby-faced Republican master advance man, is eating a cheeseburger in the Crown Plaza restaurant, relating how "letter perfect" the Ford "filler" program had worked out. The "filler" program—a last word in campaign organization for televised conventions—consisted of keeping a pool of name pro-Ford spokesmen available to rush to TV network booths for live interviews during dull interludes on the floor. Blaser is meticulous, the advance man's advance man. He has compiled a chart—down to the last fractional second—of how much exposure the President's spokesmen got on the tube, compared to Reagan's. Not through deliberate network collusion. Simply by having all-stars like Goldwater, Rockefeller, Connally available, recognizing that for the networks, the name of the game is Names . . .

REVERSE REEL   *October 1975*

"I think he's a fine fellow, but it's not clear whether or not he has the capacity of leadership to challenge and inspire the nation."

JOHN CONNALLY, on "Face
the Nation," re Gerald Ford

The Campaign(s) That Might Have Been
John Connally had it figured. Reagan would knock Ford out in the early primaries, then the call would go out for somebody

who could stop Reagan, and the man to do it would be John Connally . . . *But* . . . it didn't quite work out that way . . . so John Connally figured again. Ford and Reagan would leapfrog primary victories until they knocked each other out, then the call would be for somebody who could pull the party back together, and the man to do it would be John Connally . . . *But* . . . it didn't quite work out that way . . . so John Connally figured again. When Reagan teamed up with Schweiker, Connally raced to the White House to endorse Ford, the point being made that Ford could capitalize on the adverse impact Reagan's move had in the South if he picked John Connally as his running mate.

John Connally came to Kansas City hoping, waiting for a phone call. On the morning after Ford's nomination, he sat in his seventeenth-floor suite at the Muehlebach. And waited. At ten-fifteen the call finally came. To the suite next to John Connally's.

"Bob," said Jerry Ford, "I want you to be on the ticket."

One room away. Close, but not quite there. That's the way things have been for John Connally since the day in 1972 when he first figured that the way to the White House could be paved with Richard Nixon's good intentions.

On the morning after the morning after, Lyn Nofziger, Sears, and Keene are soaking themselves in coffee and afterthoughts at the Alameda Plaza. They are beyond might-have-beens. Their thoughts now turn to what-will-be. Ford will lose, they all agree. Dole isn't a bad choice, but he can't help the ticket that much. What finally beat Reagan wasn't so much his or their mistakes, but the political power of Ford's incumbency. The nickels and dimes added up.

A Reagan diehard from the South approaches the table.

"My *esteemed* friends," he says expansively.

"Your friends have run out of esteem," replies Nofziger.

Back in form. Old flacks heal quickly. Give him a few weeks, he'll be ready to start talking about 1978. Even 1980 . . .

Kansas City to September   Underdog Days
Ford's flacks are gloating. To beat Ronald Reagan on Wednesday, then outmaneuver Jimmy Carter on Thursday . . .

The way they had it figured in Plains: on the morning after

the Republican Convention, with Ford still unwinding, Jimmy would walk out on his lawn, smile into the cameras, and issue an "invitation" to the President for a series of public debates "on neutral ground"; that is, "outside Washington"—Jody Powell's flair for innuendo, the implication being that any debate held in the Nation's Capital, the city of painted women and wicked bureaucrats (or the other way around)—would be biased toward Ford, the native son.

Then came the leak. No Republican political espionage involved. Just routine spillage for the Carter campaign. Reporters overrated Jimmy's genius for organization during the primaries, as they did George McGovern's in 1972. The Carter camp, like McGovern's, is an informational sieve, though the source of the problem is different.

In 1972, McGovern simply couldn't control his PR operation and suffered an overabundance of campaign spokesmen. Carter likes to think he runs a tauter ship because his campaign manager, Ham Jordan, is seldom seen on TV news. Jimmy does the talking. There is, it appears, no buffer. Carter overexposes himself to reporters in answering questions about campaign strategy, his impression of what the polls show, etc.

To date, despite a Nixon-like penchant for discussing his campaign in cold technological terms, Carter has been able to maintain his nonpolitical image. But given enough television exposure replying to questions about technique—instead of addressing himself to the substantive issues and leaving the tactical questions to Jordan to answer—the impression of the calculating pol will begin to take hold, as it did in Nixon's case.

Says Frank Mankiewicz: *"I've told him, 'Jimmy, you come across great when you're talking about government, but lousy when you're talking about politics.' Not that the advice did any good."*

On the other hand, Rafshoon and Caddell, the manipulative technicians—precisely the representatives a candidate least needs out front—are still talking free-form to the media. Off-camera, all Carter aides, including Jordan, expatiate on campaign details to the end that little is decided about Plains's PR strategy that isn't known to some newsman within the next news cycle. If

Rafshoon and Caddell aren't available, newsmen can always turn to Uncle Charley Kirbo, who will confide, off-the-record, that nobody *else* around this place really knows what the candidate is thinking, which is, confidentially . . .

Inevitably, word of Carter's planned "initiative" (this year's sibling term for "momentum" in the jargon of the campaign game) came to the eighteenth floor of Kansas City's Crown Center, even as Jerry Ford was rehearsing his acceptance speech and reviewing videotapes of his practice performance with a comic, a gagwriter, and a ghost: Don Penny, the comic upon whom the Leader of the Free World relies these days for instruction in how to communicate with his followers; Bob Orben, the $40,000-a-year writer of boffo one-liners; and speechwriter Bob Hartmann. This is the scene: Penny, Orben, Hartmann, and the ubiquitous Kennerly watch the President run through his speech. They then review a videotape, like a coaching staff going over film of a preseason scrimmage.

Watch the hand, chief, watch the hand. Too much air slashing . . . Now when you get to the line, "My record is one of specifics, not smiles," pause a beat . . . Just a beat, to let it sink in . . . And when you come to the "I see Americans" part, remember the rhythm, the rhythm . . .

Even during the heat of the delegate fight with Reagan, the idea of a post-nomination challenge to Carter had been kicked around by Ford flacks, though the President's more cautious advisors were opposed to debating on any terms, whoever issued the challenge. Mel Laird, for one, thought a Ford-Carter confrontation would prove disastrous. At the least, argued Laird, a debate format would conflict with the basic strategy of placing the candidate above the battle: the "Presidential look."

But the report from Plains settled the issue. If the President didn't throw down his own glove Thursday night, he would be responding to his opponent's "invitation" on Friday afternoon. Memories of the Texas phase of the primary season, when Ford was criticized for always seeming to react to Reagan, were still fresh. Now Ford would demonstrate boldness and leadership. He would open his general election campaign with a thrust, putting his opponent on the defensive, forcing Carter to react.

The challenge, however, would not be included in the advance texts distributed to the news media. Not only was there the element of drama to consider—placating the political press's jaded desire to be stimulated by the unexpected. There was also the certainty that advance notice would give Plains a chance to prepare a response for the wires even before the "initiative" was launched. So the debate paragraph was held back. It would be dropped on the media, as well as the convention, as a surprise insert.

The President, Hartmann confided to newsmen afterward, wrote the paragraph himself. In longhand only two hours before he delivered his address.

On the back of an envelope, Bob? No such luck. Merely a Nixonesque yellow legal pad.

The challenge took Plains by surprise less than did the speech itself. For that matter, the speech took most of Jerry Ford's old friends by surprise: "Somebody must have developed a steroid for oratory," one of his former Congressional colleagues tells me the following morning. "Do you know a dealer?"

FORD SPEECH NOT AN ACCIDENT

Headline, *Washington Post*, August 21, 1976

"*. . . The President spent hours working with the speech, rewording phrases and polishing . . . He also practiced delivering it repeatedly during the last two weeks with the aid of former actor Don Penny . . . Penny, who headed his own television production company and is a former comedy writer, joined the White House staff earlier this year for the purpose of improving the President's speaking style . . .*

"*Mr. Ford went through two complete rehearsals for his speech that were videotaped, the first in Washington and the second in Kansas City. With Penny at his side to offer advice . . .*"

Even as they succeeded, if momentarily, in achieving what they had been talking about for two years—the projection of

Jerry Ford as a man grown to national leadership—the President's flacks could not leave well enough alone. Like the satellite egos in Plains, they would have to tell their friends in the press exactly how the mediamorphosis came about—the central role *they* played in shaping history; thus detracting from the image of their principle in order to enhance their own.

Guest Commentaries   Two Losers on the Making of a Presidential Image 1976

JOHN SEARS (Reagan): "Ford's staff talks about having him *act* more Presidential? You can't *act* Presidential. You have *to be* Presidential. If he has to *act*, he *isn't*. The more they talk about it, the more they defeat their own purpose."

FRANK LEE (Wallace): "Why are Caddell and Rafshoon always on camera? They're the mechanics, not the machinery, part of the woodwork, not the centerpiece of the room."

Jerry Ford should take up horseshoes. Carter is doing wonders for his home folks' image, playing slo-pitch softball with the press and Secret Service in Plains, while Ford's off-the-job sports activities bring him nothing but PR grief. It's not that Americans begrudge a leader his outdoor recreation. But there are pre-scribed ways for a candidate to take a few campaign hours off without alienating the great Middle American vote.

For incumbent Presidents, the Puritan work ethic is applied with special strictness. The standard White House line since FDR has been to portray the man in the Oval Office as the Lonely Leader Bearing His Awesome Burden. The price for that image is no time off. It worries voters: if the Lonely Leader isn't there, then *who* is?

Roosevelt and even Just Plain Harry were criticized for their high-profile vacations. FDR's use of the Astor yacht gave Huey Long six months' populist speech material. Truman's Key West sports shirts were the Forties' equivalent of Jerry Ford's ski flops at Vail. The beloved Eisenhower was rapped for golfing too fre-quently at Burning Tree Country Club. The adored Kennedy, for sailing off Hyannis Port.

PR wisdom, which no President in modern times has observed, is that if a national leader has to take a vacation or play games, let it be within a median income wage-earner's price range. Ford's country club golf and resort skiing fuel a latent populist resentment that exists even in the upwardly mobile Middle American suburb.

Carter apparently understands this principle. Early in the campaign he announced he would give up drinking *and* tennis for the duration. He will unwind low-profile, on a sandlot, shunning the high-toned. Ford could do worse than emulate his opponent. Not softball, that's taken. But find a field sport that doesn't call for special uniforms or expensive equipment. Something humanizing, down-to-earth. Touch football, whatever the frustrated Camelotian Kennerly might suggest, is also out. The Retired Flack recommends horseshoes. On the south lawn, where Ike's putting green used to be.

"All this is wrapped up in the poem by T. S. Eliot, 'The Rock,' and in that poem he says, 'And the wind shall say: "These were decent people. Their only monument the asphalt road and a thousand lost golf balls."' We can do better than that."

JOHN F. KENNEDY
October 1, 1960
Minneapolis

The Hairstyling

Should Jody Powell let them in? If not, why not? If some, why not all?

The adversary struggle isn't simply between the press and the politician, but between the press and the press. Among the press and the press. Even the word press *can start an argument. The electronic* media *don't like the word. Contrarily, the print* press, *particularly reporters over forty years of age, think the word* media *is pretentious. Print versus electronic. AM papers versus PM's. Radio versus TV. And the* news *secretary caught in the middle.*

There is a barber in Plains who *cuts* hair. Plains's leading citizen grew up having his hair cut. Now he has it *shaped* by a female hair stylist, in the Big City. When Jimmy Carter traveled to Atlanta last month, he dropped by for a styling. His news secretary, exercising good professional judgment, barred the media from entering the shop.

Why? Because if Jody Powell let the still cameras into the hair stylist's he would have had to let the television cameras in. Then the pool of print correspondents. That evening the country would have been treated to a minute and a half, two networks at least, of campaign color. Thirty million viewers would shake their heads: *Stupid politicians, they're all the same. Anything for publicity.* As far as the television audience knows it's Jimmy Carter, not the medium, that's hokey.

Then, next day, the feature stories: all about the hair stylist and what she thinks of her VIP customer (*"A wonderful person, a beautiful human being"*). What kind of tipper is he? Does he use hair dye? What do they talk about when she's styling his hair? (*"Oh, sometimes he asks my opinion on something and I tell him, straight out."*) Or, optional reply (*"We talk about fishin'. You see, mah daddy, he owned a fahm down wheah the Guvnah's daddy used to go weekends. And when Ah was a little girl, Jimmy . . . Ah called him 'Jimmy' back then . . ."*).

So Jody drew a line. He limited coverage of Jimmy's hairstyling to photos taken through a clear glass window (news management: "Mo" Udall doesn't bar close-ups of *his* hairstyling!). But nothing really bad. Bad, as if, say, the press/media were barred from covering Rosalynn's hairstyling.

A case could be made, of course, that even if the candidate's actual hairstyling isn't politically significant, his hairstyle is. In the 1970s a candidate's hair length alone—more than the buzz words his flacks put into his speeches, the slogans they concoct for his television commercials—is an unmistakable signal of how he positions himself on the political spectrum, left to right, the vote he is aiming for on election day.

Speeches and commercials are ephemeral. They are messages to be denied, modified, altered, one city to the next. A candidate can and does change clothes to fit an audience, within a three-hour period, sometimes three to five times a day. There is a business suit for the Mayor's prayer breakfast in Chicago, an open collar for a noon barbecue in Oklahoma, a Polish-American sweatshirt for a walk through a Pittsburgh ethnic neighborhood in late afternoon. And hats, the traditional American political put-on: a Stetson for the Southwest, a hardhat for western Pennsylvania.

But hair . . . hair is *an ongoing political statement*, right through the day. If too long, it suggests left-wing radicalism to Middle America; if too close-cut, right-wing inflexibility to a segment of young voters Carter considers key to his campaign's success. At some point—slightly below the ears, but above the nape—there is Jimmy Carter's consensus hairstyle for 1976.

Even when hair was a matter of personal taste, not ideological assertion, it played a part in the election of recent American Presidents. Much as Harry Truman's whistlestopping, Tom Dewey's mustache cost him votes in a close race. What was acceptable in those years in a candidate for Governor of New York somehow didn't seem "Presidential." Alice Roosevelt Longworth's "man on the wedding cake" tag was devastating to Dewey. He had the PR counsel available at that time—Jim Hagerty, Emmet Hughes—but he could not, would not shave off that mustache.

In 1976 the subliminal hair issue divides along head, not facial lines. Jerry Ford in a Jimmy Carter modified shag would be a politico-visual improbability. Candidates with shags simply don't contend for Republican nominations. The party hasn't moved that far left; though it is moving, imperceptibly, around the upper lobes.

Even Barry Goldwater is less *trim* than he was in the days I traveled with him, saving Western civilization as Teddy White put it. And Bob Dole, pragmatic conservative that he is, Dole too is reconsidering his styling, according to our mutual barber. Dole's hair, says Pietro Santoro, is in flux. It is his wife's influence.

"Mees Dole, she say when he come back from convention, 'Pietro, make eet sometheen' deefrent. Not too short thees time.'"

Santoro is a thirty-two-year-old Italian-born hairstyling maestro, who works out of the Statler Hilton shop on K Street, four blocks from the White House. He has been styling Dole's hair for about a year. Most recently, on the day following the Vice-

President-nominate's return from Kansas City when, for the first time, Santoro informs me with appropriate ethnic hand gestures, "thees bodyguard, they stand all over."

It was Pietro's first contact with a national candidate's hair, his most exalted political client until then having been a former press secretary to a former Vice-President. With Milanese flourish, as he lathers my hair, he begins to tell me about the Kansas Senator's newfound willingness, with his wife's persuasion, to experiment in hairshaping. But I interrupt before he goes too far into his story to give him a Retired Flack's friendly PR advice.

Pietro, I say, *you are now in the big time. Don't pull a Milton Pitts. Whatever goes on between you and the Doles, keep it to yourself.*

"Peets," nods Santoro, who himself used to work for Milton, one of Washington's pioneer hair stylists, the self-promoted Barber of Presidents. "Peets, you know, he cut President Ford's hair too short. I see President on television, makeen' speech . . ."

"His acceptance speech?"

"Yeah. He luke like nineteen-and-seexty. Too short."

"What did you think of the speech?"

Pietro shrugs, then runs an index finger in a quick arc around my left ear.

"I luke at hair," he replies. "You see line aroun' Ford's ears? Cut too treem. Feefteen years past style. Ford need hair more fool."

Signor Santoro now uses both hands, moving the razor and comb away from my head to demonstrate what is meant by *fool:* the President's hair, he is saying, should be thicker around and above the ears. I wonder at the infinite subtleties of making of a public image. You hire a Stu Spencer to help give you a *Presidential* look and here, from the mouths of barbers . . . for Pietro is right, of course. He isn't a public relations expert, but he does have trophies on his shelf that attest to certain image-making sensibilities. And what he has just told me is that it isn't the stumbling entrance or the fluffed speech lines, but what comes *before* even those problems. Our perception of the man before he takes a step or opens his mouth: that Bozo the Clown look that has given Jerry Ford so much trouble begins with his close-cropped hairstyling. A man with a shag could trip down a ramp, blow his lines, no problem. (Well, maybe . . . would we ask: *Is he on something?*)

"What about the President's sideburns?" I ask Pietro.

"I make a leetle longer," he says. "Ford has broad face (*the hands move this time around my jawbone, to illustrate the point*). Peets good styler, but he cut Ford too treem."

Ford inherited Milton Pitts from his predecessor, as a safe White House retainer untouched by any taint of Watergate. That part is certain. For if the Nation's First Head had ever uttered a word to his hair stylist on the subject of Watergate, Sally Quinn would have broken the story for the *Post* before Woodward and Bernstein.

Milton, you see, likes to talk to the press about his celebrity clients, from Sonny Jurgensen on down. Oddly—or maybe not so oddly—this form of advertising hasn't hurt his business at all with the National Capital Mercedes trade. What other barber/hair stylist in history can lay claim to having served not one, but two Heads of States?

Ah, but should Jerry Ford lose and Ronald Reagan come to the White House next January, Milton Pitts will be the second to go. Right after Kissinger. According to the press, Milton has been carried away by the adversary spirit of the Ford-Reagan delegate contest and made several disparaging remarks about his current client's opponent.

Reagan's coiffure, Milton has charged—an item thought significant by newsmagazines and journals looking for the truly substantive differences between the two Republican contenders—Reagan's coiffure is *pomaded.* (The report is sufficient to send Clayton Fritchey into spasms. He gives an entire column paragraph to the manipulative nature of the Reagan campaign.) But wait, the Barber of the Presidents isn't finished: Reagan also *dyes* his hair. How does Pitts know that? He is an expert on such matters, he just knows. Reagan's flacks, pressed on the issue, neither confirm nor deny. They are evasive. Milton clearly is on to something. (Gerald Ford, he tells us, doesn't use a touch of dye. Certainly not pomade. And about this, Milton speaks with absolute authority: we have a President with the Natural Look, no greasy political stuff.)

"What do you think of Reagan's hairstyle?" I ask Pietro Santoro as he holds up the mirror. Genius. The man has performed another miracle of imagectomy: the balding spot, which will reappear after the first shower, cannot for the moment be seen.

"Reagan?" says Bob Dole's expert in the field. "Nice head hair. Except, maybe, *twenty* years past . . ."

Jimmy Carter is mod, his hairstyle slightly left of center. Behind the JFK frontal sweep there is the meticulous shag slightly over the ears, with a touch of gray in the three-quarter lobe-length sideburns. Full in back, yet neat, not spilling over the collar, which would be too much concession to the young and turn off the hardhats.

Look at a photograph of Jimmy Carter six years ago, when he was elected Governor of Georgia. It tells more about the changing imagery of American politics, of the coming of the eighteen-to-twenty-one voter, or the impact of the semi-revolutionary 1960s, than a month of Pat Caddell's demographic studies. It is there, up front, on top, in the open, to be seen and measured by all.

By 1980 the country could be ready to buy a Presidential candidate with facial hair. For Democrats, a Liberal beard; for Republicans, a Conservative mustache. But not too trim. Never again a man on a wedding cake. One more lesson learned from that watershed campaign of twenty-eight years ago.

Under a Gray November Sky... Autumn 1976

Toward Super Tuesday with Dick Daley's Favorite Populist, from Warm Springs to Hugh Hefner, and Joe Garagiola's Favorite Talk Show Guest, from the Rose Garden to Earl Butz. One's Hand at the Tiller, the Other's Finger on the Pulse, the Public-Related President versus the Poll-Minded Challenger, and May the Best Image Win . . .

POLITICAL PR *Two Varying Opinions From the Past*

National news operates in twos. There are two newspapers, two wire services, two weekly magazines, and two networks. You get them all against you, you're in trouble.

LYNDON JOHNSON *to Spiro Agnew*
(circa 1968)

There's a difference between character and reputation. Reputation is what people think you are and character is what you really are inside. You can be a son-of-a-bitch, but if people think you're all right, you're in good shape. But no matter how good you are, if people think you're a rotten son-of-a-bitch, you might as well give up.

EARL LONG *to A. J. Liebling*
(circa 1956)

The Democratic nominee returns to Plains after his first post-nomination swing through Southern California. He is in a pet about that Meet the Stars party at Warren Beatty's, infuriated at Tony Randall's patronizing manner—addressing Carter as if he were a political aborigine in need of instruction on complex national issues. *Never again,* the candidate vows, *will I waste time going to meet such people.* But if Plains won't go to the mountain, the mountain can always come to Plains.

Robert Redford flies his private jet in over the Labor Day weekend to discuss, he says, Carter's position on environmental issues as well as ways he can help the Democratic ticket this fall . . .

The Retired Flack fantasizes a conversation between two leaders of the free world in Plains, Georgia, September 1976:

"You see, Jimmy, I own this property . . ."

"That's good to know, Bob. Property is where it all begins. We were the land's before the land was ours. Robert Frost. I'm extremely fond of reading Robert Frost, in Spanish translation, before I retire each evening."

"Jimmy, it's not exactly that kind of property. It's a film, all about Nixon and Watergate."

"Well, that's nice to hear, Bob, but you understand, we don't talk about those things around here. They're not part of our campaign."

"I'm sorry to hear that Jimmy, because, you see, I was thinking that as the campaign goes along . . ."

"Bob, you can stop right there. It's your property, like it's Mondale's mouth. I wouldn't presume to tell you, or him, what to do with either when it comes to N___ and W_____ . . ."

SACRAMENTO, Calif., Oct. 6 (UPI)—Warner Bros. has booked the politically sensitive movie "All the President's Men" into 600 theaters nationwide to run in the final two weeks before the Nov. 2 election, it was learned Wednesday . . .

In a television interview, Sandy Wilk, a spokesman for Warner Bros. Distributing Corp. in Hollywood, branded as "ridiculous" any suggestion that the scheduling could be interpreted as a move to possibly embarrass Republicans in the crucial weeks before the election . . .

CARTER SADDLES FORD
WITH NIXON COMPARISON

Headline, *The Atlanta
Journal*, September 30, 1976

BUFFALO, N.Y.—Jimmy Carter escalated his offensive against
President Ford here Thursday, charging that "as far as peo-
ple's lives were concerned, (he) is even worse" than Richard
Nixon . . .

THE SEMANTICS OF AMERICAN POLITICS Fall 1976

> *shacking up: screw* (shak-inup, skroo) v. vernacular used by the
> Democratic Presidential candidate during a comprehensive inter-
> view published in the October 1976 issue of *Playboy* magazine. Cf.
> Congressman Andrew Young's explanation of the candidate's use
> of the term "ethnic purity" during an interview with the *New
> York Daily News* six months earlier: *"I think it was an attempt on
> Jimmy's part to over-identify with the people he was talking to."*

Robert Scheer may not be the best one-on-one interviewer in
the country, but hands down he's the most persistent. Scheer has
a way with offbeat politicians. Jerry Brown, who last spring
demonstrated that a Presidential candidate can submit to a
Playboy interview without sticking his lustful heart in his
mouth, swears by Scheer. Brown calls the result of their taped
sessions the definitive statement on what he stands for. Or, in the
vernacular Jerry prefers, where he's coming from.

It was with the Brown interview in mind that Carter's young
inner circle—Powell, Jordan, Rafshoon, Caddell—foresaw glow-
ing possibilities in the *Playboy* interview. Caddell's polls show a
massive undecided vote among eighteen-to-twenty-five-year-olds.
Playboy beats the *Christian Science Monitor* as an entree to this
bloc—a route, through the gonads, to the hearts and minds of
young urbanites put off by the fearsome Southern Baptist image.
Far from being an oversight—a mistake on the part of Jody Powell in scheduling Scheer's extended sessions with Carter—this
was a conscious, well-considered PR ploy. And it would have
worked beautifully . . . if only Jimmy didn't have this compul-
sion to *over-identify.*

CARTER INTERVIEWER
IS SURPRISED OVER FUROR

Headline, *Boston Herald American*, October 14, 1976

"We got into the Bible because I wanted to get into civil liberties, concerning the judges he would appoint."

ROBERT SCHEER

So tell us, Bob, whom did he say he was considering? Solomon, maybe, to solve the unwanted children problem? Pontius Pilate, to work on docket clogging?

Within days after news of its contents breaks, Robert Scheer's interview with the Democratic Presidential candidate is *perceived* as the Biggest Carter Screw-up Yet. It is given a full 10 on the Evans-Novak Gasp Scale, compared, for example, to a mere 4 for the "No Embargoes" flub, a 6 for the Clarence Kelley Mix-up, and a 5 for the "median income Gaffe."

Scheer is now that most enviable of modern journalists, the reporter-become-celebrity, a giver—as well as a getter—of interviews. I meet him in the green room of "Good Morning, America," fifteen minutes before we are to debate whether his interview will damage the Carter campaign. The Retired Flack, still operating under the old strictures of political PR (*don't drink, don't cuss, don't get caught screwing*), is under the naïve delusion that, *Yes*, it will hurt Jimmy. Not because he had an interview with *Playboy* (the hypocritical Ford contention). Rather because of what he said to *Playboy*.

Scheer disagrees: *No*, he insists on the live tube, far from hurting Carter's campaign, the interview will help it. It shows Jimmy Carter as a human with human impulses. So what's wrong with being a human, with human impulses? (*Yeah*, I hear Wayne Hays growling from Ohio, *that's what I keep tellin' 'em at the office . . .*)

"My mother," Scheer tells me after the show, "my mother is a sweet Jewish lady who doesn't like bad language and believes politicians should be *dignified*. Well, she read the interview and she says, 'You know, before this I had my doubts about this

Carter. I was afraid he was one of those close-minded bigots. But now . . .'"

"That's *your* mother," I say. "She sees her son's byline, that makes everything O.K. But Carter made a mistake. Those Baptist mothers don't care for this paraphrasing Christ about shacking up. Tell me—did he really know the tape recorder was going?"

The news story had it that as Jimmy went into his New Revised *Playboy* Version of the Testament, he was told Scheer was taping. The candidate only nodded and kept on talking.

"He knew," Scheer replies. "He knew what he was saying, and it was what he wanted to say."

We are heading back to our hotel, in the big black non-bullet-proof limo ABC provides for its debate panelists. I turn to examine Scheer more closely, to see if he is smiling, even the flick of a smile, beneath the short, reddish beard. Buckley does not like beards because, he says, they tend to make all men look alike. I don't like them because they give the player across the poker table an edge. Scheer could be pulling my right leg with his left hand.

"You're telling me Jimmy Carter *wanted* to have that language —*screw, shack-up* in print, for direct attribution?"

"Carter wanted to deliver a *message*," Scheer says. "And that's what it took. He wanted to tell young people, 'Look, I'm no uptight, thin-lipped, holy-rolling bigot.' It was no mistake, no slip of the tongue. They saw the galleys, but they didn't ask for one change. Not a single change. Not that I would have changed anything, understand. Jerry Brown was on us not to run this-or-that after his interview, but I wouldn't change a word. It turned out O.K., though. He seems to be happy about it."

No, Scheer may be pulling his own leg, but I am persuaded he is not pulling mine. He is convinced that the interview is a plus for the Carter campaign. And more, that Carter and his staff are equally convinced. Are at least as happy as Jerry Brown.

"Look, Carter's a politician and he wants to go only so far to make a point," Scheer says. "And I'm an interviewer, and I'm trying to get him to be more specific. I went to them and said, 'This is an audience you need to reach,' and their polls happened to say the same thing.

"But it didn't come easy. I had to keep going back, telling them, 'You haven't made your point, you haven't given me enough.' And Carter wanted to cooperate. That last session, he came to the door with us and said, 'Do you have everything you need now?' So we asked one more thing, and—"

"Who on his press staff was there with him?" I ask.

"Rex Granum."

"Not Powell? I'd have thought Powell would be there."

"Well, this wasn't the first interview. I logged more time with Carter than any other interviewer, you know. Powell was in on some of the others. This time it was Granum."

"And he didn't say anything when he heard Carter go into the sex bit?"

Scheer shakes his head: "I'm telling you, Carter *knew* what he was doing. His *staff* knew. I'm not saying he would have gone as far if I hadn't pumped him, hadn't kept working at it, telling him I needed more. That's my job. But he knew—even with the line about Johnson, comparing him to Nixon, calling him a liar—he knew where he was headed . . ."

"I have to admit that in the heat of the campaign . . . I've made some mistakes. And I think this is part of just being a human being. I have to say that my campaign has been an open one and the *Playboy* interview has been of very great concern to me. I agreed to give the interview to *Playboy*. Other people have done it and are notable—Governor Jerry Brown, Walter Cronkite, Albert Schweitzer, Mr. Ford's own Secretary of the Treasury, Mr. Simon, William Buckley, many other people. But they aren't running for President, and in retrospect, from hindsight, I would not have given that interview had I to do it over again."

> Candidate JIMMY CARTER, headed in
> another direction, Ford-Carter
> Debate III, October 22, 1976

Flubabout is Fair Play

"There is no Soviet domination of Eastern Europe . . ."

> GERALD FORD, Debate II,
> October 6, 1976

"Let me be blunt. I did not express myself clearly when this question came up . . ."

GERALD FORD, meeting with Eastern European ethnic leaders, October 12, 1976

"Who's advising him?"

Question most frequently asked about Jerry Ford and Jimmy Carter, Campaign '76, according to unscientific poll

Who are these people?

These people with images but no identities. These candidates for the office which, we are ceaselessly reminded, is the Most Powerful Office in the World (or, variously, the Free World). These men, of whom we have heard and read so much, who have gone through, endured, the relentless exposure of the primary and convention process—and yet are constantly surprising themselves, their staffs, and us.

An election in a democratic society, we are told, is a continuing teaching and learning process, for the participants, for the people. Never has a people been fed so much information, data, minutiae about two candidates for the Presidency. Never have two candidates been fed so much information, data, minutiae about the calculated methodology of getting elected. Yet, something is missing. No, maybe the problem is that there is *too much* indiscriminate information for the people, *too much* calculation on the part of the candidates and their advisors.

Who's advising him? In the end, the answer to that question is important only as a reflection, a measure of how the candidate *perceives* himself and the Office he seeks. At the outset of the 1976 general election campaign, neither candidate seems to know that answer himself. Ford and Carter, searching for identity, image: "I don't intend to lose," says Jimmy Carter; "We are going to win," says Jerry Ford.

Of course. What other measure is there for them, or us, to determine *who* they really are and *what* they really stand for? In politics, victory is the best teacher.

Who is Jimmy Carter? Early September

By tradition, Democratic candidates launch their Presidential campaigns speaking to a labor rally in Detroit. This year, the Georgia candidate will open in the neighborhood, at Franklin Roosevelt's "Georgia White House." The change is explained in PR terms. Warm Springs, says Carter's staff, is a backyard media visual. It ties Jimmy to the Democratic past, wraps him in the aura of the Old Coalition, which ties into Caddell's poll information that tells them Carter's greatest need is to *identify* his candidacy with the party rank-and-file. Why go to Detroit to tap tradition when it's only a few miles away?

But if the decision to open the campaign with FDR's picture on the podium and a live Roosevelt by his side was made for the best of PR reasons, there were, in fact, more than one. There was a special problem with Detroit this year, one not faced by Democrats in past campaigns. Roving gangs have been victimizing large gatherings, to the point of attracting major national publicity. The possibility of a campaign kick-off either marred by violence or ringed by uniformed police out in force—in a city run by a Democratic Mayor and early Carter supporter—led Carter's staff to search for other sites. Warm Springs, for all the prime PR reasons now given, was the alternative.

Concerned at one stage during the primaries that Carter was registering as "fuzzy" on issues with large numbers of voters, Pat Caddell pleaded with the candidate to put "a semblance of substance" into his texts. He appears to have made his point. What comes through to live audiences and on the television screen these early weeks, from that very first day in Warm Springs, is not the grinning, healing "thematic" candidate of New Hampshire. It is the image of a Jimmy Carter on-the-attack, waving the bloody shirt of Herbert Hoover with a missionary zeal, preaching Republican hellfire and Democratic salvation. Somehow, the candidate doesn't seem at one with this image. But if that's what the polls show they're looking for . . .

The Quadrennial of the Holy Man Pollster

Candidates in past Presidential campaigns have used public opinion surveys, but left something to gut instinct. Not this year.

Ford holds a minimum of three séances a week with Bob Teeter to find out where his people are headed, so he can lead them. The President, they say, is "very high" on Teeter. Especially since his house pollster shows him only six points behind Carter, compared with Gallup's thirteen.

In Plains, the irreverent say that when Caddell catches cold, Jimmy starts sneezing. The Carter campaign is the most poll-ridden in history: nothing will be left untracked. The Caddell operation will be linked directly to two computers on the campaign plane. Scientific-manipulative politics elevated to new levels. In the pre-computer days, candidates were brought up to speed on regional and local issues by means of a briefing book containing data gathered by the research staff and, for late material, the political advance men. Under the Carter computer method, last-minute fluctuations in public attitudes will be flashed to the candidate even as the plane's landing gear swings down.

Carter and Ford look for different things from their pollsters. Jerry takes comfort in whatever good news Teeter brings him, any scrap of data to sustain him through a day when he's not on the road being warmed by the crowd. Jimmy, however, looks at the bad news first. Shown an eighty percentile approval rating on a given issue, he will fret about the missing twenty.

There is a thesis going the Washington rounds—being pushed, ironically, by Republicans—that Carter exhibits Nixonian character traits. In the case of reacting to public opinion, however, the comparison is not to Nixon but LBJ. Jimmy seems to hunger for mass, Total Consensus, nothing less. It is the characteristic of a driven, a winning, yet as Johnson demonstrated, an ultimately vulnerable politician.

Trumanphilia, Trivia & Irony

"President Truman, like Abraham Lincoln, had a great faith in the ultimate good sense of the people. He liked them, he liked their language—and in 1948 they went to the polls and proved that his faith was fully justified."

GERALD FORD, *running campaign theme, 1976*

"My favorite modern President is Harry Truman. He exemplified the kind of administration I would like to have. I admire his honesty, his vision in foreign policy, his closeness with the American people."

JIMMY CARTER, *running campaign theme, 1976*

TRIVIA: Harry Truman, the Presidential candidate, despised public opinion polls. Not that it makes any difference. In 1976, Truman is cited like the Good Book, to prove any point.

IRONY: That in the year of the anti-politician Harry Truman should emerge as the historical image even his old enemies embrace. Truman, the machine-produced pol, the exemplar of Washington Old Clubism, now the hero of the seventies. Alive, Truman would have bitterly opposed the upstart from Georgia, as he did the upstart from Tennessee in 1952. Carter, the student of modern Presidential campaigns, knows this, yet recites the litany, speaks the historical lie.

Ford's hypocrisy is worse. Truman was his political contemporary. Young Congressman Ford, as a dutiful party hack, opposed the Democratic President in the White House with Booster zest. Now, in working to tie his contemporary image to the idealized public memory of Truman, Ford not only Orwellizes that past but repudiates the memory of an old political friend and ally. The people's *"faith . . . fully justified"* consisted of their rejecting Thomas Dewey, Ford's old party leader, a University of Michigan product who, in 1948, campaigned to help Jerry Ford win his first term in Congress.

At the Iowa State Fair, the public Jimmy brings cheers from a rural audience by promising "no embargoes" on grain shipments. This is the same pledge—the same words—Ford used in his Kansas City acceptance speech. But following his appearance at the Fair, another Jimmy, in the mahogany quiet of the newspaper board room, tells Des Moines editors that under the stress of national emergency he would make exceptions to his embargo on embargoes. This qualifier to his public utterance is headlined the next morning, perfectly timed for Bob Dole, speaking at the Fair that day, to wave the paper as demonstrative evidence of Carter's speaking in double tongues. Jody Powell complains that the headline distorts what Jimmy actually said. Where? Which Jimmy?

The PR principle here is not necessarily *Never say Never*. It is *Never say Maybe in the same circulation area where you've just said Never.*

At Brooklyn College, in his first swing through the Northeast, the public Jimmy criticizes Ford for retaining Clarence Kelley as FBI director following revelations that Bureau personnel were used to decorate Kelley's apartment. This is Powell's brainstorm, raw meat fed the candidate aboard his campaign plane en route to the speaking site. It is Jody's greatest PR contribution since the *Playboy* interview, and Carter delivers it with the moral passion his press secretary recommended, symbolically linking Kelley's freebee valances to Nixon-Watergate. An FBI director, Jimmy says, must be "purer than Caesar's wife."

It is a hard-hitting campaign bit, delivered in populist shirt-sleeves on a bare campus stage. But following these remarks, the other Jimmy, in the relatively calm atmosphere of a post-speech interview with reporters, is specifically asked whether, as President, he will fire Kelley.

The question is standard reportorial pushing to the outer limits, intended only to provide—if the candidate is willing to help along—a more eye-catching headline: CARTER WILL FIRE KELLEY is harder, crisper, for news purposes, than CARTER SAYS FORD SHOULD FIRE KELLEY.

There would seem to be no difference. Except that this Carter would like to keep options that the public Carter doesn't contemplate in the finality of his utterances. And then there is the matter of Jimmy Carter's campaign catalogue mind flipping through index cards and coming up with Nixon's gratuitous *"I will fire Ramsey Clark"* line at the Republican Convention in 1968. So the second Jimmy—relating now to his reportorial rather than his public audience—hedges: "I'll cross that bridge," he tells his questioner, "when I get to it."

This is the backing-and-filling of a candidate suffering some San Andreas fault in self-identification. Two Jimmy Carter images pulling in different, if not always opposite, directions. It is the same split-image problem that plagued McGovern four years ago after he won the nomination and was faced with the challenge of forging a general election majority rather than a mere primary plurality: McGovern, the populist prairie preacher/urbanized college professor, given to, first, the sweeping statement; then a hedge. As distinguished from the problem that plagued Goldwater in 1964: the sweeping statement, followed by an amplification . . .

In terms of media relations alone, Andrew Young's perception of Jimmy Carter's over-identification with whatever "people he's talking to" can also be distinguished from Jerry Ford's search for the elusive image.

Ford, from an older political school, sees the reporters he talks to as conduits to constituencies, the "people" who read the papers, watch the evening news. In replying to questions, Ford isn't reaching so much for the interviewer's approbation as that of his readers and viewers. The "newsies" are only flesh-and-blood extensions of their typewriters and microphones.

Carter, on the other hand, views the members of the news media—educated, sophisticated, politically savvy—as a peer constituency in their own right. Scheer may be right in saying that Carter's interest was in breaking through to the *Playboy* constituency. But he was also working to break through to Bob Scheer (and, as in the case of Hunter Thompson, he succeeded). Carter sees individual reporters as more than mechanical conduits: as a special audience who, if influenced, can bring political benefits longer-lasting than that of a single favorable interview. Jimmy wants the vote and commitment of the individual reporter as much as he wants that of his/her general audience.

This technique, similar to that of John Kennedy in 1960, has been highly successful in acquiring the respect, and support, of certain members of the traveling press. Carter cultivates his individual journalistic targets with the same calculation he employs in wooing other important constituencies. The Thompson conversion was a demonstration of the use of thematic buzz words on a one-to-one basis as impressive, in its own way, as any of

Jimmy's primary wins. But it is precisely this approach—that the news media covering him represent an independent constituency, separate from their readers and viewers—that leads one Carter to get another Carter into hot political water in his/their after-speech editorial boards and news conferences.

"President Ford's Labor Day strategy was to select the *pose* of a President at work."

BOB SCHIEFFER, CBS-TV
White House correspondent,
(emphasis supplied)

Who is Gerald Ford?

Jerry Ford, when last seen impersonating Harry Truman in 1948, is now working on a re-creation of Eisenhower in 1956. *Give 'em hell?* No. *Give 'em the Presidential seal.*

PRESIDENT DISPLAYS STRATEGY
CAMPAIGN PLAN
CALLS FOR USE
OF WHITE HOUSE

Headline, *Washington Post*,
September 1976

The President's flacks, obviously fearful that Jerry's impersonation of Ike might not be all that good at first, are busy spreading word of exactly what he's trying to do. They talk of "strategy," "tactics," the terminology of public relations so dominant in their conversations with reporters that it dominates the coverage of the eventoids they are staging. It isn't *what* Ford does that now attracts the media, but *how* he does it . . .

ED WALSH, *Washington Post:* "In the White House Rose Garden and press briefing room, President Ford began yesterday to implement what has been *described* as a 'Presidential' campaign strategy against Democratic nominee Jimmy Carter . . ."

JIM NAUGHTON, *The New York Times:* ". . . While none of these events was unusual, each was *described* as an element in a Presidential campaign strategy through which Mr. Ford will make his case for staying in the White House by staying, for the most part, in the White House . . ."

The Associated Press: "President Ford is continuing to *test-market* his stay-at-home campaign with an assortment of events designed to keep him in the news and *play up the fact* that he lives in the White House."

This is the wind-him-up-but-not-too-tightly President. Just Plain Jerry, the President who uses no makeup when going before the cameras. The *Times'* Naughton captures the spirit of the Ford campaign, in all its contrived naturalness, recalling for the Retired Flack a Don Penny-written line Jerry used in a speech during his primary run against Reagan the Actor: "There are no retakes in the White House," said Jerry. Writes Naughton:

> This morning Mr. Ford's aides arranged a small desk, straight-backed chair and fiberglass floor mat on the lush White House lawn so that television cameras could film the President striding to them from the Oval Office to sign the Teton Dam Measure.
> An hour later the desk chair and mat had been moved and the television cameras repositioned so that Mr. and Mrs. Ford could be filmed striding into the garden from a different White House door.

The "Jerry & Betty Show." But on the initial walk, it seems, the performers don't quite hit their *marks* at an angle suitable to the needs of cameramen present. The scene will be reshot. The President of the United States and his First Lady moved back to the doorway. They are recued. They redo the scene. Cut! It's a take . . .

Adjoining the Naughton story the *Times* runs both photos, with the caption: "*President Ford shaking hands with his wife, Betty, in the Rose Garden . . . and doing it again for photographers who asked for a better angle.*"

Skip Watts doesn't know the name of the advance man working Texas who phoned in the idea about plugging into the CB vote. But he says he'll check it out if I want. Not necessary, I tell him, but it was an advance man's idea, right? Not Susan Ford's, as Sheila Weidenfeld said when she told the press that Betty Ford was getting a Citizens Band radio put into her limo.

"Oh? Is that what they said over there?"

Watts flicks his chin in the general direction of the White House, ten blocks away from his work hole in the PFC on L Street. "Well, she probably had the idea too. It's a helluvan idea. What I heard is that some advance man—the advance men, they know the scene—called in to say CB's were big in the Southwest. It made a great shot."

"Why Betty? Why not the President himself?"

Watts laughs and tunes the question out. I don't blame him. Besides, I know the answer. Sure, Jerry Ford, the old Congressional campaigner, would have jumped at the idea. But how *Presidential* would it have seemed? No, this was a sidebar, something for a member of the family. Jack or Betty. And the best shot was the mother, not the son. Jack's using a CB would be something for the regional wires. But the First Lady could go national, all the way. But what would she be called? "Apple Betty," as the President suggested, or "First Mama," Susan's choice? Really Susan's. Not the advance man's.

"Is Mrs. Ford still using her CB?"

"Her what?"

"Her CB, Citizens Band radio."

"You want me to check *that?*"

"I'd appreciate it, I tell the female Voice on the other end of the phone. It is the closest Voice the Retired Flack can get to Nessen or Weidenfeld these days. Or am I coming down with a case of Media Paranoia? No, something is wrong. Somebody must have gotten around to reading that prediction I wrote for the *Washingtonian*, the one about Ford's losing the election and writing his memoirs, *Years of Judg-e-ment*. It has to be that. Last month Sheila passed me in the corridor at the Kemper Arena as if I were Richard Reeves in full cry. No matter. I will dig more deeply into the Great CB Sham.

Not digging, really. Just a follow-up, something the campaign press seldom does, once a gimmick gets played. Which, of course, makes it easy for the working campaign flack. He/She can pull off the most blatant, contrived publicity stunt, it gets its ride and that's the end of it. You never need to worry about anybody coming back next week to recheck the story. Or, if anybody does, that any editor will think it important enough to run the follow-up copy.

The editors *want* to go with "First Mama"-type *shtiks*—especially the photo editors—as much as campaign flacks want to push them. So who needs a follow-up? To find out that Betty Ford really isn't a CB fan, that she doesn't use her equipment, that it was just a one-shot stunt, wouldn't embarrass the flack that manipulated the media as much as the media that went along with the gag.

"I'll have to check," says the Voice in the White House news office. "Let me get this right now. You want to know whether Mrs. Ford is still using her Citizens Band."

"Right," I say. "Anything you can tell me about where, when was the last time she used it. How much she uses it. Whether she's had any interesting CB conversations lately—"

"Well, Mrs. Ford is on the road now, but I'll get back to you as soon as I can get your answer. O.K.?"

My answer. The operative possessive. Like, *you* ask a piddling question, we'll get *your* piddling answer.

I call Skip Watts's office. He is unavailable, on the road. And Doug Blaser, the electronic gimmick whiz of Republican advance men. If it's something you plug in, ask Blaser, he'll know. Doug is also on the road. No, specifically, on the *water*. A special project. Advancing media arrangements, they tell me, for the President's trip down the Mississippi on a riverboat.

A riverboat trip? Jesus, I'm sorry. If I'd only known . . . No wonder they don't have time around the Ford campaign for piddling questions about CB's. I mean, with so many *big* things going on . . .

But isn't that what they always taught us back in flack school? I should have remembered: *There is nothing older than yesterday's media event.*

Who's advising him? This then is Campaign '76: two hyper-mediatized staffs, each reflecting its candidate's obsession with different aspects of the campaign process. Ford, fascinated with the mechanics of appearance, the political value of visual availability, a candidate continually in *pose*. Carter, fascinated by the calculation and measurement of the dynamics of a winning campaign.

This is the choice: Ford will stand still for a photo with a clown costumed as a giant chicken; Carter may not. But Carter will, if asked, give the inquiring photographer a ten-minute expatiation regarding why, at this particular point in the campaign, that sort of picture would prove counterproductive, because the polls show that chickens . . .

"Obviously, to the extent that I would be ahead in acceptance among the voters, if there was no dramatic change at the conclusion of the debates, if the won-lost analysis was conjectural or doubtful, then I would not have disturbed a lead among voters.

> JIMMY CARTER in pre-
> Debate I interview

Watching, listening to Jimmy Carter conduct seminars for newsmen on the technology of modern campaigning, I am reminded of the title of Edward Bernays' classic handbook on public relations: *The Engineering of Consent*.

Jimmy complains about the press incessantly asking questions on the nuts and bolts of the campaign. But he never fails to reply to them, sometimes in exhaustive detail. Why? Here the answer lies not in dissecting the *persona* of Jimmy the Candidate, but of Jimmy the Engineer. Carter talks technology. He isn't the political organizer so much as the mechanical specialist, putting nuts and bolts together. By instinct and training he is impelled to reply to reporters' questions about the hows and whys of constructing a political campaign, and does so with the fervor for detail of an engineer describing the construction of a bridge, a building, a ship.

Given the 1976 news media's absorption in the technology of the campaign, this Carter penchant can lead to what, in former campaigns, would have been considered absurd dialogues between reporters and the candidate.

Asked how he intends to address Ford during the debates, Carter doesn't dismiss the question as an incidental bridge that will be built, and crossed, when he comes to it. Instead, he replies with painful specificity: *I will call him,* says Jimmy, without the trace of a saving grin, *"Mr. Ford."* Then commences a meticulous discourse on the history of political decorum . . . *Thomas Jefferson, you see, preferred being called "Mr. Jefferson," and then there was James Madison who was called "Mr. Madison."*

Within a news cycle the question takes on major operational significance in Carter's high command. Now comes Jody Powell to say that he has conferred with Jimmy about the problem of what to call Whatzisname during their face-to-face exchanges, and as chief flack and advisor on such matters has pointed out and recommended the following: (1) "Mr. Ford" might be *perceived* by viewers as too informal, disrespectful of the office; (2) while "Mr. President" would sound too reverential, which would also be bad for Jimmy's image; Jody, therefore, has made a pitch for "President Ford."

A nice interim solution. Awkward but good for a holding operation until Caddell has taken a sampling on the subject . . .

CELEBRITY QUIZ   Washington Squares

QUESTION: *Paul Lynde, what did John Kennedy call Richard Nixon during the 1960 debates? (a) Vice-President Nixon; (b) Mr. Nixon; (c) Tricky Dick . . .*

Skillfully, Carter and Jody Powell maneuver for the role of underdog. From Lincoln-Douglas to Kennedy-Nixon, there have seldom been any genuine winners in face-to-face debates between political candidates. What we have then is another version of the High-Low Expectation scoring system used by the news media to gauge success-or-failure in primaries. Did Lincoln "win" his debates with Douglas? Certainly. So every American high school student learns because (1) the "unknown" Lincoln was going up against the "national figure" Douglas, and (2) Medill's Republican *Chicago Tribune,* even then touting Lincoln as a future Presidential possibility, was the prime news source covering the event.

The rule is that the candidate who is expected to do well because of experience and reputation (Douglas, Nixon) must do *better* than well; while the candidate expected to fare poorly (Lincoln, Kennedy) can put points on the media board simply by surviving.

Thus, with his candidate enjoying a wide lead in the public opinion polls, Powell must do something to project Carter as something less than a front-runner. Jimmy is to be portrayed as limping gamely onto the field to do battle with Gerald Ford, the President, formidable and fearsome amid his Presidential aura.

This is a first. To date, no Carter spokesman has ever conceded that Jerry Ford is, in any respect, "Presidential." But Powell understands the difference between long range PR strategy and short-term PR tactics.

Carter himself embellishes his press secretary's poor-mouth act by asking that the first debate be held in a "neutral" city, i.e., not Sodom-on-the-Potomac. If held in the National Capital, says Jimmy, network TV cameras would almost certainly focus during the pre-debate hour on such visuals as Ford's "leaving the White House in a limousine."

It is a straw man—or, as it were, straw site—since, to date, no one has been heard to suggest that the first, or any other debate, be held in Washington. And in any case, what more could Populist Jimmy ask to make his main campaign theme than the Imperial President pictured arriving at the debate site in one of those fancy, black limousines?

In San Francisco (Jerry Brown Country), late August, Carter upsets the Secret Service with a directive: he doesn't want to ride in any more limousines. The order goes to the crux of the problem of how any modern American leader can fend off imperial trappings even if he tries to.

The Secret Service isn't concerned about imperialism. Only protection. Carter's limousine (like Ford's) is superprotective bullet-proof. But Jimmy limo'ed into Los Angeles yesterday and had to drop a cheer line from his speech there. One about bigshot politicians who ride around "isolated" in limousines. The Service's alternative is to provide a specially made superprotective bullet-proof *sedan*, which costs approximately the same as your ordinary run-of-the-country-club limo. No, it won't solve the isolation problem. But it *will* help Jimmy keep that cheer line in his speech.

Ford spokesmen will have a tougher time pushing the line that the candidate they've been projecting as THE PRESIDENT will go into the debates with that inexperienced one-term Georgia Governor at any disadvantage, despite Carter's lead in the polls. The White House strategy, in any case, is to downgrade the importance of the polls. But this once, the Chevy Chase head-bumping image may work to Jerry's benefit. Viewers will tune in to watch the Klutz fall over the podium—and be surprised when he doesn't.

"The debate challenge is a mistake," Elizabeth Drew tells me on the convention floor in Kansas City last month. She foresees Ford as unable to cope with the confrontation format, stumbling on screen, blowing the advantage of incumbency.

Though not a public speaker (his acceptance speech aside), Ford has actually done well in stand-up, statistical recitation sessions with the press and small political groups. He prepares, has a low-key delivery, and is deadly dull in spewing forth facts and figures. His handicaps as a speaker before large audiences become assets in a modern TV debate format (which differs from the nineteenth-century variety in which oratorical flourish and wit scored with live audiences).

Physically, Ford and Carter are toss-ups coming off the screen. Ford will not suffer Nixon's handicap with JFK. Carter, though he can be photographed to remind us of Kennedy, doesn't project Kennedy, either in terms of youth or sex appeal, as a TV speaker. The Retired Flack therefore disagrees with Liz Drew (who, it now develops, will be a member of the Debate I news panel). Ford, given a chance to demonstrate knowledgeability and an assured presence, stands to gain by the debates. Not that Carter stands to lose. He can dispel the notion that he is fuzzy on the issues. *All he has to do is tie to keep from losing, which will be a win, understand. Or if not, there is always the second debate, in which what was perceived as a loss in the first will work to his advantage in that people will then expect more from Ford . . .*

FALL FASHION NOTES *Populist Chic vs. the Vested Interests*

Jimmy Carter now travels with an entourage of dozens including Secret Service personnel. He attends Beverly Hills parties given by Warren Beatty, plays host to Robert Redford in Plains, is very large with Tony Randall and the Gucci Populist set. Still he wants to be remembered as the lonely late-hour sock-washer of his Jimmy Who primary days period.

In the early going, there was this candid wire service photo that featured Carter rinsing his footwear over a hotel washstand after a hard day's campaigning. Unless Jimmy was sharing room space with the wire photographer—unlikely, even for a candidate determined to accommodate the press—the shot was about as "candid" as Jerry Ford's English muffin toasting. But it ran nationwide, with a cut line that told readers how Jimmy had learned to wash his own socks when he attended Annapolis. Great appeal to the Middle American ethic, the sort of sales pitch, as PR men remind advertising men, that money can't buy.

Sock-washing is a one-time photo opportunity, however. What Jimmy needs is a running populist *shtik*, something Middle American viewers can savor every day. And he has one. A bit the candidate developed himself, no inspiration furnished by professional flacks. He carries his own suit garment-bag, held over his shoulder as he walks across the landing strip to board the plane, and as he walks down the ramp, deplaning.

Most of Carter's luggage, like that of his staff and the press, is delivered from plane to hotel. Not the garment-bag, however. The Carter airport scenarios call for Jody Powell or some other aide to hand Jimmy the bag on landing. The candidate appears at the top of the ramp and is seen by the crowd, filmed for video and photographed with the bag slung over his shoulder. He walks down the ramp, then passes it to the advance man as he hits the ground. Variations have the candidate carrying the bag through airport lobbies, being interviewed with it slung over his

219

shoulder. If the bag is indeed filled, I give Carter credit for Spartan indifference to the excruciating pain of Travel-Bag Finger Cramp. The man really does want it bad.

Asked the rationale for this contrivance, Carter's aides defend it in terms of its "symbolism." A realistic simulation, as the TV spots say. Like Ford's toasted muffins, it sells. Equally important, it keeps the photographers happy.

"If I were doing the President's clothes, I'd like to see him wearing tweed jackets, nice gray flannel slacks, a buttoned-down shirt and tie, even a turtleneck on weekends. But no vest. That's a frivolity. Not too much 'rigueur,' because a too refined look could turn off some people."

> *Fashion Designer* GEOFFREY BEENE
> *on the Tailoring of the President*
> *1976, to Eleni,* Washington
> Star, *May 9*

Jerry Ford opted against a suitbag-carrying image long ago. When he steps off *Air Force One*, he wants to look like THE PRESIDENT. More recently, thanks to his clothier Harvey Rosenthal, Just Plain Jerry has taken a sartorial leap forward. He is wearing a vest.

Whatever Milton Pitts, Ford's Secretary of Tonsure, may or may not be doing to enhance the Presidential image, Ford from the neck down is overcoming the *lumpen* sartorial habits which were dear to him as a schlock-wearing Congressman from Grand Rapids.

Mrs. Ford has been the mover in this area. First, Jerry was torn away from his favorite broad-checked sport coats: his Ralston Purina Look. But even after working the President into sober solid colors, Rosenthal had to solve the problem of Ford's Open Coat Policy. Jerry has a habit of unbuttoning his single-breasted suit coats as he moves. This reveals a broad expanse of linen, along with a flapping tie: the Willie Loman Look, a traveling salesman on the fifth call of a hot afternoon in Sioux City.

Despite recommendations from his clothier, Ford clung to the habit. He would begin working crowds with his middle button hooked, Presidentially, into its assigned hole. But as the warmth of the welcome increased, the hand would, out of long habit, move to the midriff, and out of the Presidential image would pop —Surprise!—the Congressman from Michigan's Fifth District.

The answer, despite Designer Geoffrey Beene's stricture on the subject, was a vest. Not because it pleased conservative Republicans in the heat of the Reagan delegate fight, but because it eliminated the flapping tie. Now Jerry Ford can keep his middle button unbuttoned and *still* look like THE PRESIDENT.

"He looks like Superman in a three-piece suit."

> BILL CARRUTHERS, described
> as Ford television "coach,"
> on plans for the President's
> mode of debate dress, pre-
> game, September 1976

Mid-September   The Return of Roger MacBride

It's been a long time between Cokes. Roger MacBride, the Libertarian Party standard-bearer, is back in touch, through his national campaign chairman, Ed Crane. I last saw MacBride in the lobby of the Carlton . . . how long ago? Thirteen months. He was on the market, I vaguely recall, for professional public relations help. I advised him to forget it, to do it his way, the way the Founding Fathers would have wanted. No multicolored balloon rises, no contrived media events (though, come to think of it, what was the Boston Tea Party if not a media event?).

Obviously, Roger has taken my advice to the letter, talking straight issues and substance. No gimmicks. Obviously; because neither I nor anyone of my acquaintance has heard much about Roger MacBride's candidacy, except for an occasional squib in *National Review,* since the campaign began.

"They're jobbing us out of the debates," Crane tells me. (Roger is on the road, campaigning in third-party limbo somewhere west of Charlottesville and east of Flint, Michigan.) "Not only that, they're jobbing us out of talk show appearances. I've called "Today." No answer. You know, Tom Snyder put Gus Hall on, but I can't even get through to his producer? Why not?

Roger is on more state ballots than McCarthy, Maddox, or Hall. But they're making the talk show rounds, getting the publicity, and we can't get diddly. Tell me, why not?"

Crane's tone is insistent, not livid. He isn't angry, only perplexed by the fact that his candidate can't crack the national news media. Roger MacBride's campaign manager has nothing against Gus Hall's appearing on national talk shows. All he wants to know is how to get *his* candidate on.

Does Hall have professional PR counsel? No, and he doesn't need any; though he does have professional advertising help. In fact, Communist TV spots this year are on a slick Madison Avenue par with what the major party capitalist candidates are packaging. Hall's attraction to talk shows, however, derives from his notoriety. He may be a dull, *lumpen* performer. But a one-on-one with the Communist Party Presidential candidate is the sort of freak meat that talk show hosts relish.

Crane and I are in the Libertarian Party's cramped, barebone offices in northwest Washington, out of the high rent district. On the wall is the Libertarian orange sunburst on deep blue, the party insignia with the message A NEW DAWN IN POLITICS FOR AMERICA. Crane, a large, spectacled political amateur, has taken leave from his San Francisco insurance business for the campaign's duration. Like his candidate, Crane could be taken for your average Middle America weekend lawn-tender or golfer. Yet, why should I expect him to look otherwise? The Retired Flack, though he should know how political stereotypes work, has been brainwashed to regard minor party membership as the way of the kook:

Two parties good, three parties bad. The only thing worse—a category with special significance this year—is the Apathist: the citizen who doesn't vote. For while voting third party is deviant behavior, we're all taught from high school civics that nonvoting is worse—nothing less than a malignancy on the body politic.

Nevertheless, Ford versus Carter has brought the Apathists out of the closet like no Presidential contest since Coolidge-Davis. Some argue that the voters are apathetic (or seem so . . . could even *this* be a media-warped perception?) because of Vietnam-Watergate. Others blame the personalities (or lack of same) of

222

the major party candidates. MacBride, Crane, and the Libertarians believe that the *perceived* disinterest in this year's election is the culmination of a gradual loss of public faith in the Democratic and Republican parties. They see the Apathy of '76 as an opportunity to expand their own third party base; which, for Crane, makes MacBride's failure to attract media attention all the more frustrating.

"We must rise above the left-right spectrum by advocating a consistent policy of individual liberty. Conservatives and liberals differ only in the manner *in which they would use government to intervene in voluntary human activities."*

"MacBride on the Issues," Libertarian
Party pamphlet

Crane and I sip office coffee, a hot bean passed through cold water, and contemplate his dilemma. My feeling for the Libertarians is one of personal sympathy, not political ardor. As with the first time I met with Roger MacBride, what brings me here this morning is the instinct of a lifelong flack who can't resist a call for technical counsel. No charge for talk. A cup of dishwater will do just fine.

"If it makes you feel any better," I inform Crane, "Gene McCarthy is having the same problem. He's complaining about lack of coverage."

"What's *he* got to complain about?" Crane objects. "At least he's on the talk shows. We're getting *blanked*."

"For one thing, McCarthy's complaining, just like you, because he's shut out of the debates," I tell him. "He's filed a suit. Even Maddox has gone to Federal Court. There's your opening. File a suit. You won't get anywhere legally, but it's publicity."

Ed Crane is sitting across the surplus-sale 1947 vintage desk, shaking his head. "No," he says. "Roger can't very well do that. A candidate can't go around the country saying he's against government intervention, then file a suit asking for government intervention, can he?"

He can't? (the Retired Flack is thinking) *Since when?*

"But we wrote a letter to the League of Women Voters and to

223

the networks," sighs Ed Crane. "We've asked them to let Roger in on the debates. In fairness, you know."

"And?"

"We're waiting for an answer."

"The first debate," I say, "is tomorrow night."

"I realize that," replies Ed Crane, "I realize that . . ."

Great Ideas of Southern Man
On Matters of Political Principle, etc.

There was the time (the Retired Flack recalls from his youthful study of the uses of power) when Governor Huey Long wanted his Louisiana Legislature to approve funds for a new State Capitol. But the program was held up by a bloc of principled lawmakers who thought a building good enough for their fathers was good enough for them. A Principled Member of the bloc sat in a chair directly under a leak in the old domed roof. One rainy morning in Baton Rouge, while the Governor was visiting the legislative chamber, the Principled Member waved Huey to his desk, where a torrent drained directly onto his chair.

"When are you going to repair that?" asked the legislator, pointing upward.

"Are you in favor of the new Capitol?" asked Long.

"Hell, no!" roared the Principled Member. "Never!"

"Then," said Long, walking away, *"die, damn it, in the faith . . ."*

Partial Script of Afternoon Rehearsal to test stage sound system   Debate I   September 24, 1976

CAST OF CHARACTERS

Moderator Edwin Newman	Edwin Newman
Panelist Elizabeth Drew	Elizabeth Drew
Panelist Frank Reynolds	Frank Reynolds
Panelist James P. Gannon	James P. Gannon
President Gerald R. Ford	John Kostic, in real life, a truck salesman from Wilmington, Delaware

224

Jimmy Carter   Bob Salica, student,
                                Temple University

Q. (REYNOLDS): Governor Carter, what is your position on
               your position on your position?
A. (CARTER):   My position on that is that I have a position,
               and I have researched that position.
REBUTTAL (FORD): My position on that position is the opposite
               of his position.

Source of excerpt, JAMES P. GANNON,
Wall Street Journal

*The news media in rehearsal. The news media reporting on the
news media in rehearsal . . .*

"For us, the first debate, in Philadelphia, was a lot of little
headaches," says Mike Miller, account executive for Wagner &
Baroody, the Washington PR firm that represents the League of
Women Voters. "Not so much big problems, just a mass of details, nitty-gritty. We didn't have to worry about whether there
should be a Presidential seal, that sort of thing. The candidates'
staffs worked those out with the producer. Our headache was the
press covering the event."

"The event," he says, to be distinguished from *the debate*. Or
are the two synonymous? No. A *debate* is defined as "*a systematic contest of speakers in which two points of view of a proposition are advanced . . .*" But here the debate is only the catalyst
for the *event*, which is a confrontation not merely of *points of
view* but images and perceptions.

"Then you didn't have to worry about camera angles favoring
one candidate over the other?" I ask Mike Miller. "The things
they complained about in 1960?"

"Oh, we had to worry about camera angles, all right," Miller
replies. "But not TV cameras, and not from the candidates' staffs.
Our headache was the still photographers. The Walnut Street
theater, you see, was small and there was no way we could get all
the still cameras in."

"So you made up a pool."

"Right. A photographer from each wire service, one at the back of the theater on the left side, the other on the right side."

"Didn't that solve your problem?" I ask.

"Hell, no," says Mike Miller. "The AP, on the left side, said, 'Look, our angle will favor Carter,' while the UP on the right said, 'Look, our angle will favor Ford.' So we had to settle for four photographers. One AP and UP on the left, a matching pair on the right. Then, in the second debate, the photographers were putting their film in crackling paper bags, which distracted the audience. And the local papers and national magazines were raising hell, so we had to go to eight photographers, two on one side, two on the other, four in the middle . . ."

"Today" Show   October 22, 1976

Tell me, Tom Brokaw asks NBC Political Correspondents Don Oliver and Marilyn Berger, why haven't some issues been discussed in greater detail during this campaign? For example, why hasn't national health care become a major issue? Well, replies Oliver, the reason national health care hasn't become an issue is that Jimmy Carter keeps making the same speech about it but he never says anything new about it . . . Well, says Berger, neither candidate wants to get specific on the issues because he would lose voters either way he went . . . But wait a minute, replies Brokaw, isn't that the press's job? To keep driving in on issues and not get sidetracked into personalities? . . .

The news media criticizing the news media's performance (while in the act of performing) . . .

The Retired Flack, by now in a condition of advanced mediascopia (suffering temporal dislocation and terminal apathy), catatonically considers what might have happened had the networks offered each candidate forty-five minutes apiece—divided into opening statements, rebuttals, and closing statements—in separate studios, with no physical confrontation, i.e., "a systematic contest of speakers in which two points of view of a proposition are advanced" . . .

226

But that, of course, would have been a prime-time bore. The clash of issues isn't what we mean by "debate," regardless of the media's (and the people's) pious assertions to the contrary. Only the physical confrontation—a clash of personalities rather than ideas—can be expected to draw our interest. So that if we the people get the government we deserve, it is because we get the election formats we want: the contest, the shoot-out, the battle, the skirmish, the showdown, the horse race, the game . . .

"Carter's handlers say . . ."
> Debate coverage reference, ABC, CBS

". . . the President's trainers . . ."
> Debate coverage reference, *Newsweek*

"It's a completely controlled environment."
> ELLIOT BERNSTEIN, electronic pool producer, describing both logistical and political conditions within the Walnut Street Theater preceding Ford-Carter Debate I.

In the lobby outside, Jody Powell, with a sly Country Boy smile, is telling NBC's Doug Kiker that *It sure is funny, Jimmy was just about to answer that question about the CIA, when BLAP! The sound conks out.*

Are you suggesting, asks Kiker, going for the bait, *that there's more here than meets the camera's eye?*

Well, gollee, no! smirks Jody, the boy who has just sold Tom Sawyer watered paint, *Ah haven't heard nuthin' like that? Why? Have you?*

It is fill time for network commentators. Tell old campaign vignettes. The Uncontrolled has occurred. Stretch it out, Harry, Walter, David, until, inside the theater, the environment is recontrolled.

For 27 of the total 117 minutes, the six characters on stage are freeze-framed, like wax figures at Madame Tussaud's. That the two leads do nothing—just stand there, gripping their lecterns— is much criticized by media PR critics when the judges total up the score afterward (the Reasoner System, ten-point-must per Question, is patterned after that of the New York State Boxing Commission and seems to catch the Roone Arledge spirit of the occasion).

Why (the question is asked) didn't they at least sit down? That would have been the *natural* thing to do. In Ford's case, there was this answer: the President was advised/programmed to stand throughout the debate, ignoring the chair behind him, in order to emphasize his four-inch height advantage over his opponent. (Could *that* have been Lincoln's edge over Douglas?) In Carter's case, he simply couldn't afford to be seen *sitting* while THE PRESIDENT was standing. You can get points taken away for bad decorum.

Atlanta, October 1976

A Republican matron approaches at a socio-political gathering.

"I understand," she says, "that you're the one who knows Bob Dole."

I nod, agreeably. She bears in, disagreeably.

"How well?" she asks. "Well enough to give him some advice?"

"I tried to give Bob Dole advice ten years ago," I reply. "He didn't take it and got elected to the Senate. What do you have in mind, ma'am?"

"Tell him," she says, "to do something about that *posture* of his. Slouching over his lectern that way."

"You mean, during the Mondale debate?"

"Yes, and let me ask you, if you're such an expert. What kind of an appearance is that for a man running for Vice-President?"

"Dole," I explain, "has this war wound. His arm is withered. He tends to *lean* to the right, both politically and physically."

A small joke to lighten the conversation. But no use. The Republican matron is displeased. Bob Dole has leaned on his lectern. He has looked *natural* on television. And paid, I begin to think, a price.

"What about the debate itself?" I ask, knowing that Dole, by being his natural quick-tongued, acerbic self has been *perceived,* by Democrats and Republicans alike, as coming up short in his confrontation with Mondale.

"Oh," she says, "I don't think he did very much for himself there either. But what got me was that awful *posture*. Somebody ought to tell him about it . . ."

REVERSE REEL

The morning after the first Ford-Carter debate, Marshall McLuhan is at his jabberwock sharpest, attributing the twenty-seven-minute breakdown in communications to a Revolt of the Medium against the Message. The debate, says McLuhan, was sterile, the format turgid, the stage setting absurd, the characters themselves unreal in their rote recitation of data and statistics. All of which contributed to a psychic short-out of the sound system. In brief, it serves them right: twenty-seven minutes of enforced silence on two banal politicians is simply a case of the punishment fitting the crime.

McLuhan is too modest. What was wrong with the political science melodrama of Debate One was that the central characters, their "trainers" and "handlers" had studied their McLuhan. Ford, Carter, and their flacks have taken for Scripture what the Professor has been preaching, in his own special glossolalia: that the Medium is omnipotent. It can make or destroy a public figure with the vengeance and dispatch of the God of the Old Testament.

The sound system is broken? (thinks the candidate at his lectern). Remember what the experts have warned. The slightest gesture may be *perceived* in exaggerated, distorted form. If I move toward the chair, how will it be interpreted? As a sign of weakness? No, if HE doesn't move, I don't move. Stay cool. Very cool. *Freeze* . . .

First Two Debates Analyzed

. . . four researchers in communications at the State University of New York at Buffalo attempted to quantify the process by what they described as "an analysis of 4,458 specific nonverbal behaviors and 628 verbal references" in the first and second debates . . .

229

After 500 hours of work on the subject, they have now reported that Mr. Carter looked at the camera 85 percent of the time in the second debate compared to only 26 percent in the first . . .

The researchers reported that Mr. Ford increased his quantum of smiles from a meager eight "slight smiles" in the first debate to 42 slight smiles in the second, plus four broad ones . . . Mr. Carter . . . managed, the researchers said, 95 slight smiles in the second debate and 14 broad ones . . .

Excerpt, *The New York Times*,
October 22, 1976

CARTER SEEKING TO REGAIN ORIGINAL FLAVOR OF CAMPAIGN

Headline, *The New York Times*,
October 2, 1976

Early October, The Reborn Candidate

The measure of how Jimmy Carter's campaign has gone since it commenced at Warm Springs a month ago is that his spokesmen in Plains-Atlanta spent the first days of October passing word among members of the press corps that from here on in there'll be a New Carter. A page torn out of the opposition's campaign lexicon. It is as if Jerry began to refer to one of Jimmy's proposals as a *dis-grace*.

New Fords we've seen. But until now, no New Carters. None, at least, that had to be presold as such to the media. Never before have Jimmy's flacks, like those at the White House, stepped from the campaign sanctum to make the concession that, *Yes, things have been going badly, but we've reappraised our campaign, pinpointed our errors, and put our act together.*

Presold New Fords have come in several shapes and sizes, all "Presidential." But what will a New Carter be like? The change, says Jody Powell, is simple. In the future, Jimmy will be . . . *Jimmy*. O.K. So who is it we've been watching these past thirty days?

"We've tried," acknowledges Powell, "maybe without realizing it, to make Jimmy into Hubert Humphrey. Jimmy's strength is that he is Jimmy . . . That's basically where we're going."

Who are these people? A President trying to act like a President; a Jimmy Carter trying to act like a Jimmy Carter . . .

In a series of confessionals to various friendly members of the press corps, Powell shuffles his verbal clods as he tells of the Pilgrim's Progress of a simple Country Boy campaigner from Georgia going up against the supersmooth city slicker Jerry Ford.

"You know," Jody says, "we completely misfigured Ford's ability to pull off his Rose Garden campaign. That was really a surprise to us. They've worked it to perfection."

And more: of a sudden we learn that Jimmy Carter, who was first inspired to run for President after being unimpressed with the national leaders he met while serving as Governor, is *awed* when in the awesome presence of Gerald Rudolph Ford: "Jimmy," says Powell, "was too deferential to Ford. He won't be next time."

In an interview with Cronkite, Jimmy himself gives his version of the same line. The old image of Jimmy the nuclear engineer is scrapped for the moment: What happened to him in that first debate, says Carter, is that as "a country farmer" he was overwhelmed by the magnitude of being on the same platform with THE PRESIDENT.

Score one for Stu Spencer. No, make that for Jack Carruthers and Ford's haberdasher. The three-piece suit strategy succeeded beyond their fondest expectations.

According to Powell, the candidate and his key advisors—Jordan, Kirbo, Rafshoon, Caddell—spent the dwindling hours of a bad September in self-criticism sessions. The central theme of the discussions? At this stage of the campaign neither Carter's nor Ford's people can be expected to tell us they talked about anything other than imagery. It is no longer a surprise to hear a candidate's press secretary admit, on the record, that the campaign's first and foremost concern is the efficacy of a particular imagic strategy.

The "Warm Springs strategy," as Powell terms it, has proven to be "a failure." Everyone, including Pat Caddell, whose polls first pointed to the use of that strategy, has concluded that linking Carter to the Democratic past by campaigning in the image of Franklin Fitzgerald Truman was "a mistake, a big mistake."

Even Bob Strauss, the party regular, got on *Peanut One* to counsel the candidate to return to his winning thematic image of the early primaries.

The Best-Laid Plans, etc.

"No more mistakes. No more, at all."

HAMILTON JORDAN, author of the Jordan
Memorandum on How to Run a Perfect
Presidential Campaign, October 1, 1976

September 1–30, 1976: *"The place for a President to be is in the White House, doing his job."*

GERALD FORD; ROBERT DOLE;
JAMES BAKER; RON NESSEN;
STUART SPENCER; JOHN CONNALLY . . .

Old Horses, Old Tricks Dept.

PRESIDENT TO FLY
WEST ON MONDAY
ON A 6-DAY TRIP

Headline, *The New York Times*,
October 2, 1976

"Nessen said the President would leave San Francisco early Thursday for Los Angeles, where he will tour a plant of North American Rockwell Corp. set aside for production of the B1 bomber. Later Thursday . . . Ford will take part in a 'voters convocation' on the campus of the University of Southern California . . . On Thursday night, the President will join Ronald Reagan . . . at a black-tie fund-raising dinner . . . Friday morning will be devoted to meetings with civic leaders . . . followed by participation in a civic festival in suburban Glendale . . . Early Friday afternoon, Ford will fly from Burbank, Calif. to

Lawton, Okla. for an overnight stop . . . On Saturday, the President will fly to Dallas to take part in the opening of the Texas State Fair, and in the afternoon, is expected to attend the Texas-Oklahoma football game . . ."

Once You're South of Washington, News Travels Slow Dept.

CARTER-FORD IMAGE WAR MAY ERUPT

Headline, *Atlanta Journal-Constitution*,
October 3, 1976

The Mediascopic Blur

Ford is up, Carter is down . . . Carter is up, Ford is down . . . Charles Ruff, the Watergate Prosecutor, tells CBS he has "nothing to say" about the Grand Rapids investigation of Congressman Ford's campaign finances . . . "If the sonofabitch had nothing to say, why did he say it on camera?" asks a bitter PFC flack. And John Dean is back, on two fronts: with the charge that Congressman Ford worked to quash Wright Patman's investigation of the financing of the Watergate break-in; and as a purveyor of the Wit & Wisdom of Earl Butz . . .

"I call upon the American people to force Ford to tell the truth."

The New, Unawed JIMMY CARTER,
post Debate II

REVERSE REEL

"I'm going to disturb his little playhouse."

EARL BUTZ, re Jimmy Carter's
peanut subsidy, March 28, 1976

"Everybody understands that Earl is engaged in a bit of political flackery."

JODY POWELL, March 29, 1976

BUTZ RESIGNS;
FORD CALLS HIM
"DECENT, GOOD"

Washington Post, October 5, 1976

John Dean? Well, why not? If a Republican Cabinet officer can't trust a former Republican Presidential staff aide, who *can* he trust?

And here things were going so smoothly, Carter making all the flubs . . . Ah, well . . . Once the substantive decision was made that Earl Butz would have to go, following the news break about his telling Pat Boone and Dean a vulgarism about "the colored," there were two media options still to be weighed by the surviving flacks in Jerry Ford's disturbed little playhouse.

First, how should Butz go? By execution or by handing him a pistol with one silver bullet, the gentleman Cabinet officer's way? Outright firing held the possible PR benefit of spotlighting the President as forceful, decisive. But there were arguments on the other side.

Earl, the President tells his advisors, deserves better than a firing squad. He's been loyal, stayed on the job after 1974 only at Ford's request. He can't be bounced, just like that. Besides, Bob Teeter's surveys show Butz as having the highest "favorable" rating among Midwestern farmers of any Secretary of Agriculture in the past thirty years.

Earl, then, will be handed the pistol. But who'll pass the word? For credibility's sake (the press will ask questions about White House pressure) the signal ought to come from outside.

No problem. That's what Vice-Presidential candidates are for. Let Dole do it. Despite his execrable taste in airplane humor, Earl is a politically sensitive man. When the Vice-Presidential candidate goes to the cameras to criticize a Cabinet officer and no criticism-of-that-criticism comes from the White House, the Secretary will get the message. But to make sure—isn't Bill Scranton due to go on "Meet the Press" this Sunday?

He's bound to be asked about the impact of Butz's remarks at the UN. No need to program Scranton. When he checks in, just tell him to follow his own instincts; that he doesn't have to dodge the question when it comes.

The second media decision, following Butz's use of the pistol (denying, of course, that there is "any pressure from the White House to do this"), involves the resignation scenario. The President turns down the suggestion that he accept the resignation with a pro forma letter. He says again that Earl deserves better. So after a full-dress meeting with the Secretary in the Oval Office, Ford will bid him farewell with deep regret, before the cameras.

But *not* together, at the same news conference. Let Earl go first, and leave. *Then* bring in the President. Separate news packages. The prospect of an evening news featuring Jerry and Earl together—a chummy two-shot photo for the morning papers—is too much of a bad thing. *Decent, good*, sure—but let's not get carried away.

Mid-October, 1976

It is Kennedy versus Nixon on Cuba, 1960: the Democrat turned hawk, the Republican incumbent dovish. Carter uses the trigger phrase "Iron Curtain" which, used by Ford, would send Kissinger into spasm. The Democrat is tough on Panama, an issue Ford thought he had buried at Kansas City. The White House is hoist by its own pregame boast about getting Jimmy on "our natural turf," foreign policy and national defense. But it is not *his* turf. It is Henry's. For a quarter century, Jerry Ford was the Cold Warrior and the language of "d—e" does not come naturally.

"The decision was made, right at the top, not to be defensive about Helsinki," says a White House aide. "We thought that by tying it to the Vatican, we could put Carter on the defensive with Catholics. It wasn't a bad idea—oh, hell, who's kidding who? There was no way he could bring it off . . ."

FORD IS QUIETLY GETTING THE JOB DONE

Headline on controversial PFC ad, run
in twenty-one black weeklies, but withdrawn,
with apology, after protest

"I don't think the President of the United States ought to have
an interview in a magazine featuring photographs of unclad
women."

Candidate FORD, October 20, 1976,
defending controversial PFC ad on
Carter *Playboy* interview, run in
350 dailies.

Earl Butz wasn't exactly on the money when he told Dean,
Pat Boone, and Sonny Bono that the Ford administration wasn't
doing anything to attract black votes. At the PFC there's been
a symbolic effort. Like the Nixon campaigns, Ford's appeal to
blacks and other minorities centers around the activities of special
"ethnic" subcommittees. It is big-name-oriented and personalized,
face-card symbolism designed to show that some of Jerry's best
friends are . . .

Jack Carruthers' campaign film shown closing night at Kansas
City featured not only a predictable clip of Transportation Secretary Coleman lauding the Boss, but of one of Ford's black
Michigan Wolverine teammates of the thirties describing how
Jerry put the leather pads to a racial bigot playing for an opposing team one afternoon, knocking the offender out of the game.
The footage was not without a subliminal crackback at the opposition this year. Carruthers didn't mind in the least when Jerry's
black teammate threw in the fact that the bigoted opposing ball-
player that Saturday forty years ago played for Georgia Tech,
Jimmy Carter's alma mater. It was a glancing reference, one
likely to go past most white viewers of the film, but which might
register with blacks who feel uneasy about Carter's Southern
background.

Now the PFC, trying to reach blacks through positive visual
symbols, is under fire for using a two-year-old White House
photo, which shows Ford with Vernon Jordan of the Urban

League and the Reverend Jesse Jackson. Jordan and Jackson are protesting the ad because it implies they're endorsing Ford, which is anything but the case.

Though nailed in this instance, the PFC has never been particularly reluctant to lift stock Oval Office photos for campaign purposes. For this reason a group of two hundred Indian leaders turned down a special invitation to visit Ford back during the primary months. The meeting, ostensibly, was for the purpose of discussing Indian problems with the Department of Interior. But what gave Chief Goodbear and Chief Driving Hawk pause was that smoke signal memo from the White House flacks advising that they arrive at the Oval Office wearing "traditional native costume."

Vic Lasky, the conservative warhorse (who still stays in touch with N— in San Clemente), is shocked that Ford has turned down the annual Al Smith dinner in New York City. The President's "trainers" explain that the dinner comes the night before Debate III. They want to keep the Boss rested. Besides, they point out, Carter hasn't accepted either, for the same reason.

Now Lasky is doubly shocked: first, that Carter, who needs every Catholic PR point he can score, should pass up what in past Presidential campaigns has been a ritual for Democratic candidates; second, that Ford won't take time off to exploit Carter's lapse.

"I think they've finally lost all their marbles at the White House," says Lasky, whose large oval face, glasses, and oversized cigars often get him mistaken for Art Buchwald (everywhere but the Sans Souci). "I'm a New Yawkah," says Vic, redundantly, there being as little phonetic doubt about his origins as about Jimmy's or Jody's. "I just know the impawtance of this dinnah. Fa' Foahd not to go to the Al Smith is just plain *meshugah*."

I ponder the infinite variety of that last political insight. Only in America. No. Only in New Yawk. Lasky assuahs me he intends to "keep talking to those people . . . the President can't pass this one up. It's crazy, just crazy."

I think he means *meshugah*.

237

Ford's "trainers" have re-examined his schedule. The President will attend the Al Smith dinnah. Lasky is happy.

Following the White House announcement, Carter's "handlers" have re-examined his schedule. Jimmy will attend the Al Smith dinnah. "So?" says Lasky, "*What's new?*"

The Mediascopic Blur

If ever there was a debate in which Roger MacBride should take part, this is the one. Quaint, historic eighteenth-century Williamsburg . . . *Watch out, bud, you don't get hit by that dolly* . . . *Testing, one, two, three* . . .

The present violates the past, but all in a good cause. The Founding Fathers would have wanted it this way, even if McLuhan doesn't.

In the third and final debate, Jimmy sits down between questions, as he began doing in the second confrontation at San Francisco. The President, ever-mindful of that height advantage, remains standing, like Ali between rounds when he's out to do a psych job. Standing, and *appalled*. To think that Walter Mondale would compare General Brown to a sewer commissioner! The Retired Flack is also appalled. What does Mondale have against sewer commissioners?

Ford is also *aghast*. Aghast that Carter would say that if elected he will not send American troops to Yugoslavia, in the event that country is invaded by the Soviet Union. For his part, Carter thinks that Ford should be *ashamed* of a statement he's just made, and that the present tax structure is: *Choose 1 of 2:* (*a*) a *disgrace;* (*b*) same as (*a*).

And so forth . . . on inflation, unemployment, welfare, housing, Vietnam, Watergate, *Playboy*, gun control, strip mining, and apathy. Except for the last-mentioned, the candidates find nothing to agree on. Apathy they're against (though Ford's people, looking at comparative voter registration, in fact feel that a little apathy on election day wouldn't be all bad).

In this finale, the rubber match, as the wire services term it, there are no major gaffes, no real surprises. And like Ali-Frazier, after three confrontations, no one—not the networks, not even a trainer or handler—is clamoring for a rematch.

Late October, Milwaukee

This is not a city of fond campaign memories for the Retired Flack:

In 1964 the Goldwater traveling press and staff arrive late on a cold, rainy night to find ourselves *tripled* in hotel rooms. The only reporter not bellowing to be changed is Nofziger, then with Copley Press; he draws the plane's two stewardae.

Six years later, with Spiro T., in Campaign '70, there is the near-brawl at the auditorium when one of our party patriots berates a network soundman for working his equipment, instead of standing at attention, while the national anthem is played.

No, Milwaukee in October is not my favorite city during campaign years. But there are undecided votes here, so this is where the action is. Milwaukee this day is at the vortex of the Second Campaign, the one just behind the front lines. Ford is in Washington, Carter in New York. But roving cadres of Secret Service agents walk the corridors of the Pfister Hotel, because the two quickest tongues in the campaign are here simultaneously, one of those scheduling coincidences that often occur in the final frantic days of a close campaign. Wisconsin is now classified as a swing state. Both Ford and Walter Mondale will be here next week. Today we have the advance team; Bob Dole, just flown in from Jackson, Mississippi, where he was symbolically pictured waving a hatchet; and Joan Mondale, who, on hearing that her husband's counterpart is in the area, opens the insult bidding: "*I loved the comment by the Mayor of Houston,*" she says. "*If we wanted a comedian for a Vice-President, Bob Hope would be better than Bob Dole.*"

The political wife as something other than a platform mannequin is a novelty on the Presidential campaign level, though in past years wives like Eleanor Roosevelt and Martha Taft (Mrs. Robert, Sr.) were prototypes for the activist four of the 1976 campaign. That, however, is one of the revolutionary PR features of this year's race. It is the first Presidential contest in history in which not one or two, but all the four candidates' wives are regarded as political assets for substantive rather than decorative reasons.

In past campaigns, with few exceptions, the candidate's wife was limited in her activities to one-dimensional ceremonies and cotton-candy interviews concerning Home Life with the Great Man. But Joan Mondale, her counterpart Elizabeth Hanford Dole, Betty Ford, and Rosalynn Carter are now routinely called on to address general audiences and meet the press as basic working members of the campaign team, like any other official party spokesman. Nothing so impresses the Retired Flack with the extent of this change in political public relations mores as the nature of the controversy surrounding Elizabeth Hanford Dole's campaigning for her husband this fall.

It had nothing to do with Bob Dole having divorced his first wife to marry a younger woman—an act of political suicide twenty-five years ago. Rather, it concerned the legality of an independent regulatory commissioner, who also happened to be a candidate's wife, taking time off to campaign for her husband.

With Agnew's disgrace, the Eagleton episode, and recent Presidential history, the Vice-Presidential race was expected to come under intense scrutiny this year. In fact, copy coming out of the Dole versus Mondale campaign has a familiar ring. Nothing noticeably different from past campaigns.

The Republican Vice-Presidential nominee, as has been the case since 1952—with the single exception of Lodge in 1960—is typecast as the political Hatchet Man par excellence. Considering that the position was once played by Nixon and Agnew, it is a hard media stereotype to escape under the best of PR conditions. Unfortunately for Bob Dole, a sharp tongue and aggressive style fit the media mold all too easily.

Dole, in the Retired Flack's opinion, owns one of the quickest political minds in the Republican Party. That, however, isn't the reason Jerry Ford picks him as his running mate. The Kansas Senator is chosen for the reason most Vice-Presidential candidates in history have been selected. Not so much for his campaign assets as his lack of liabilities compared to other possible selections.

In the atmosphere of the Kansas City convention following Ford's nomination, someone with Dole's acceptability on the Republican right is needed to keep the Reaganites placated, if not happy. Dole can fill that gap. If he doesn't bring geographical balance to the ticket, he can at least recite the party catechism without abrading either the Republican right or, such as it is, left. More importantly, Dole meets one of the President's most-used criteria whenever a choice has to be made for a key political position on the White House team; the same credential held by Rumsfeld, Callaway, and Morton, among others. Jerry knows Bob from his days as a Congressman. He feels "comfortable" with him.

Carter's choosing Mondale as his running mate is the culmination of one of the best conceived and handled PR operations of the post-primary campaign: the separate visitation to Plains of each Democratic Vice-Presidential hopeful. This achieves two desired publicity objectives. First, it emphasizes that this year's surprise Democratic Presidential nominee is using the time between the primaries and the convention to organize his campaign and avoid the errors of 1972; second, it sustains public interest in the Democratic Convention and Carter at a time when, without Jimmy's Vice-Presidential game, the Republicans' Ford-Reagan contest would totally dominate the national news.

Thus, although Mondale may be a disappointing choice for Democrats who believe the ticket would benefit from having a Catholic running mate (a point made by Caddell, stressing Muskie's assets), no one can fault Carter for running a sloppy, loose-ended operation. Jimmy's flacks can argue that unlike most VP nominees, Mondale's was not a name picked by a tired Presidential candidate as a desperate last-minute compromise; though in the broader, strategic sense, compromise he is, like Dole.

For balance, to placate the losing faction in his party, the anti-Washington candidate has picked a member of the Establishment, a link to Capitol Hill and the traditional national Democratic power base. Yet, despite his Establishment credentials and the old liberal record that disturbs some of Carter's conservative Southern constituents, Mondale is not an old, but a new face on the national scene. Like Dole, he can also recite his party's catechism to the satisfaction of a consensus of its members. He has the extra advantage of being popular with the Washington press corps. And, oh yes: Grits does feel "comfortable" with Fritz . . .

Family Honesty Is the Best Politics Dept.

PLAINS, Ga. (AP)—Rosalynn Carter says her three sons have told her they have tried marijuana, but she says their behavior does not worry her because they are honest about it . . .

The Mediascopic Blur

All right, let's see now. If Susan had an affair, Betty wouldn't . . . I forget which, wouldn't be *surprised* or wouldn't care if she was *honest* about it. And Jack Ford used pot once, but *he* was honest about it. And Steve—or is it *Mike* Ford?—thinks that the Carter interview with *Playboy* wasn't all that bad because, at least, *Jimmy* was honest about it . . . And Jeff *Carter*—or is it Jack Carter (is there a Jeff *Ford?*)—says that the Reverend Billy Graham bought his religious doctorate for two dollars . . . But then Jeff, Jack, whoever, apologizes for having said that, while at the same time defending his father's mixing religion and politics. Proving once again that the families that politick together stick together. Honestly.

Late October, Atlanta

The Retired Flack is at the Omni, watching a Jimmy Carter one-minute TV spot. The candidate, standing before a microphone, appears to be delivering an address in a banquet hall. But there is something too *even* about the sound, the atmosphere. Video clips of candidates speaking to live crowds, even those taken while the crowd is hushed and unseen, exude a hidden electricity. It could be the speaker himself exuding his kinetic quality in some subliminal way he flexes his vocal chords or moves his eyes. Whatever the clue, the texture is different from film on videotape taken in a closed studio.

And then there is another sign: the periodic flashing of a strobe light, always from the left side of the screen, apparently an effort to give the scene an added dimension of reality. It's a ringer. The cheering heard when Jimmy finishes his statement has to be dubbed. Because not even a Country Boy press aide is going to let photographers pop strobes under his candidate's lectern while a speech is going on. It blinds the speaker and distracts the crowd.

No, there should be a superimposed notice: SIMULATED

ADDRESS inserted at the bottom of the TV screen; the kind of notice the FTC requires of detergent advertisers whenever they run ersatz "real life" enactments. This is *politique* not quite *vérité*.

I call Carter's advertising offices at 100 Colony Square and talk to one Joanne Herbert, an executive adperson working directly with Rafshoon. She informs me that all Carter spots are handled by the Magus Corporation, the outfit that produced that clever film on Jimmy which was featured closing night at the convention.

"To my knowledge," she says, "there's no simulation. All our spots are done by cameramen and technicians traveling with the Carter campaign. The clips are from actual footage."

Ms. Herbert herself has the sound of the campaign spokeswoman reciting what she believes to be the truth. Yet . . . something . . . something I read somewhere. Oh, yes. Now I remember.

Excerpt from *The New York Times*, April 18, 1976:

> An extended hand holds a microphone before the candidate's face, thereby simulating a TV news interview. (The body attached to the hand, which is never visible on the screen, belonged not to a newsman, but to Gerald Rafshoon, the Atlanta advertising man who designs Mr. Carter's ads.)

Maybe Joanne Herbert doesn't remember that bit, written in those early months of a campaign year when flacks like Don Penny at the White House and Jerry Rafshoon in Atlanta were busy promoting their own professional reputations as much as their clients' candidacies. Odd that Rafshoon would keep his own people in the dark about the way those things are done. Or maybe it's just that Joanne Herbert has more PR sense about how to handle this sort of question than he does . . .

"We're now outspending the Democrats about three to two. They started too early and now they're running out of money."

STU SPENCER elucidating on why
Republican flacks are smarter than
Democratic flacks . . .

243

The premise being advanced is that in these closing days of the campaign the only way the candidates can get their message through the din is by way of paid TV spots. Sander Vanocur writes in the *Post* that the spots actually tell us more about the candidates than the news clips we see and hear on the evening news. Extending this premise, it is the consensus of astute political media critics like Jim Perry of *The National Observer* that if Jerry Ford wins next Tuesday it will be because John Deardourff and Malcolm MacDougall, the PFC's TV spot-makers, have done a better job than Rafshoon and Tony Schwartz in their authentic TV simulations . . .

The Stepford President

Katharine Ross has just had it on the miniscreen in my living room. She is no longer Katharine Ross. Just this Stepford Wife model that looks, talks, and moves like Katharine Ross. A programmed robot.

Pause for commercial. It is, what do you know, one of those Deardourff-MacDougall productions. Jerry Ford, in the Oval Office, rapping with a visiting contingent of blue collar workers and hard hats. Only—wait a frame: democracy is democracy, but you'd think the guy would at least have the courtesy to take his hard hat off in the Oval Office! Except that Ford himself seems a trifle out of uniform. His collar is loose, his tie at half-mast. This is the way a President greets visitors in the Oval Office these days? Only when we're trying to drive home a point. Simulated Jerry da simulated woiking man's fren' . . . Or is what I'm watching the last frame of that flick? The images blur. Those hard hats are robots, and Katharine Ross is going to enter, stage right . . .

The Crowd Pleaser

On the stump, the unsimulated Jimmy Carter has, engineer-like, reduced the art of campaign rhetoric to its most efficient form. Jimmy can now get more cheers per minute than John F. Kennedy. He does it by the simple expedient of transferring the old Jack Benny Azuza-Kukamonga bit, of getting easy laughs, to the political stage.

"How many of you here like Franklin Roosevelt?" he asks,

after a few minutes of low-key-issues rhetoric. The crowd roars. Then, "Harry Truman!" Another roar. Then, "John Kennedy!" Another roar. Then the blood-curdlers: "Herbert Hoover?" ("Boo-oo-oo!") *"Richard Nixon?"* ("BOO-OO-OO!")

Finally, the peroration: "Don't we have a wonderful country?" ("Yeeaahhh!")

It's like what Adlai Stevenson said: All you have to do is talk sense to the American people and they'll respond . . .

The Mediascopic Blur

"You know, a boss is a political leader on somebody else's side." (MORRIS UDALL, responding to Jimmy Carter's attacks on "bossism," April 1976) . . . "I believe in tight, carefully organized political structures." (JIMMY CARTER, introduced by Mayor Richard Daley, October 1976) . . . "I shall go to Korea." (DWIGHT EISENHOWER, October 1952) . . . "I intend to visit Israel." (GERALD FORD, October 1976) . . .

A Bicentennial Moral

One day, Pogo, Albert, and Churchy are lost in the swamp during a torrential rain. After several days spent wandering in circles, Albert announces that he, not Pogo, is now the leader of the group. After several more days moving in circles, Churchy challenges Albert's leadership.

"If you're the leader," says the turtle, "do something *leaderful*."

"But I have," replies the alligator. "Look, it's stopped rainin'."

"So what?" asks Churchy. "You didn't have anything to do with *that!*"

"HAH!" roars Albert, "IT HAPPENED DURIN' MY ADMINISTRATION, DIDN'T IT?"

A BICENTENNIAL WINDFALL FOR FORD

Headline, *The New York Times*, July 8, 1976

"Something wonderful has happened in America," the Deardourff-MacDougall TV spots tell us during the final weeks. Video shots of fireworks, crowds, the Bicentennial celebration. *"A new spirit has moved across the land since Gerald Ford . . ."*

FORD HAILS WISCONSIN
MILK AND FOOTBALL

Headline, *The New York Times*, pre-Wisconsin primary

"While the tourists gawked, Indiana University's undefeated NCAA basketball team was escorted around the White House yesterday . . ."

Washington Star, pre-Indiana primary

Washington, July 13 (AP)—President Ford will join the "Bird" watchers at baseball's All-Star game tonight to cap a series of appearances that may be designed to steal some of the nation's attention from the Democratic Convention . . .

PRESIDENT FORD TRIES
ON BEAR BRYANT'S
LUCKY FOOTBALL HAT

Photo cutline, *Birmingham* (Ala.) *News*, September 27, 1976

JERRY & JOE: It is a match made in that Great Locker Room in the Sky . . . Just Plain Jerry and Everyjock, Ford and Garagiola. In 1968 and '72, Nixon's grand television tour aimed at regional and local audiences and featured a retired football coach turned sports announcer in meticulously planned Q. and A. sessions with selected audiences. The PFC's variation is to bring the "real Jerry Ford" to local audiences in talk show sessions featuring a retired baseball player turned sports announcer.

In the final hours of the campaign, as at its outset, the Nixon motif is the One. It worked twice before, so do it again; with a slightly new twist here, a variation there, to make up for whatever differences there are between the personalities of the two clients. Bud Wilkinson's crisp self-containment blended with that of Nixon; Joe Garagiola's Gee, folks chumminess, all hot dogs and apple pie, is the perfect catalyst to bring out the President's common touch.

The Jerry & Joe Show is the centerpiece of the PFC's display of sports imagery, a Jocks for Jerry campaign (officially, "Athletes for Ford") that includes an All-Star roster to appeal to every area of fandom. There are George Allen, Bart Starr, Don Shula, Fran Tarkenton; Chris Evert and Billie Jean King; Al Kaline, Mickey Mantle, Rocky Graziano . . . and to counter Jimmy's appeal to race car buffs (he has Professional Athletes for Carter-Mondale recruiting for the Democratic team), the PFC has signed up Mario Andretti, Richard Petty, and the Unser Brothers . . .

But the big find is Joe Everyjock, up there in the cabin of *Air Force One*, not only a great Middle American image to have going for you in what looks like a down-to-the-wire, game-of-inches, split-decision finish, but the sort of man the President is—to coin a phrase—"comfortable with" . . .

The Mediascopic Blurrrrrrrr . . .

FORD RAPS CARTER ON FOREIGN POLICY . . . CARTER CLAIMS FORD AUTHORIZED "SLANDER" . . . "Too many Federal agencies are insensitive" . . . "A tax increase of this kind would place an unfair burden" . . . CARTER FLATLY VOWS . . . FORD UNVEILS . . . *"momentum"* . . . *"perceived"* . . . CARTER LEAPFROGGING ACROSS U.S. . . . FORD PREDICTS WIN . . . A Look Behind Gaffes . . . "CBS projects . . ." . . . "disgrace" . . . "appalled" . . . Reverend Clennon King . . . FORD AIDE DISAVOWS . . . "We have Dick Scammon here" . . . "We have Lou Harris here" . . . "Too close to call" . . . SLIGHT EDGE TO CARTER . . . *The Mini Page:* WHO WILL BE THE NEXT PRESIDENT'S DAUGHTER? AMY OR SUSAN? . . . "momentummomentummoMENTUMMOMENTUMMOME . . ."

Apathy.

"When I went to vote this morning," Roger Mudd is saying as we board the Washington-to-New York shuttle," the turnout had already exceeded four years ago by . . ."

"Heavy, huh?"

"It looks very heavy. If this keeps up . . ."

HEAVY EARLY VOTE REPORTED

Consensus headline, first edition,
afternoon dailies

"Surprising," I tell Rowland Evans as we share a cab to the hotel midafternoon. "After all this talk of apathy, they're reporting a heavy turnout."

"I hear that every four years," replies Evans. "And every four years, after it's all over, it turns out only—what?—fifty-or-so percent actually voted. You know what happens, don't you?"

"No, what?"

"Reporters go to vote early morning, they have to stand in line, so they go to the office and write that there's a big turnout . . ."

"Well, here's one who didn't stand in line," I tell Evans. "This time I passed."

"You didn't vote?"

I tell him, no, I didn't.

"Well, I'm not going to ask you why you didn't," says Evans. "But you're wrong, dead wrong. You should have voted."

It is a short cab ride. I like talking to Evans, but am just as happy when we split at the hotel.

November

"The ball game is Michigan, Ohio, Texas, and Pennsylvania. We need to win three out of those four to win the whole thing, unless we win Iowa and Wisconsin . . . That is, assuming we win California and Illinois. If we lose Illinois, we have then got to . . ."

Campaign Manager JAMES
BAKER, slowly losing his grip,
circa 11 P.M., EST, November 2,
1976

President Gerald R. Ford
and
Senator Robert J. Dole

request the honor of your company
at the Victory Celebration
on Tuesday evening, the second of November
from eight-thirty
Sheraton Ballroom
Sheraton-Park Hotel
2660 Woodley Road, Northwest
Washington, District of Columbia

hors d'oeuvres   *cash bar*

Send regrets. On second thought, I doubt we were missed, since, by the time our invitation arrived through the mails, the party was over. The one at the Sheraton-Park as well as the other one that featured the precocious little eight-year-old, yawning and squinting into the blinding television lights at 4:03 A.M., Atlanta time. So it ended: an invitation one-day late and a case of child exploitation; two disjointed PR traumas, equally administered, one from each team, to jar the Retired Flack's overmediatized psyche.

The FORD/DOLE Victory Party will be held at the Sheraton-Park Hotel, November 2, 1976. Admission will be by ticket only. Individuals wishing to obtain additional tickets may do so prior to . . .

Ah, but was RMN invited? Spiro T.? John Dean? Earl Butz? For surely this invitation derived from that old Nixon-Agnew Victory Party mailing list used Election Night, 1972, when the Retired Flack (then Hyperactive) was asked to the Shoreham, to help orchestrate the celebration of the Slaughter of the Innocents.

That this quadrennial's invitation didn't arrive until the morning after the event might be perceived as a bad omen, assuming omens were retroactive. But that the President Ford Committee had used that, of all lists, was more than a random omen. It was a symbolic nexus explaining why, in the end—after the stratagems and the gaffes, *Playboy* and Butz, the Bishops and the Poles, Dole versus Mondale, Debates I, II, and III, Rafshoon's *politique vérité* versus Deardourff's—why the Victory Celebration took place in Georgia, not Washington.

"I shall be content if those pronounce my History useful who desire to give a view of events as they really did happen, and as they are very likely, in accordance with human nature, to repeat themselves at some future time—if not exactly the same, yet very similar."

THUCYDIDES, pre-instant replay